THE
CURTAIN
DESIGN DIRECTORY

THIRD EDITION

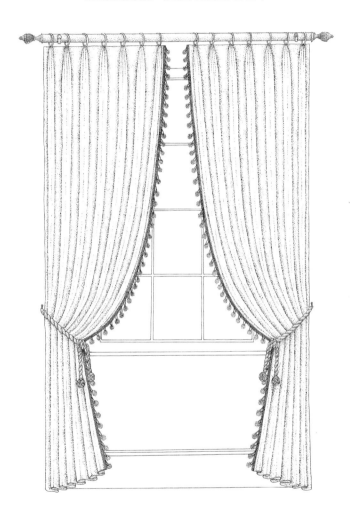

by Catherine Merrick and Rebecca Day

Illustrations drawn by Clare Elwes

MERRICK & DAY

THE CURTAIN DESIGN DIRECTORY
THIRD EDITION

Printing history
First published 1991
Second edition, revised and expanded 1994
Third edition revised and expanded 1999

ISBN 0 9516841 67 Bound version
ISBN 0 9516841 91 Ring binder

A CIP record for this book is available from the British Library.

The publishers have made every effort to ensure that all the instructions and measurements given in this publication are accurate and safe, but they cannot accept liability for any resulting injury, damage or loss to either person or property, whether direct or consequential and howsoever arising.

The measurements in this publication are approximate, as are the conversions of measurements from metric to Imperial.

Third edition edited by Caroline Brandenburger
Cover by Richard Hannaford

Printed by Butler & Tanner, Caxton Road, Frome, Somerset BA11 1NF

For JOD and EMD

Acknowledgements
Our thanks to Penny Dixon FAMU of Penbrice Interiors,
George Jewitt, everyone at Merrick & Day and our family.
Heartfelt thanks to Clare Elwes for her beautiful drawings.

Merrick & Day
Southfield, Redbourne, Gainsborough
Lincolnshire DN21 4QR
England
Web site: http://www.drapes.u-net.com

FOREWORD

Every year, when it might have been thought that the variety of curtain designs had reached its final limit, yet more styles and finishes manage to evolve. In the course of our work over the years, we have, as it were, test-driven a huge and ever-growing range of designs.

This Third Edition of *The Curtain Design Directory* aims to bring up to date fresh and inventive ways of dressing windows, allowing you to benefit from the hard-earned knowledge we've gained in our workroom. Every window really is different, and it is an awareness of that difference which leads to such a multiplicity of possibilities.

We hope you will find inspiration here, whether you wish to reproduce our designs, or use them as a springboard for a greater flight of fancy, or simply draw key elements from them. A window to dress is, after all, an exciting challenge!

Catherine and Rebecca, Redbourne, January 1999

MERRICK & DAY BOOKS AND PATTERNS

THE ENCYCLOPÆDIA OF CURTAINS

Packed with inspirational full colour photographs, over 600 clear line diagrams and step-by-step instructions, this is an indispensable curtain-making guide. With graded projects, from quick and easy to elaborate swags and tails, many techniques are explained here for the first time.

THE SWAG AND TAIL DESIGN AND PATTERN BOOK

Everything you need to make beautiful swags and tails in one book. Over 70 swag designs to choose from, supported by make-up notes and full-sized swag and tail patterns.

SUPPLEMENTARY SWAG PATTERNS

To complement *The Swag and Tail Design and Pattern Book*, this Master Pattern Sheet contains a further 8 swag patterns graded in size up to 170 cm (67in) wide. The pattern sheet and tracing paper are presented in a wallet.

PROFESSIONAL PATTERNS FOR TIE-BACKS

Patterns for plain, banana and scalloped shaped tie-backs, each in 8 sizes. Each style has clear step-by-step instructions on the pattern sheets; presented in a wallet with tracing paper.

THE FABRIC QUANTITY HANDBOOK

The essential tool for anyone involved in curtain making and design. Accurate and easy to use — for fabric, fringe and trim quantities. Includes quantity tables for curtains, valances, pelmets, swags, blinds, bed valances, covers, tablecloths etc.

MAIL ORDER SERVICE AVAILABLE FROM:

Merrick & Day Orders Department
Southfield, Redbourne, Gainsborough, Lincolnshire DN21 4QR England

Credit card orders
Telephone +44 (0)1652 648814 Facsimile +44 (0)1652 648104
e-mail: merrick.day@drapes.u-net.com Web site: http://www.drapes.u-net.com

All books are subject to availability

CREATIVE CURTAIN COURSES

MERRICK & DAY run a range of curtain-making courses at their Lincolnshire workroom. Based on practical tuition, they offer a wealth of professional hints and tips.

CONTENTS

INTRODUCTION
TO THE THIRD EDITION

The first edition of *The Curtain Design Directory* gave interior designers, curtain makers and clients the chance to browse through pages of detailed sketches, helping them to judge and compare the effect of particular designs. The brief and simple text simplified the explanation of ideas and techniques —a genuine case of a picture being worth a thousand words.

This new and completely revised edition of *The Curtain Design Directory* offers even more inspiration. It contains 300 design ideas. Of the 246 pages of black and white line drawings drawn to scale, 53 are completely new. These illustrations form the core of *The Curtain Design Directory*, showing dressed windows and accessories. At a glance *The Directory* offers a huge range of ideas which can be reproduced exactly, or adapted to individual requirements.

Step-by-step, it acts as guide to a complete range of design details, types of window treatments, window shapes and sizes, beds, accessories - even baths! What could be a daunting and baffling choice becomes an exciting and rewarding venture.

The 12 clearly-defined sections all include details of specific design benefits, concise illustration notes, and discussion of both formal and informal designs. All of which helps to make communication between clients, interior designers and curtain makers that much easier.

After all, creating a window treatment is one of the most exciting and effective ways of enhancing a room. Curtains add elegance, proportion and harmony to room schemes which might otherwise seem unfinished. You can complement proportions and decorative style — and at the same time emphasise special features. For an even bolder effect, curtains can become really dramatic focal points in their own right.

The choice of fabrics, trims, accessories and decorative curtain hardware now available is wider than ever before. This means that the perfect solution really can always be found for every window — from the huge bay window with a panoramic view of the countryside to the small, awkwardly placed skylight in a city flat. But careful planning and the correct choice of design are essential to all successful window treatments, no matter how simple the final effect. You need imagination and flair, an eye for balance and detail. With so many possibilities to choose from, and so many window shapes and sizes to suit, *The Curtain Design Directory* is the invaluable source of design ideas.

HOW TO USE THIS BOOK

Simply browse through the illustrations and choose the designs most appropriate for the windows you are dressing. Then choose the design details which complete the overall effect.

The drawings can easily be photocopied for use on sample boards. To display colour and patterns, simply photocopy the chosen illustration onto clear acetate film and lay it over a fabric sample. Designs can also be combined by tracing different details onto the illustration of your choice. Or you can use an illustration as the basis for your own interpretation.

However you use them, try and imagine the line drawings in three-dimensional fabric. The drawings are diagramatic to help construction, but, after all, fabric hangs in softer, fluid folds. Then again, each fabric has its own look — silk with its glorious light play will look different from a crisp linen.

To calculate fabric quantities, see *The Fabric Quantity Handbook* for quick, easy-to-use tables. You will find some of the make-up techniques required here are explained in *The Encyclopædia of Curtains*.

QUICK STYLE GUIDE

DESIGN
DETAILS

CURTAIN & VALANCE HEADINGS

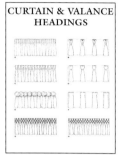

34

CURTAIN & VALANCE HEADINGS

35

HEADINGS FOR POLES

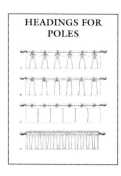

36

HEADINGS FOR POLES

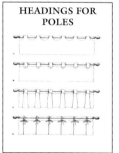

37

TIE-BACK DESIGNS

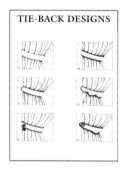

38

TIE-BACK DESIGNS

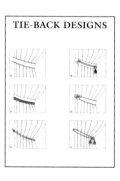

39

TIE-BACK DESIGNS

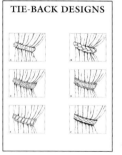

40

TIE-BACK DESIGNS

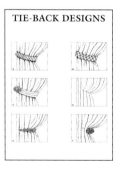

41

FABRIC TRIMS

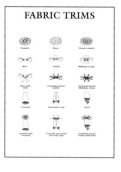

42

PASSEMENTERIE

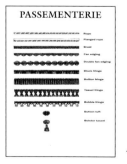

43

FRILL DESIGNS

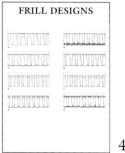

44

FRILL DESIGNS

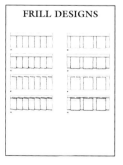

45

FABRIC-COVERED LATHS

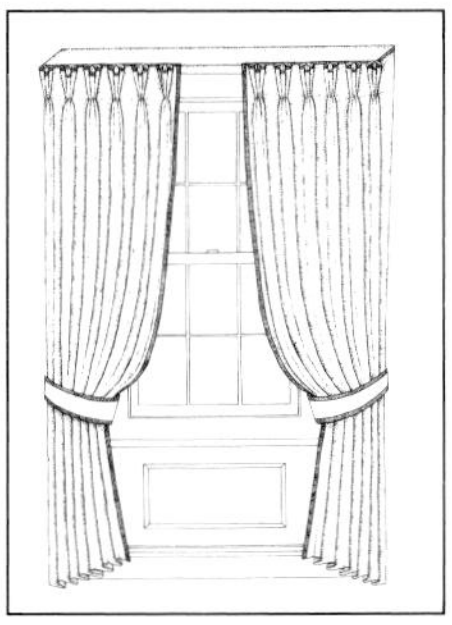

48

49

50

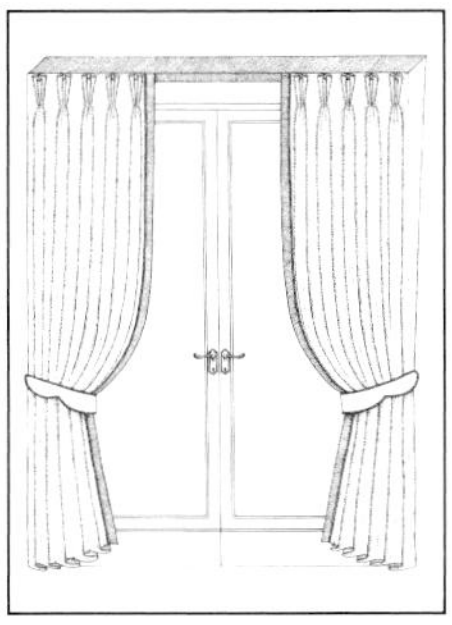

51

POLES

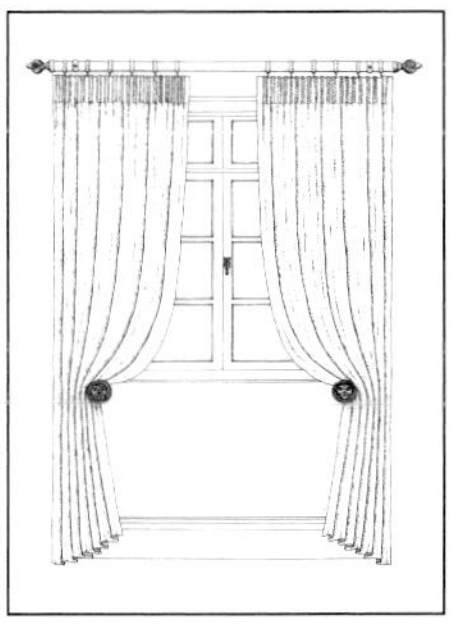

57

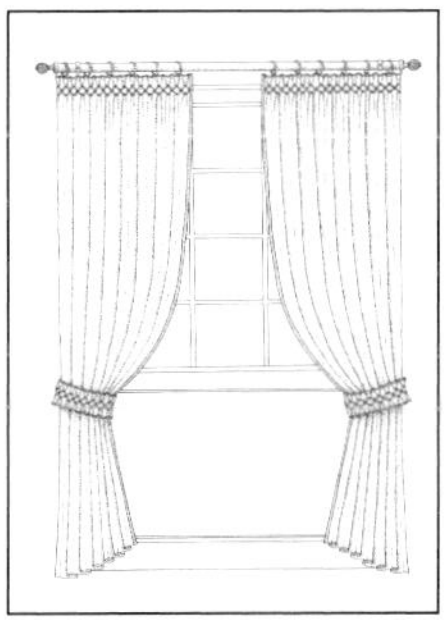

58

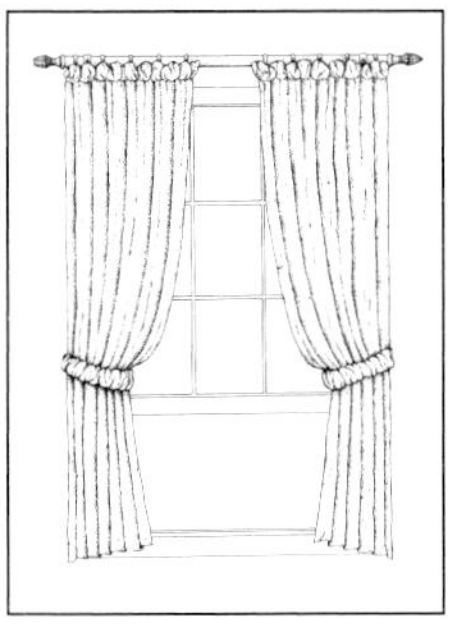

59

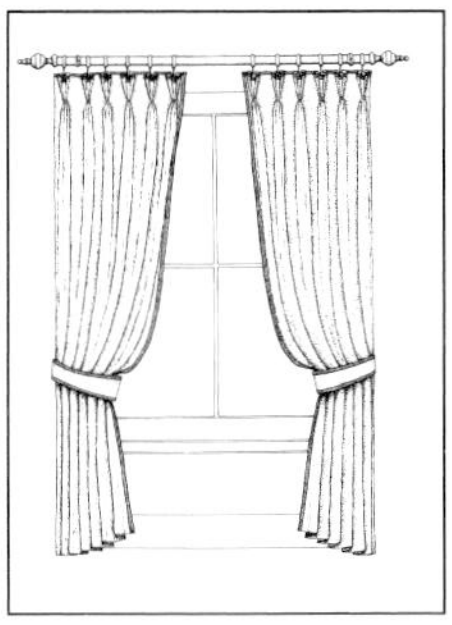

60

61

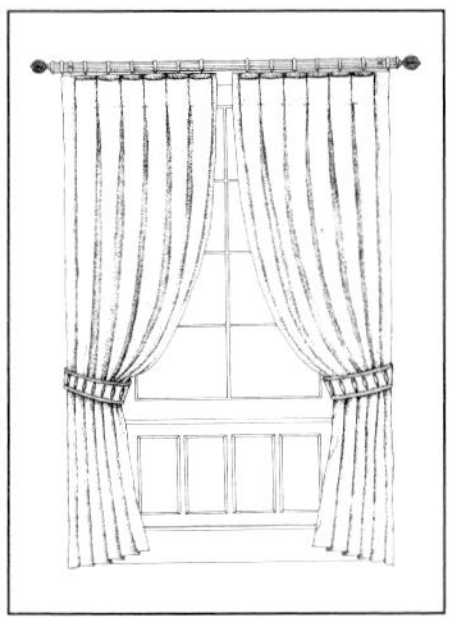

62

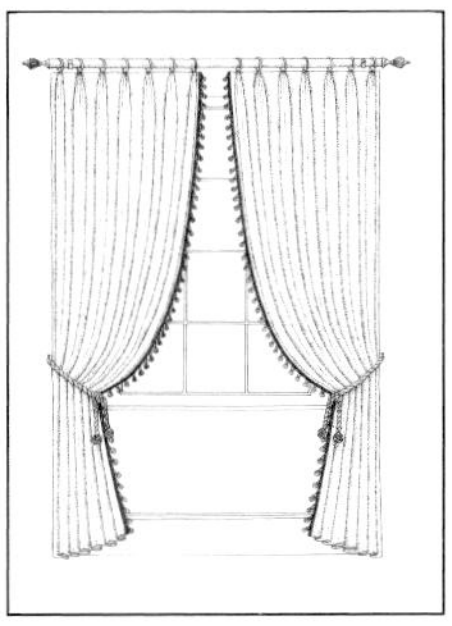

63

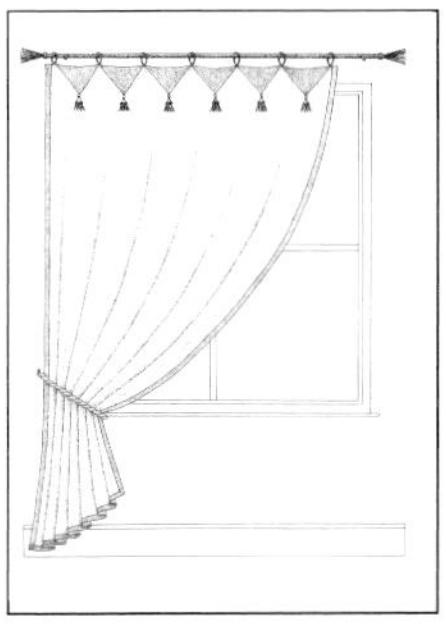

64

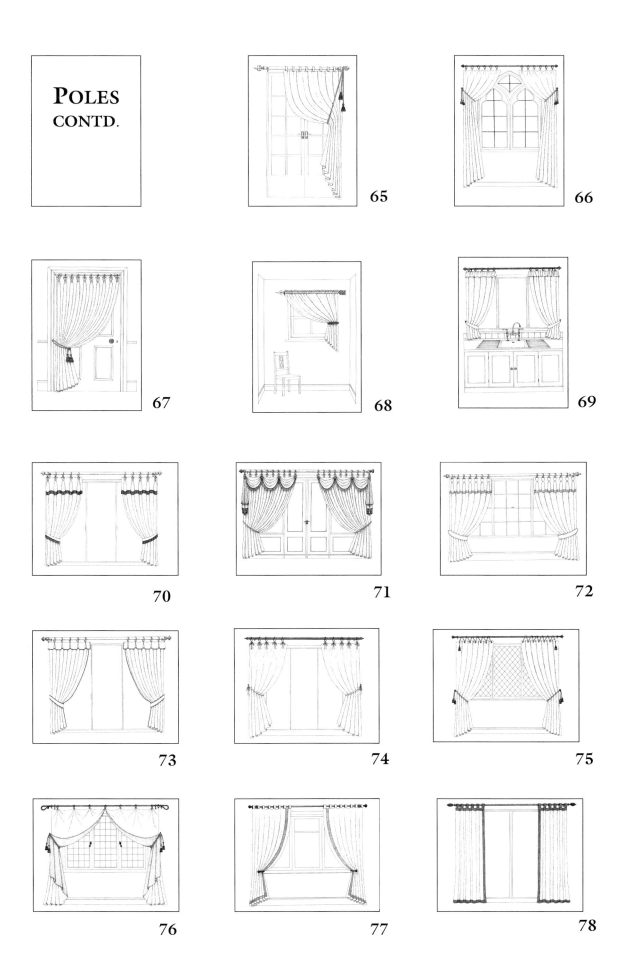

POLES
CONTD.

65

66

67

68

69

70

71

72

73

74

75

76

77

78

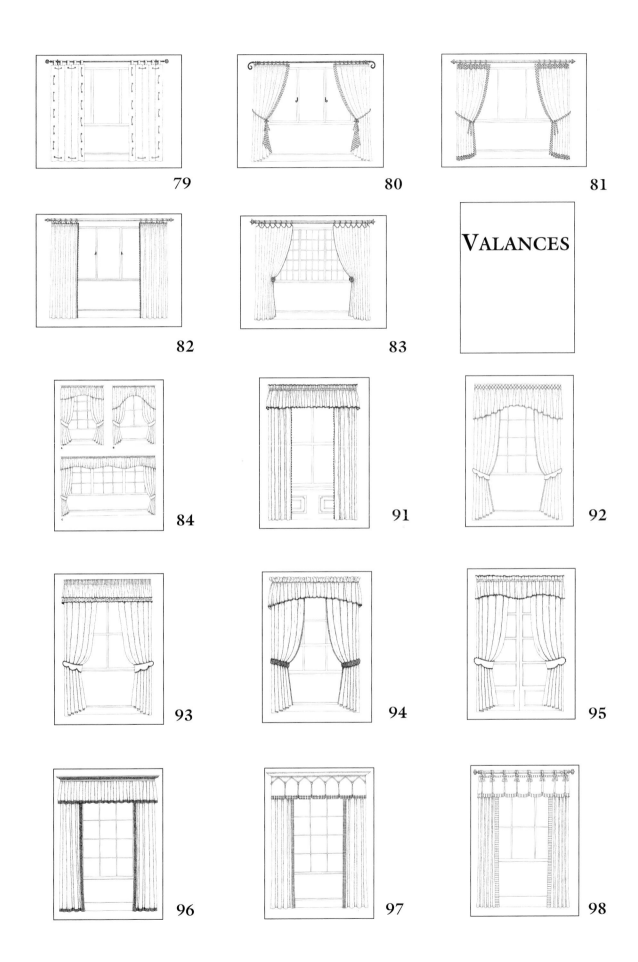

79

80

81

82

83

VALANCES

84

91

92

93

94

95

96

97

98

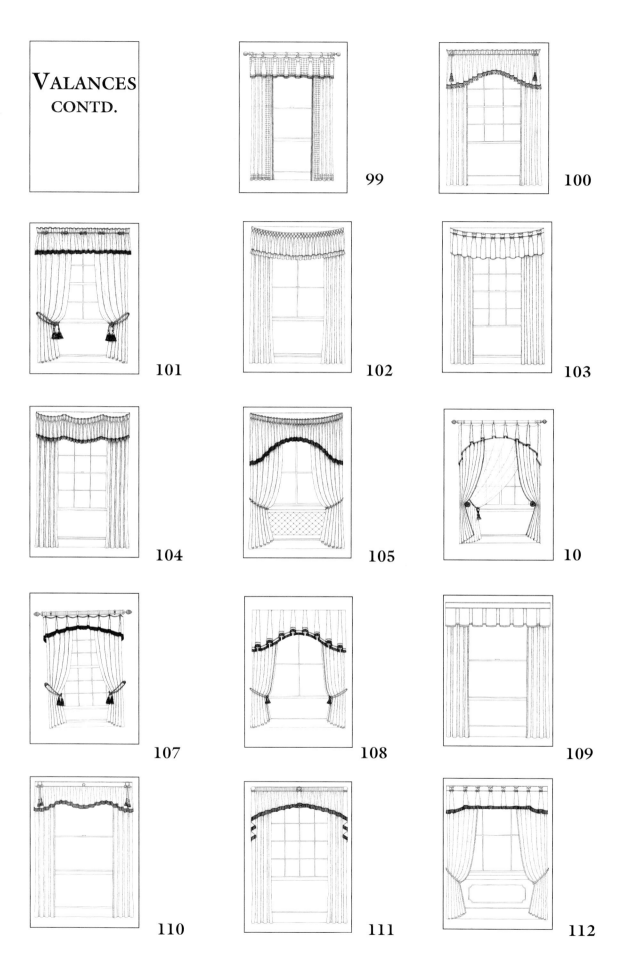

VALANCES
CONTD.

99

100

101

102

103

104

105

10

107

108

109

110

111

112

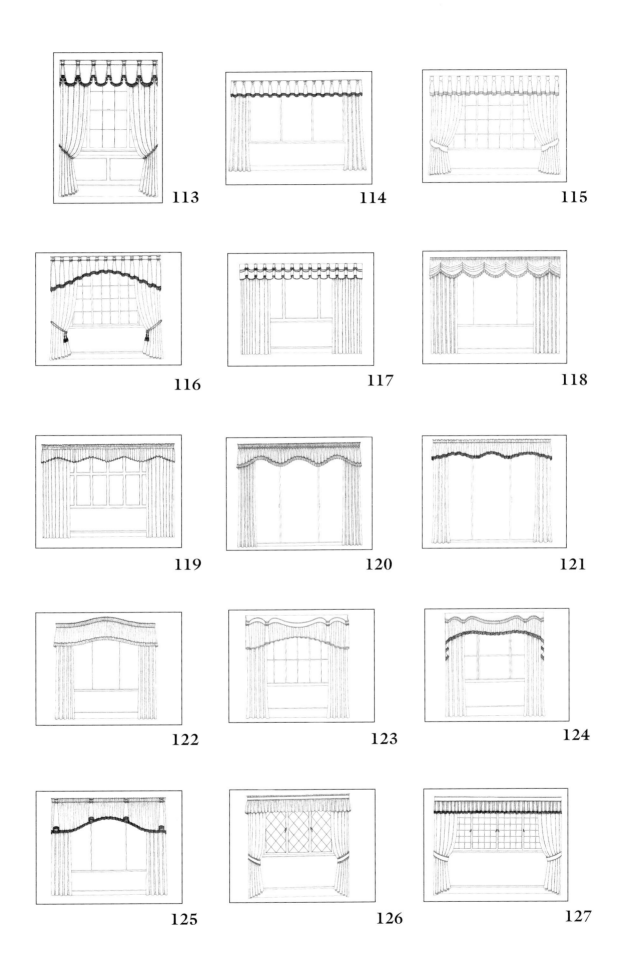

113

114

115

116

117

118

119

120

121

122

123

124

125

126

127

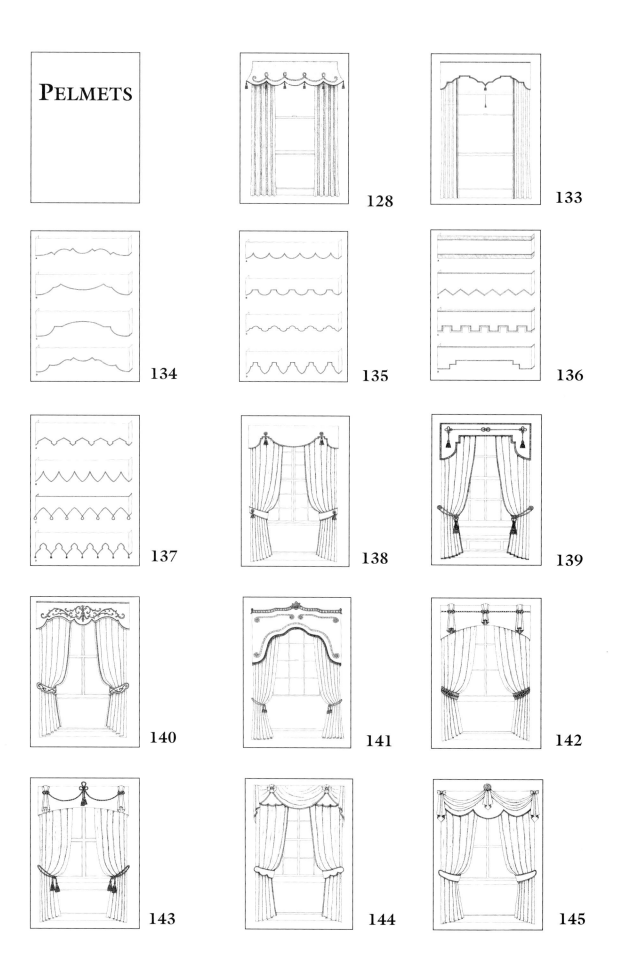

PELMETS

128

133

134

135

136

137

138

139

140

141

142

143

144

145

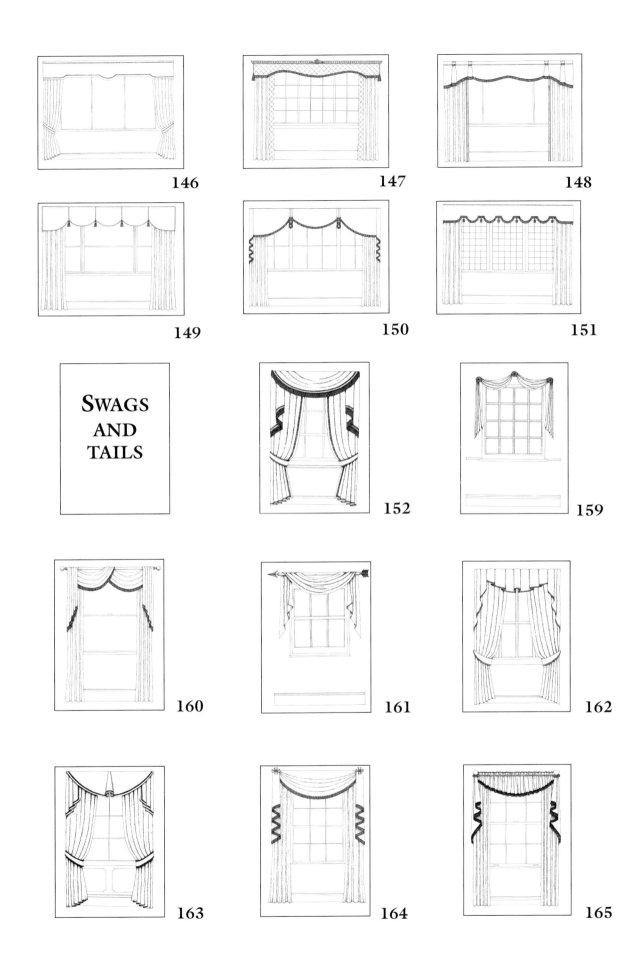

146

147

148

149

150

151

SWAGS AND TAILS

152

159

160

161

162

163

164

165

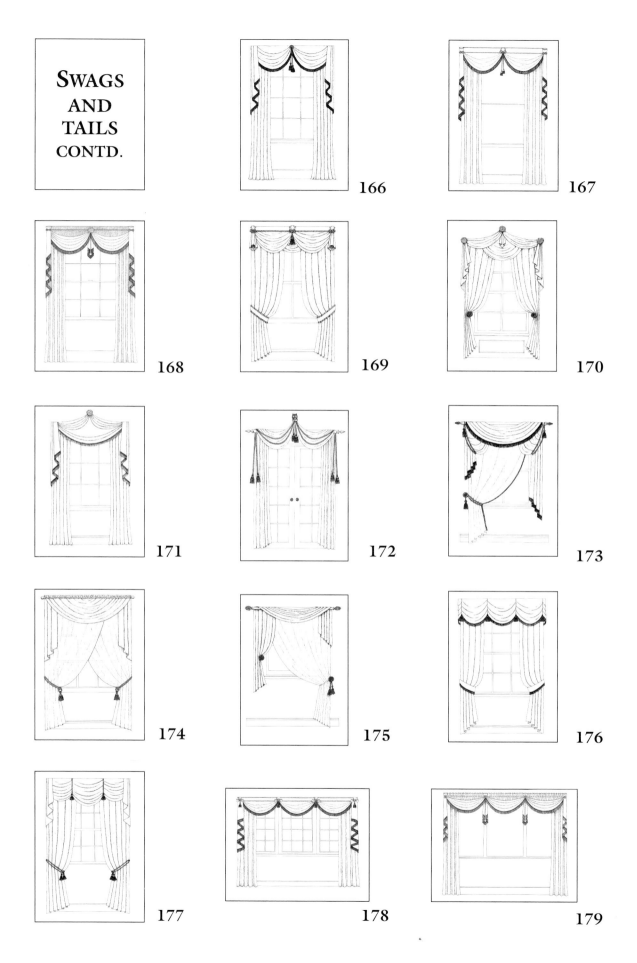

**SWAGS
AND
TAILS
CONTD.**

166

167

168

169

170

171

172

173

174

175

176

177

178

179

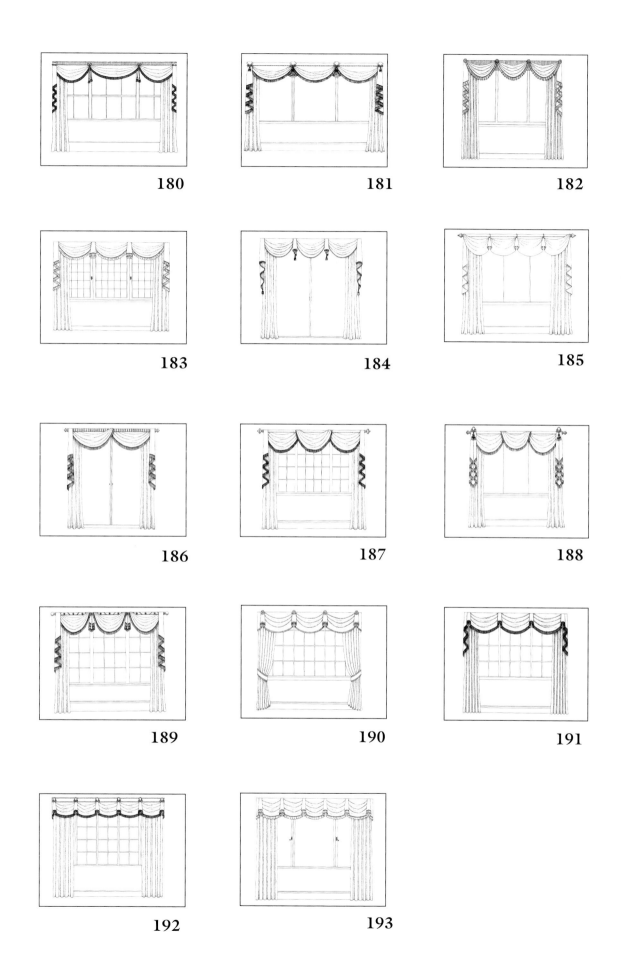

180

181

182

183

184

185

186

187

188

189

190

191

192

193

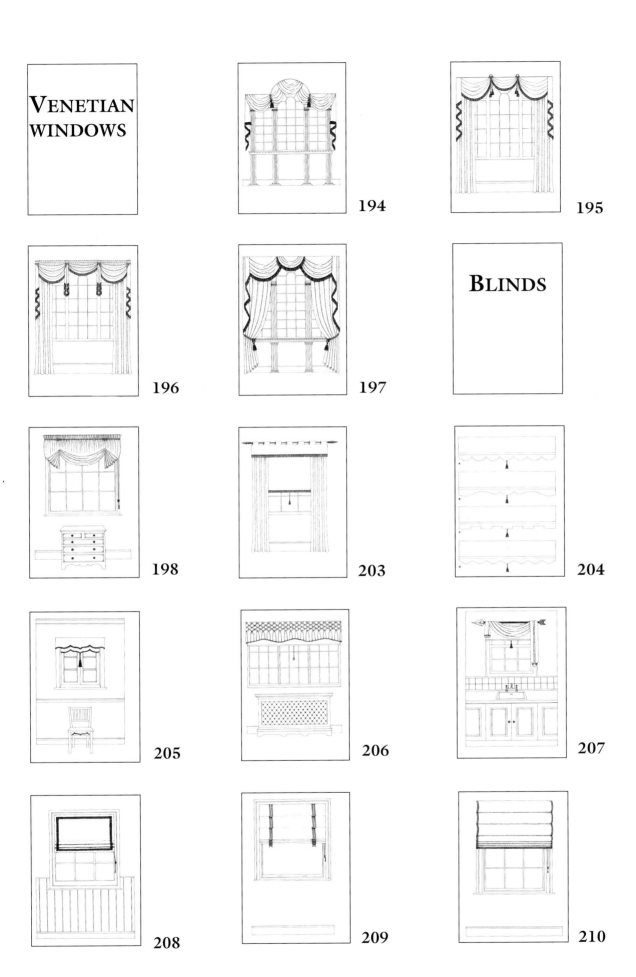

VENETIAN WINDOWS

194

195

196

197

BLINDS

198

203

204

205

206

207

208

209

210

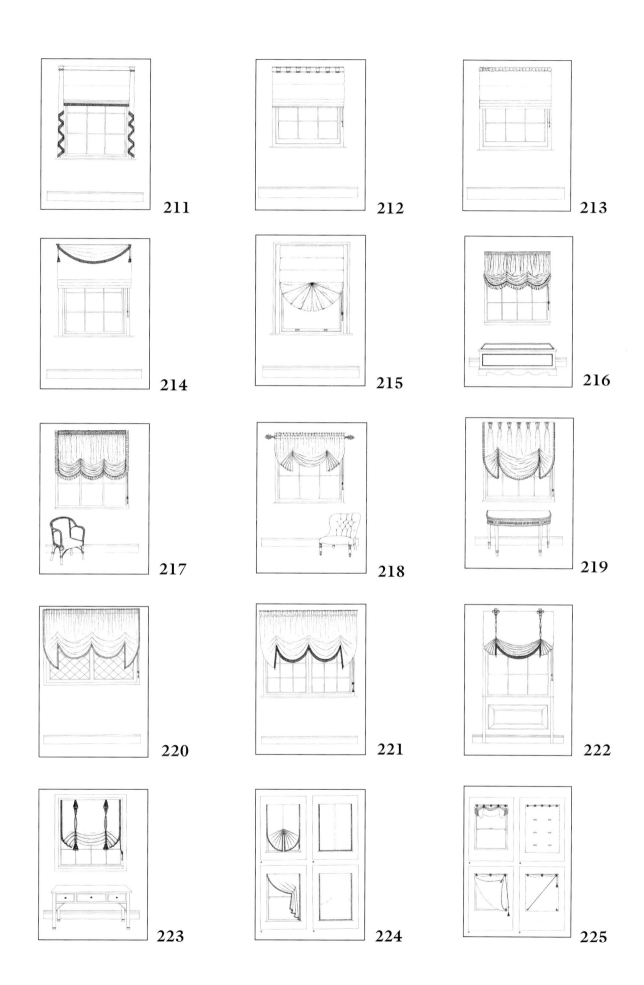

211

212

213

214

215

216

217

218

219

220

221

222

223

224

225

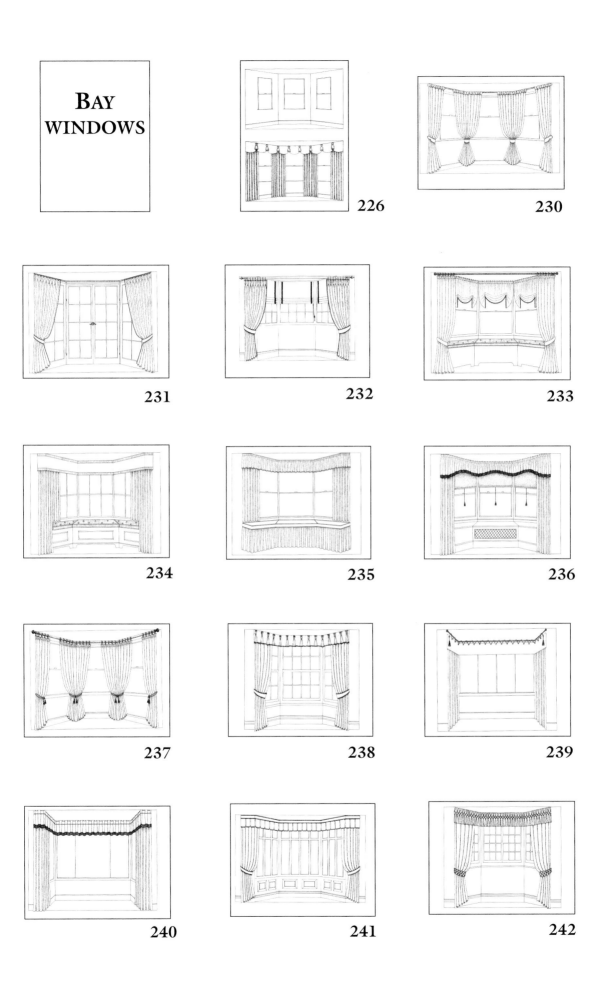

BAY WINDOWS

226

230

231

232

233

234

235

236

237

238

239

240

241

242

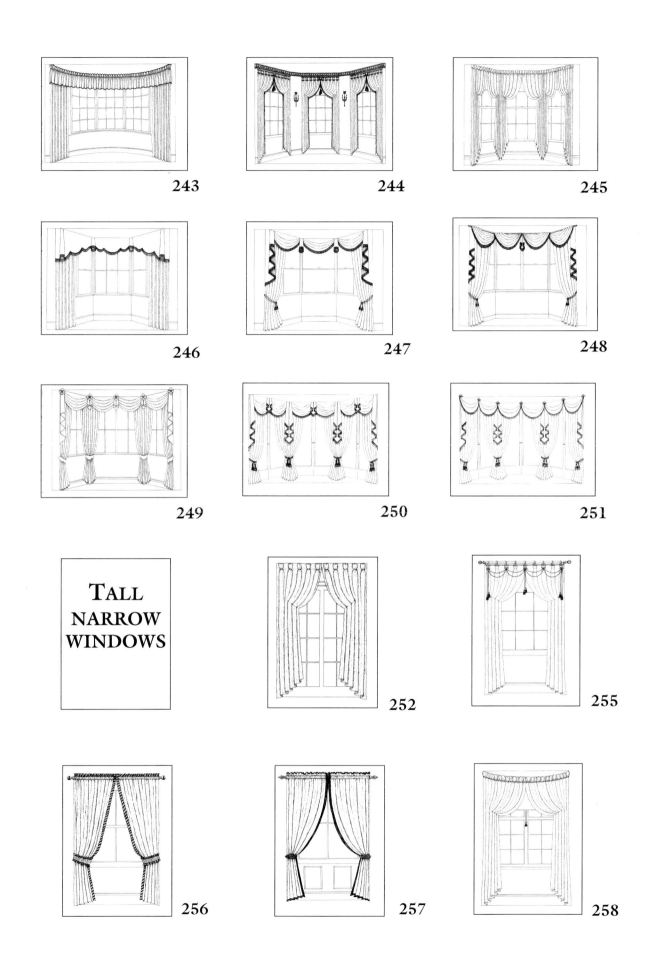

243

244

245

246

247

248

249

250

251

**TALL
NARROW
WINDOWS**

252

255

256

257

258

**TALL
AND
NARROW
WINDOWS
CONTD.**

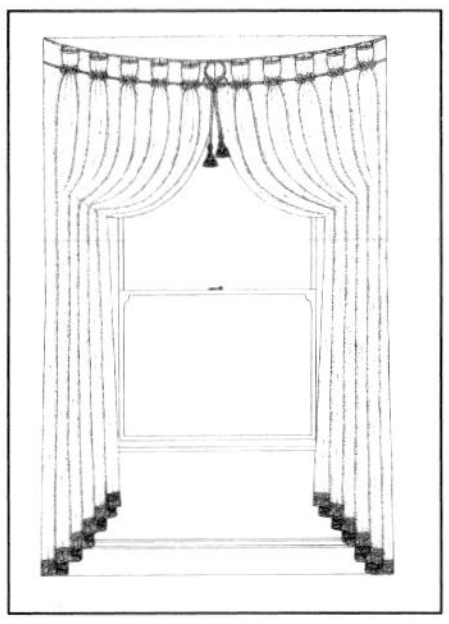

259

260

261

**ARCHED
WINDOWS**

262

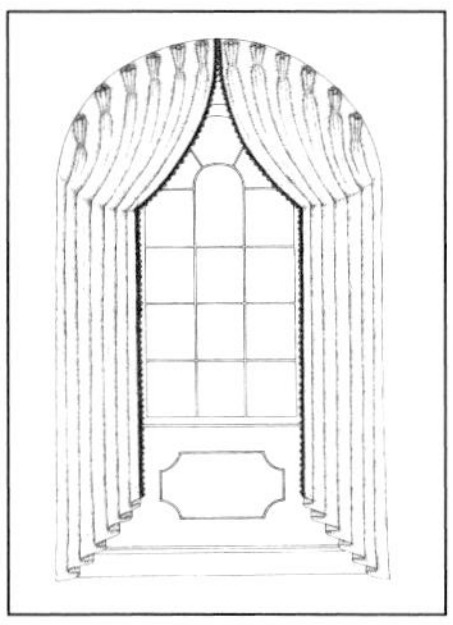

263

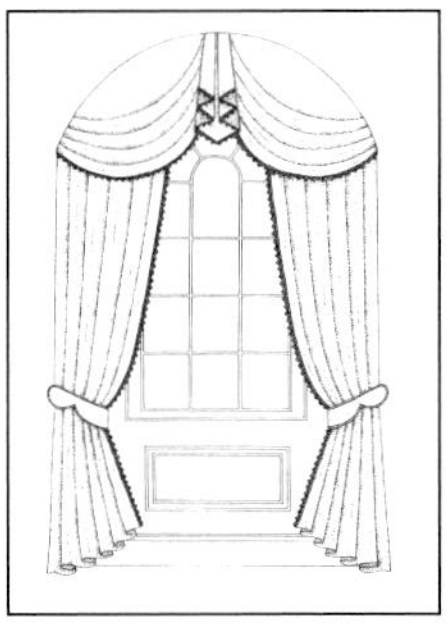

264

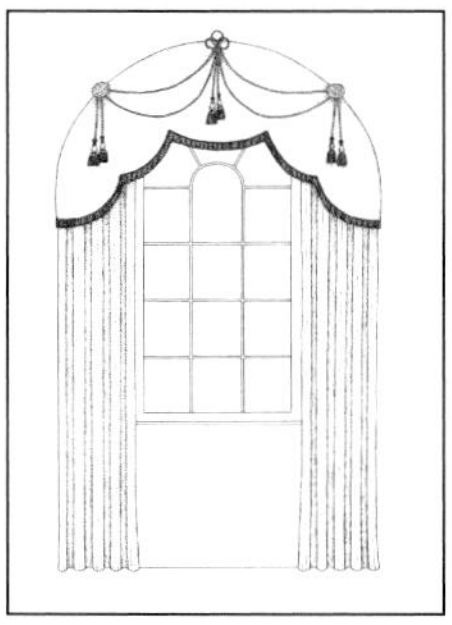

265

266

267

268

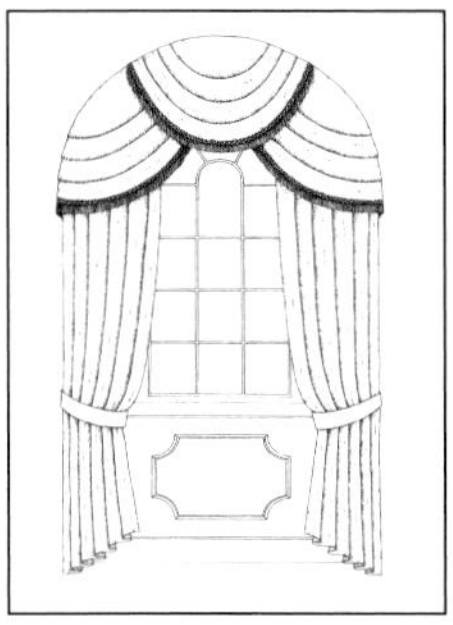

269

PROBLEM WINDOWS

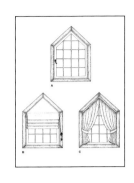

270

DORMER WINDOWS

274

DORMER WINDOWS

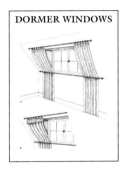

275

SKYLIGHTS

276

ATTIC WINDOWS

277

DESIGN SOLUTIONS

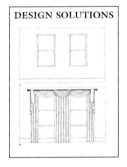

278

DESIGN SOLUTIONS

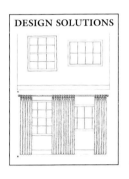

279

DESIGN SOLUTIONS

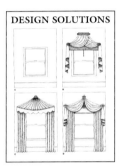

280

DESIGN SOLUTIONS

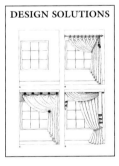

281

DESIGN SOLUTIONS

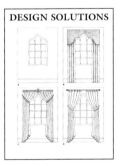

282

DESIGN SOLUTIONS

283

DESIGN SOLUTIONS

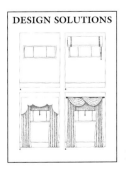

284

DESIGN SOLUTIONS

285

BEDS

QUILT STITCH DESIGNS

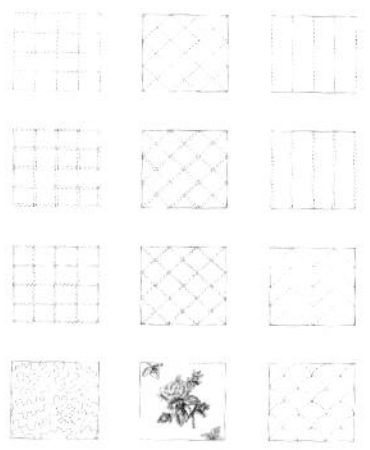

286

HEADBOARDS

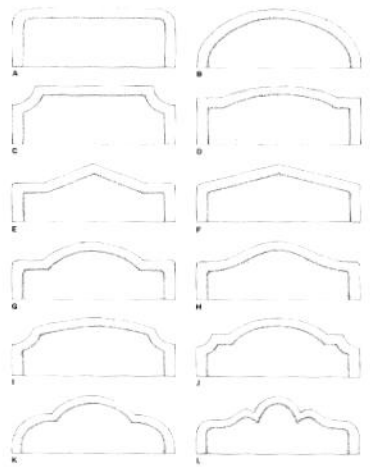

291

BED COVERS

292

BED VALANCES

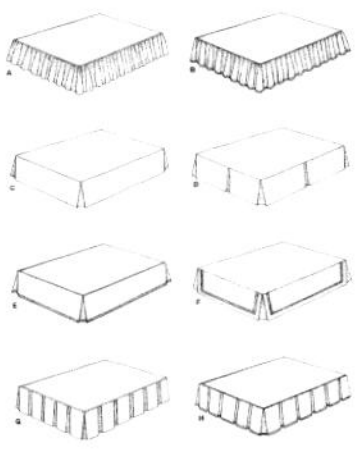

293

WALL DRESSING

294

WALL DRESSING

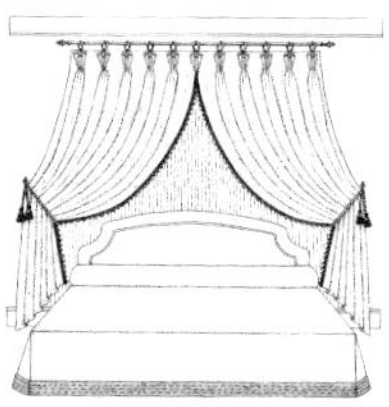

295

CORONAS

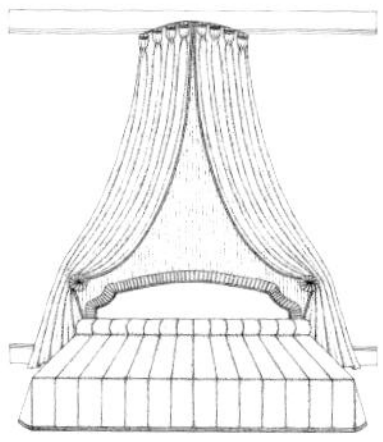

296

CORONAS

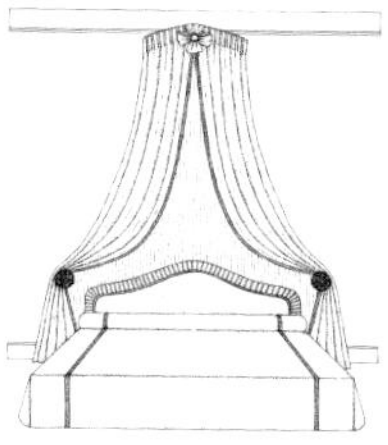

297

CORONAS

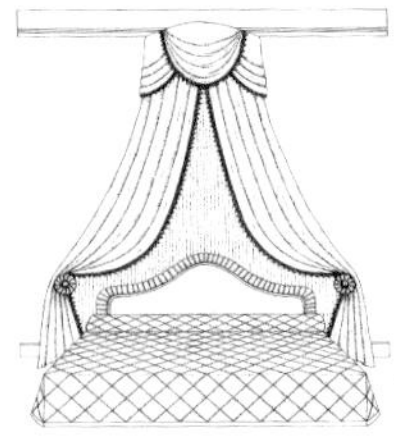

298

CORONAS

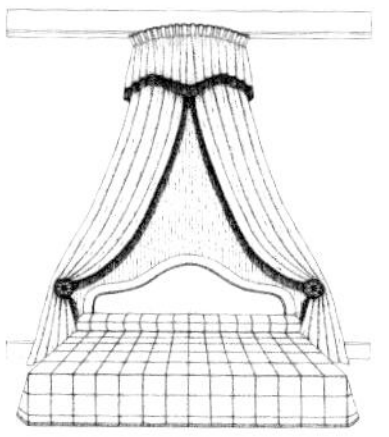

299

CORONAS

300

CORONAS

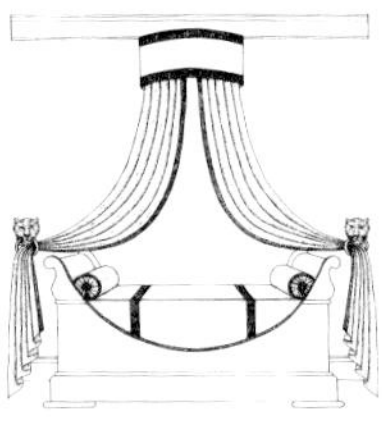

301

HALF-TESTERS

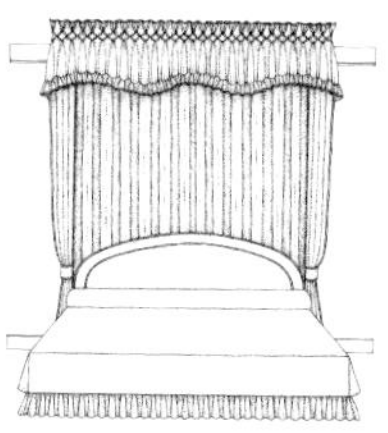

302

HALF-TESTERS

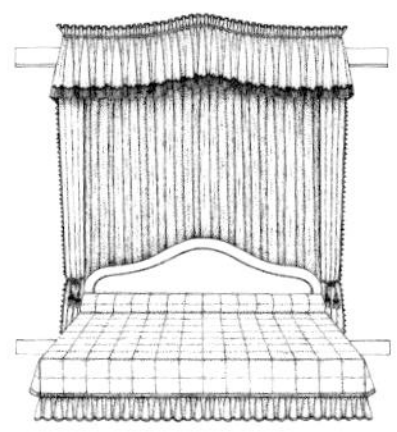

303

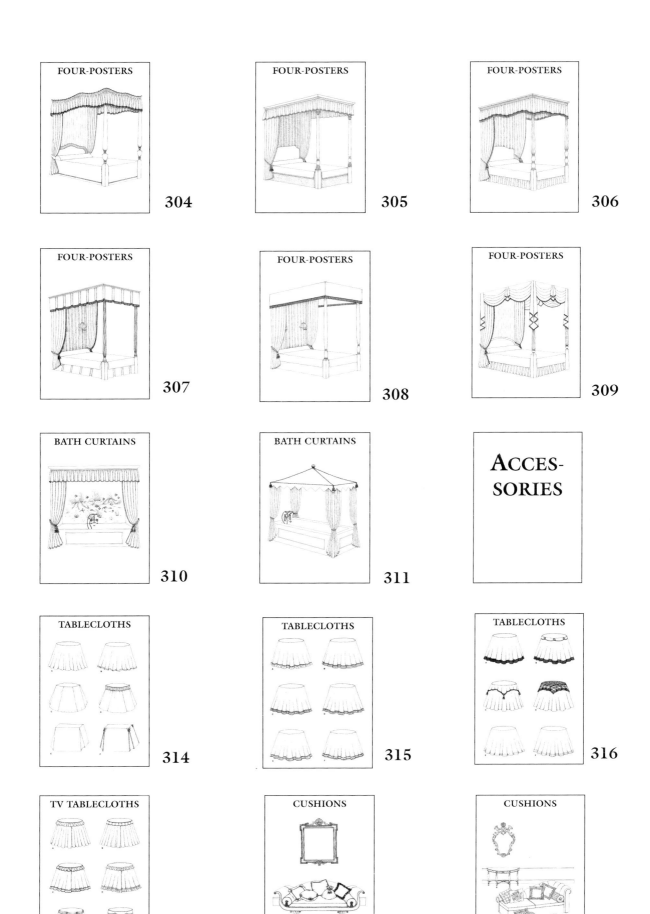

FOUR-POSTERS

304

FOUR-POSTERS

305

FOUR-POSTERS

306

FOUR-POSTERS

307

FOUR-POSTERS

308

FOUR-POSTERS

309

BATH CURTAINS

310

BATH CURTAINS

311

ACCES-SORIES

TABLECLOTHS

314

TABLECLOTHS

315

TABLECLOTHS

316

TV TABLECLOTHS

317

CUSHIONS

318

CUSHIONS

319

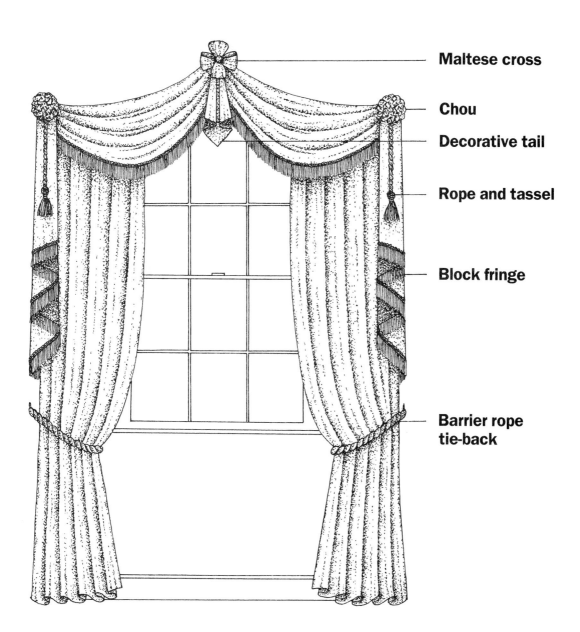

Maltese cross

Chou

Decorative tail

Rope and tassel

Block fringe

**Barrier rope
tie-back**

DESIGN DETAILS

Design details are the important finishing touches. Careful use can lift a window treatment from the ordinary to the distinctive. Headings for curtains, valances and poles, the design of tie-backs and frills, and the use of fabric trims and passementerie all help to create a unique curtain design.

CURTAIN AND VALANCE HEADINGS

Headings for curtains, valances and gathered blinds can be made up in a wide range of styles. For example, they can be pleated, gathered, smocked or informally assembled. They may be made with machine tape or they can be hand-sewn.

Headings that stack back well are used on curtains. If the heading chosen for curtains does not stack back very far then they can be held open by tie-backs, but this may restrict the light. Valances and gathered blinds have static headings, so any type of heading can be chosen.

Machine tape headings
A wide range of machine tapes is available, so most types of heading can be achieved by using the appropriate tape. While machine tape saves time, it is not as flexible as gathering or pleating the headings by hand. Tape headings usually require double fullness. They stack back well and are suitable for curtains, valances and gathered blinds.

Pencil gather tape is either 7cm (3in) or 15 cm (6in) deep with several drawcords which when pulled will form a heading of small pencil pleats.

An alternative gather tape is the 2.5cm (1in) standard tape which gives a softer look. The tape can be placed below the top of the curtain to make a small stand-up frill. Special tape for a smocked effect creates a pretty heading.

For a more tailored look, French and goblet pleat tape is available. The tape is usually 7cm (3in) deep, and pleats and spaces are each approximately 14cm (5½) wide. Because the pleat and space measurements are fixed, the French or goblet pleats cannot be altered to work with the pattern of the fabric.

Hand-sewn headings
Although time-consuming, hand-sewn headings are the ultimate finish to a curtain, valance or gathered blind. Hand-sewn headings offer total flexibility compared with machine-tape headings where the depth, pleats and space sizes are pre-determined.

Most hand-sewn pleated or gathered headings require a minimum of 2¼ times fullness and preferably 2½ times fullness. Less than 2¼ fullness tends to look mean and does not do the heading justice. Informal tab or eyelet headings require only 1½ - 2 times fullness.

Hand-sewn pleated headings
French, goblet and box pleats are stiffened with heading buckram and then individually pleated. The pleats allow the curtains to fall into even, organised folds. For this reason it is a good idea to French-head curtains hung under pelmets and valances, even though the decorative heading is not visible.

French pleats stack back extremely well, goblet pleats nearly as well. Because box-pleated curtains do not stack back very well they will need to be held open with tie-backs or ombras.

Where the fabric has a strong vertical pattern, it is critical to pleat the fabric to the horizontal pattern repeat. Surprisingly, even floral fabrics have horizontal patterns that can be brought forward in the pleats. When a French-, goblet- or box-pleated heading is not pleated to the horizontal pattern repeat, the effect is rather jangling. You may in this instance prefer to gather the fabric for a softer look.

When using, for example, a blue-and-white striped fabric with a hand-pleated French-goblet heading, if the blue stripe makes up the pleat and the white stripe is in the space, then the curtain will be pre-dominantly blue and vice versa.

Headings can be effectively trimmed with a contrast binding along the top to define the edge. The contrast binding should be about 1cm (½in) wide to give a subtle effect. The base of French- or goblet-pleated headings can be finished with hand-sewn knotted rope, or trimmed with button tufts or small rosettes.

Proportions
For French-headed curtains the buckram is usually 10-15cm (4-6in) in depth. For valances with French-pleated headings the depth of the buckram should be in proportion to the depth of the valance, usually 7-10cm (3-4in) deep. The deeper the valance, the deeper the heading.

For goblet-headed curtains and valances the buckram can be as little as 7-10cm (3-4in) deep to echo the shape of the goblet wine glass (the effect which gives this heading its name).

As a general rule of thumb there should be four pleats in a width of fabric, but on patterned fabric the number of pleats may be dictated by the print. Pleat sizes can be between 15-20cm (6-8in) with spaces of 10-15cm (4-6in).

Hand-sewn gathered headings
These headings have parallel rows of running stitches which are then drawn up to the required width. The depth of the gathering varies from 2.5cm (1in) to 15cm (6in). As an extra finish the gathers can be smocked. It should be noted that hand-gathered headings do not stack back as well as French-pleated headings.

ILLUSTRATION NOTES

Page 34
A Simple pencil heading which can be gathered by hand or with tape. It is usually 7cm (3in) in depth.

B French or pinch pleats which can be gathered by hand or with a tape. For valances, pleats should be approximately 10cm (4in) in length. An excellent hand-sewn heading to use on curtains hung underneath valances, pelmets, or swags and tails as the French pleats encourage them to hang in organised folds.

C Dropped down 2.5cm (1in) tape which creates a frill above the gathering. The tape is usually dropped down 7cm (3in). This is a pretty heading, especially suitable for simple sill-length curtains and also for valances.

D Goblet heading which can be used on curtains and valances. The goblets are usually 10cm (4in) in depth. If they are any deeper they lose the wine glass shape which gives this heading its name. They stack back well, but not as well as French headings.

E A puff heading is a pretty heading, either hand- or tape-gathered leaving a 15cm (6in) frill above the gathers. The frill is stuffed with net and stab-stitched to organise the puffed effect. This heading works particularly well in silk fabrics but not so well in heavy cottons. It does not stack back very well and so curtains will need to be held open by tie-backs.

F Box-pleated heading where the pleats are flattened to form a smart tailored heading. Box-pleat headed curtains will need to be held open by tie-backs.

G A 7cm (3in) deep smocking heading. Smocked headings are effectively a pencil heading that is then embroidered with smocking stitches. Special smocking tape can be used, but the machine lines of the tape will be visible. With hand-sewn smocking, the depth of the heading is a matter of personal preference.

Honeycomb or trellis stitch can be worked in embroidery silk, cotton or wool, depending on the fabric. Coloured yarns can be threaded through the stitches to emphasise the smocked effect.

H A dropped-down 5cm (2in) smocked heading which creates a frill above the embroidery stitches.

Page 35

A Hand- or tape-gathered pencil heading with a 1cm (½in) contrast bound top.

B Hand-gathered trellis heading that is softly gathered to form alternating 'v's, with a 1cm (½in) contrast-bound top.

C French pleats with a 1cm (½in) contrast-bound top.

D French pleats with a 1cm (½in) contrast-bound top and hand-sewn knotted rope at the base of the pleats. Avoid using really stiff rope to ensure the curtains will still stack back well.

E Goblet heading with a 1cm (½in) contrast-bound top.

F Goblet heading with a 1cm (½in) contrast-bound top and hand-sewn knotted rope at the base of the pleats. The double overhand knot sits well over the rounded base of the pleat. Provided the rope is not really stiff, the curtains will still stack back well. Soft wool rope is particularly good for this purpose.

G Wool button tufts sewn at the base of each goblet.

H Small rosettes with a covered button in the centre sewn at the base of each goblet.

HEADINGS FOR POLES

Goblets, French pleats and gathered headings can all be hung from a pole, but other more unusual headings can also be used. The pole rings can be sewn directly onto the curtain, but for cleaning they will have to be taken off and then re-sewn! This type of heading can also be used for café curtains (see page 285).

ILLUSTRATION NOTES

Page 36
A French pleats with scooped-out spaces between the pleats.

B Box-pleated heading hung from rings.

C Pleats formed by sewing the rings onto the curtain at wide intervals and then placing them closer together on the pole. 1½-2 times fullness required.

D The curtain has a channel heading which is slotted onto plain dowelling. This is a non-functional fixed heading.

Page 37 None of these will run along the pole well.

A Scooped-out heading with no fullness. Often used as café curtains where only the lower half of the window is dressed.

B Tabs are sewn on the curtain and secured with a button. This is a casual tailored heading and suitable for situations where no fullness is required. Tab curtains can have 1½-2 times fullness.

C Box-pleated curtain attached to the pole with fabric loops.

D Pleated curtain attached to the pole with ties rather than cornice pole rings.

TIE-BACK DESIGNS

Tie-backs add the finishing touch to curtains and therefore deserve careful consideration. The design of fabric tie-backs should be sympathetic with the design of the window treatment. They should be 'bow' shaped so that they sit neatly around the curtain and do not stand away from the curtain at the leading edge. Tassel tie-backs introduce texture to the window treatment, while brass ombras and curtain bands add sophistication.

ILLUSTRATION NOTES

Page 38
A Plain tie-back.

B Contrast-bound tie-back.

C Contrast piped banana tie-back.

D Contrast-piped scalloped tie-back.

E Contrast-bound tie-back with a bolster tassel trim.

F Sweetheart-shaped tie-back, contrast-bound with a chou trim.

Page 39
A Rope-trimmed tie-back.

B Tassel tie-back set on a fabric tie-back.

C Bullion-trimmed tie-back.

D Contrast-bound tie-back with a contrast-bound Maltese cross trim.

E Barrier rope tie-back usually made from 2.5cm (1in) diameter rope giving a smart finish.

F Double tassel tie-back. Using double

tassels as opposed to single tassels gives a sumptuous look.

Page 40
A Ruched tie-back.

B Plaited tie-back which can look effective if the curtain fabric and two plain colours are plaited together.

C Ruched tie-back with bound edges.

D Ruched tie-back with ruched bound edges. An appropriate design for puff-headed curtains.

E Box-pleated tie-back with bound edges.

F Quilted tie-back with bound edges.

Page 41
A Pencil-pleated tie-back.

B Smocked tie-back.

C Pleated tie-back with rosette trim.

D Italian-strung curtains are permanently joined together at the heading and are drawn apart by draw cords. The resulting scalloped effect created by the leading edge is particularly attractive.

E Acanthus-shaped brass curtain band.

F Brass or wood ombra.

FABRIC TRIMS

Trims are an attractive and subtle finish that should be an accent rather than overpowering the window treatment. They can be used on tie-backs, valances, pelmets, swags and blinds.

It is important to consider the size of the trim in relation to the window treatment. Rosettes and choux trims with a diameter of 9cm (3½in) will look smart whatever the size of the window. Maltese crosses and trefoils should be graded in size according to the use. For example, as a tie-back trim the Maltese cross could be 9cm (3½in) wide but as a centre trim on a pair of fixed headed curtains at a tall narrow window (see page 184) it can be as much as 20cm (8in) wide.

Trumpets, decorative tails and flutes should again be in proportion with the valance or pelmet treatment over which they are to hang.

ILLUSTRATION NOTES

Page 42
Identification chart for fabric trims.

PASSEMENTERIE

It is worthwhile investing in good passementerie as this detailing can make or break a window treatment. There is a huge range to choose from, made in either natural fibres such as wool, cotton and linen, or in man-made fibres such as rayon and viscose.

If stock colours are not suitable, then there are specialist companies who will dye and make up passementerie in specified colour mixes.

ILLUSTRATION NOTES

Page 43
Rope can be run along the tops of swags and tails to define the edges, knotted at the base of goblets, made-up into rope clovers, and used to trim pelmets and tie-backs. The most commonly used size is

12-15mm ($\frac{1}{2}$-$\frac{5}{8}$in) in diameter.

Flanged rope may be seamed into the leading edges and hems of curtains and onto the edges of tie-backs and cushions.

Braid can look stunning set in from the leading edges of curtains and along flat pelmets. It is also an effective trim for Roman blinds.

Fan edging is a delicate finish for curtains, valances, bed curtains and cushions. It can either be set into the seam so that only the actual fan edge shows, or it can be onset so that the straight braided edge is also visible. Approximately 20-30mm ($\frac{3}{4}$-$1\frac{1}{4}$in) in depth, it is often two tone in colour.

Double fan edging is not used as much as fan edging as the effect is heavier, but once again it is a very pretty finish.

Block fringe is about 4-10cm ($1\frac{1}{2}$-4in) deep and is a smart finish for the leading edges of curtains and the bases of valances and blinds. It is often made as a two- or three- colour fringe.

Bullion fringe is a thick fringe made from twisted drops of yarn usually 10-15cms (4-6in) long. It is used for trimming swags and tails, valances and sometimes the hems of curtains. It gives a sumptuous, rich finish to a window treatment.

Tassel fringe Tassels are tied onto a braid giving a more delicate fringe than bullion fringe. It can be used to trim valances, swags and tails, and sometimes cushions.

Bobble fringe A short fringe with bobbles made out of cotton, or sometimes wool. Cotton bobble fringe can look very effective on light-weight muslin and cotton sheer curtains

Button tuft A small bow of yarn. They can be sewn to the base of the goblet or French pleats and can also be used to trim cushions. They are traditionally used on bed mattresses.

Bolster tassel A small tassel sewn onto a braided circle. They are attractive when placed between swags and can also be used to trim tie-backs.

FRILL DESIGN

Frills are a pretty, light finish to window treatments. They can be used along the base of valances, on the leading edges of curtains, on tie-backs and cushions, and even along the hem of swags and tails. Austrian blinds look attractive with frills along the hem and the sides. Frills should be twice to three times fullness and 8-10cm (3-4in) deep. They are either inset into a seam or onset on top of the fabric.

ILLUSTRATED NOTES

Page 44
A In-set gathered frill with contrast piping.

B In-set gathered double frill with contrast piping. The under frill is also in a contrasting fabric.

C In-set and gathered frill with contrast-bound lower edge and contrast piping.

D In-set gathered frill with a pinked edge. Pinking gives a light finish.

E On-set gathered frill with the gathering set down to create a pretty finish to the top of the frill.

F On-set gathered frill with pinked top and bottom edges.

G On-set gathered frill with contrast-bound lower edge.

H On-set gathered double frill with pinked lower edges. The underneath frill is in a contrasting fabric.

Page 45

A In-set knife-pleated frill with contrast piping.

B In-set box-pleated frill with contrast piping.

C In-set knife-pleated frill with contrast piping and a contrast-bound lower edge.

D In-set box-pleated frill with contrast piping and a contrast-bound lower edge.

E On-set knife-pleated frill.

F On-set box-pleated frill.

G On-set knife-pleated frill contrast-bound edges.

H On-set box-pleated frill contrast-bound edges.

CURTAIN AND VALANCE HEADINGS

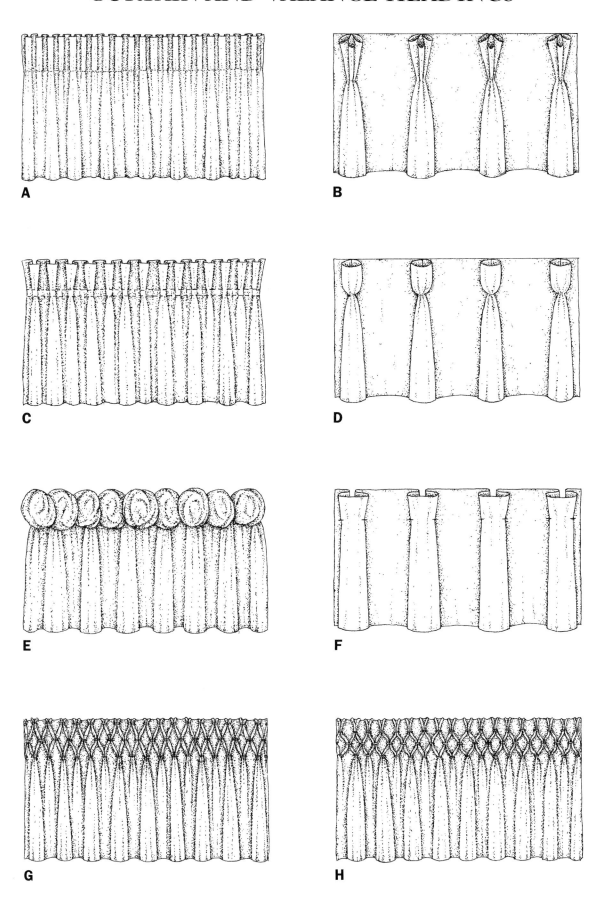

A

B

C

D

E

F

G

H

CURTAIN AND VALANCE HEADINGS

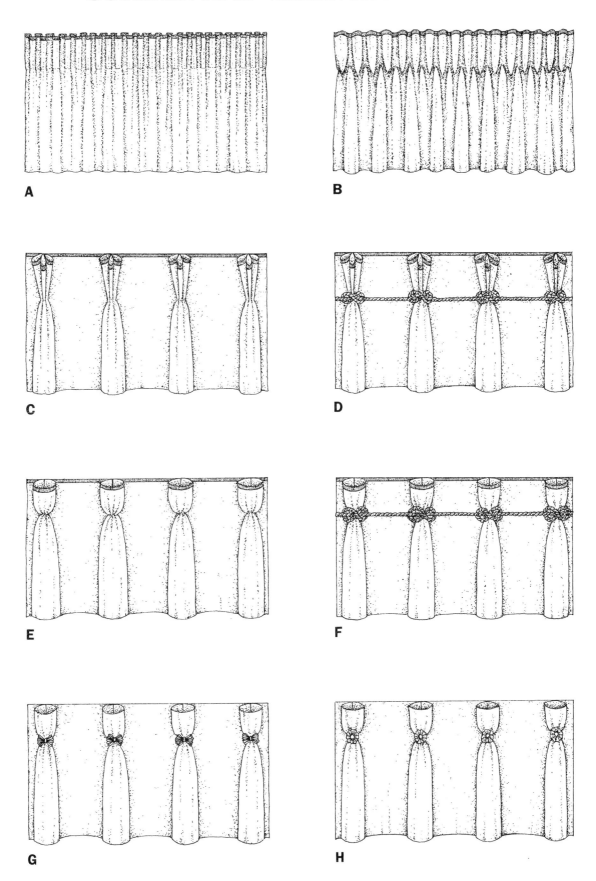

A

B

C

D

E

F

G

H

HEADINGS FOR POLES

A

B

C

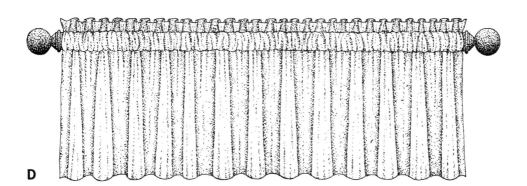

D

HEADINGS FOR POLES

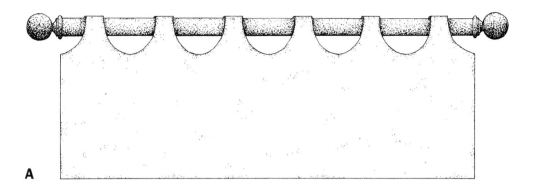

A

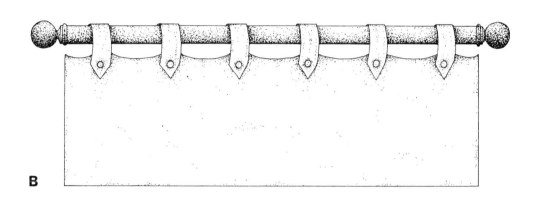

B

C

D

TIE-BACK DESIGNS

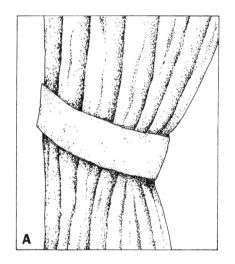

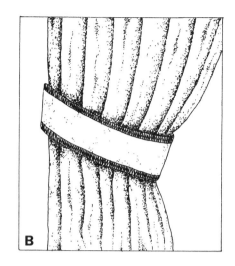

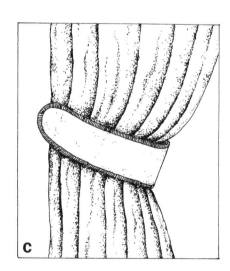

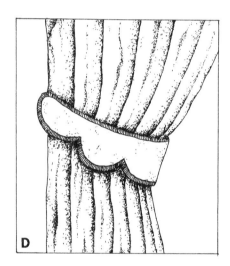

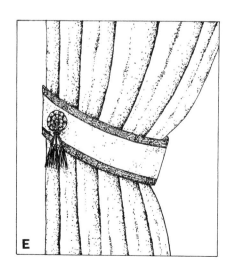

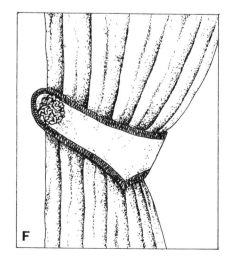

TIE-BACK DESIGNS

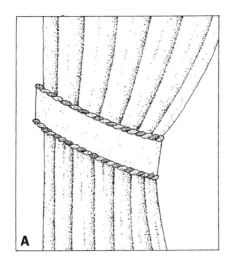

A

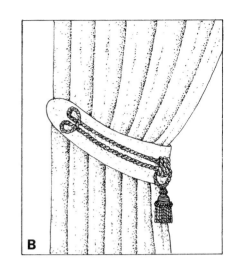

B

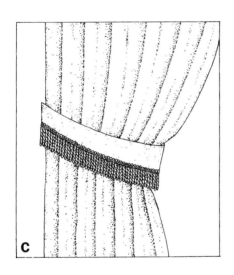

C

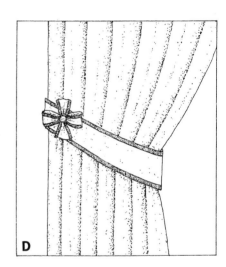

D

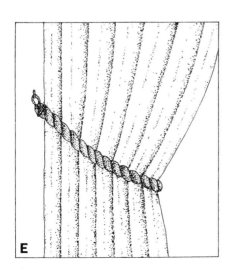

E

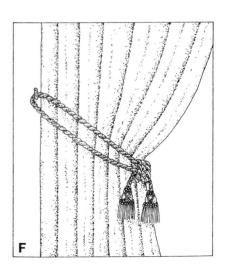

F

TIE-BACK DESIGNS

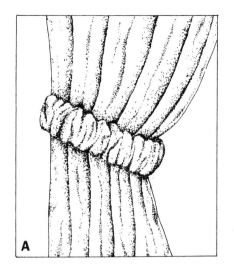

A

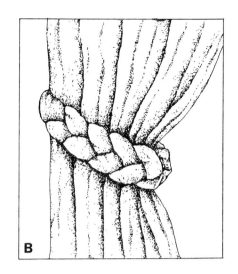

B

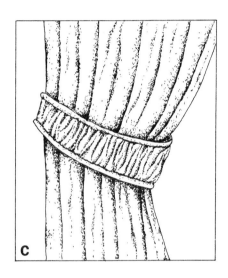

C

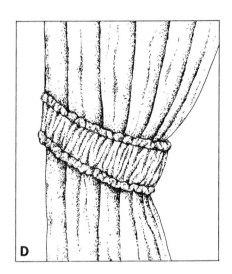

D

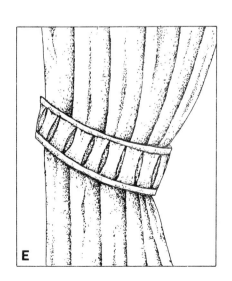

E

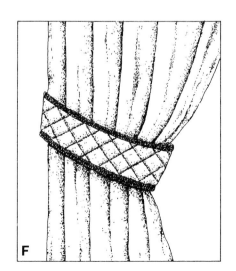

F

TIE-BACK DESIGNS

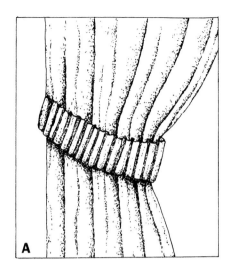

A

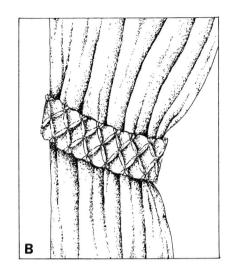

B

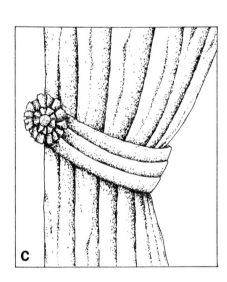

C

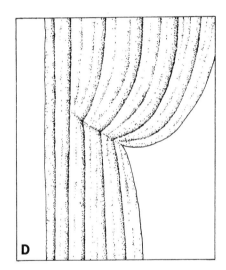

D

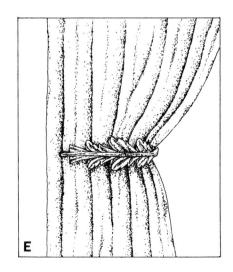

E

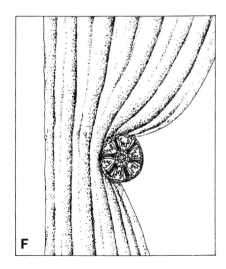

F

FABRIC TRIMS

Rosette

Chou

Tiered rosette

Bow

Trefoil

Maltese cross

Bow with tails

Contrast bound trefoil

Contrast bound Maltese cross

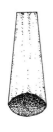

Trumpet

Decorative tail

Flute

Rosette and trumpet

Coronet and small tail with rope

Contrast bound trefoil with flute

PASSEMENTERIE

Rope

Flanged rope

Braid

Fan edging

Double fan edging

Block fringe

Bullion fringe

Tassel fringe

Bobble fringe

Button tuft

Bolster tassel

FRILL DESIGNS

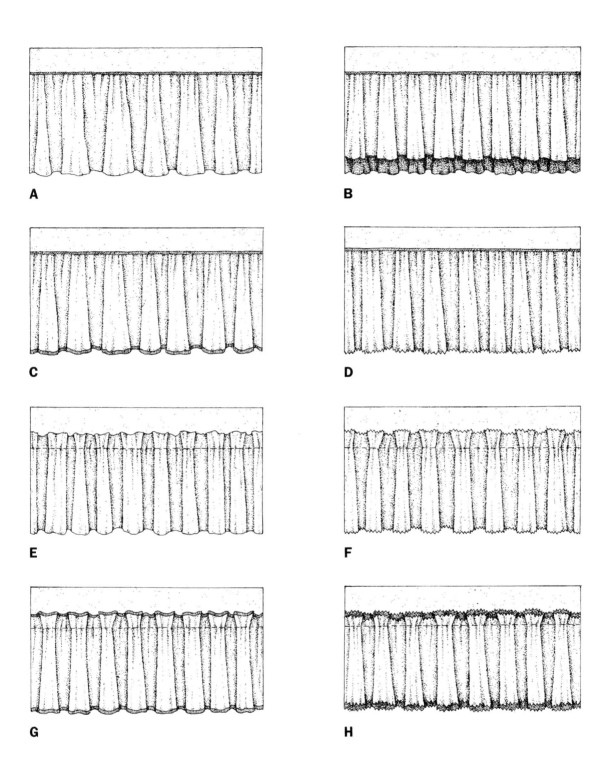

A

B

C

D

E

F

G

H

FRILL DESIGNS

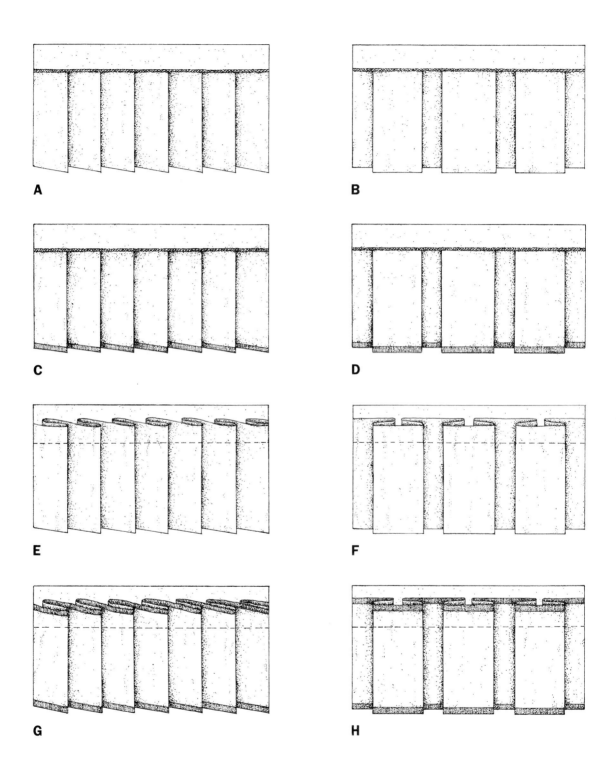

A

B

C

D

E

F

G

H

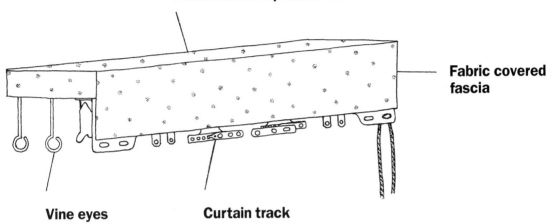

Fabric covered pelmet board

Fabric covered fascia

Vine eyes

Curtain track

Attach the hardboard or buckram fascia to the front of the wooden pelmet board with nails or tacks. Cover neatly with a strip of fabric, turning in all the raw edges and staple in place. Screw the curtain track onto the pelmet board directly behind the facsia making sure that the gliders run freely below it. Screw vine eyes into the ends of the board. These enable the curtains to be wrapped around the ends of the board, and allowing the curtains to return to the wall, to exclude light and draughts.

The covered lath is secured to the wall with angle brackets in the same way as a pelmet board.

FABRIC-COVERED LATHS

DESIGN BENEFITS
- A smart and discreet method of concealing the curtain track
- Do not restrict light
- Good treatment when no dead wall space above window
- Can be ceiling fixed

Curtains hung from a covered pelmet board and fascia are a simple but smart window treatment which can be fitted to both small and large windows. On a pelmet board with a fascia attached to the front edge, the track is top-fixed onto the underside of the board just behind the fascia. The fascia is made from a narrow strip of either pelmet buckram or hardboard, roughly 4.5cm (1¾in) in depth.

The pelmet board and fascia can be covered either in curtain fabric or with wallpaper. The fascia only conceals the track; the gliders hang below it which allows the curtain free movement. The top of the curtain should be flush with the top of the fascia and the curtain hooks should be set down approximately 7cm (3in) from the top of the curtains.

The usual width of the pelmet board is 10cm (4in). However, where for example full length curtains are to be hung in front of large radiator covers, the pelmet board can be up to 20cm (8in) wide to allow the curtains to hang vertically.

Fitting fabric-covered laths
A fabric-covered lath is fitted in the same manner as a pelmet board. They are especially suited if there is little or no wall area above the window as pelmet boards are only 5cm (2in) in depth. In recessed areas, the pelmet board and fascia can be fitted flush to the ceiling.

ILLUSTRATION NOTES

Page 48
French-headed curtains hung from a fabric-covered pelmet board and fascia, with a 1cm (½in) contrast-bound top and 2cm (¾in) contrast-bound leading edges. The curtains are held by contrast bound tie-backs. The spaces between the French pleats are dressed forward.

Page 49
Goblet-headed curtains hung from a fabric-covered pelmet board and fascia. They have a 1cm (½in) contrast-bound top and 2cm (¾in) contrast-bound leading edges, held by contrast-bound tie-backs. Spaces between the goblet pleats are dressed forward, a simple smart treatment.

Page 50
Puff-headed curtains hung from a fabric-covered pelmet board and fascia and held by tie-backs. As the puff heading does not stack back well it is essential to use tie-backs. The puff heading gives a softer look than a pleated heading.

Page 51
French-headed curtains hung from a fabric-covered pelmet board and fascia with 5cm (2in) contrast-bound leading edges which have piping inset in the seams. The curtains are held by scalloped tie-backs which have been piped in a contrasting fabric. The spaces between the French pleats are dressed forward.

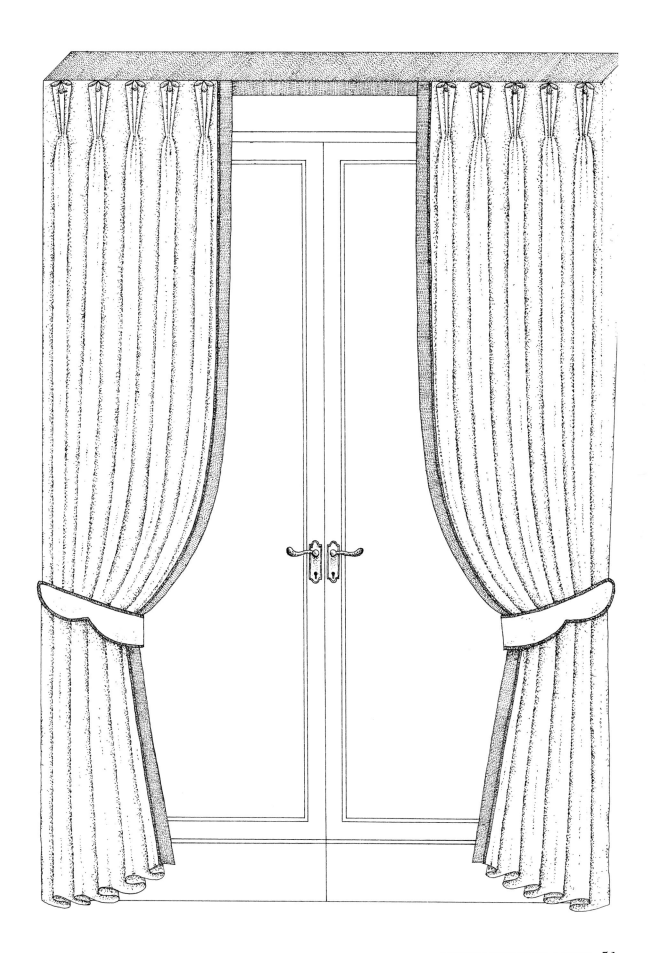

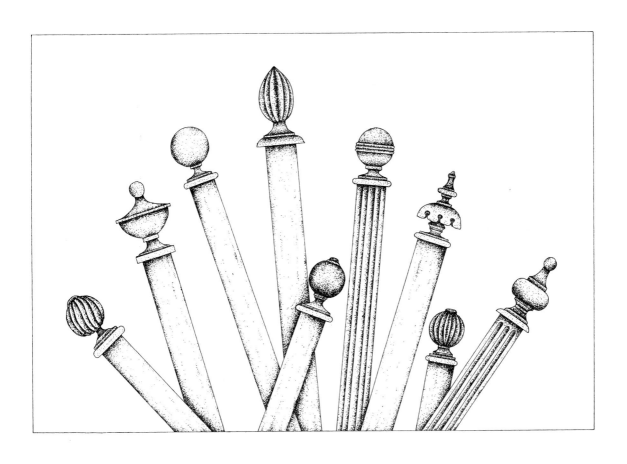

POLES

DESIGN BENEFITS
- A simple window treatment
- Do not restrict light
- Good treatment when no dead wall space above window
- Suitable for most types of room

Poles are a decorative, versatile curtain fitting, suitable for all types of rooms and sizes of windows. They can be made from thin iron, brass or wood dowelling. The dowelling can be painted, stained or gilded, and even reeded as well.

The type of pole used can set the mood and tone of the room so the design and diameter of the pole should be in keeping with the style and proportion of the interior.

If the pole is extended beyond the window frame, light will not be restricted provided that the curtain heading chosen draws back well. Tape-headed curtains and curtains with hand-sewn French and goblet pleats will stack back well.

The spaces between the hand-sewn French and goblet pleats should be dressed backwards when the curtains are stacked back. Hand-gathered, smocked, puff and box- pleated headed curtains will not draw back far and will usually need to be held open by tie-backs.

Other more informal headings include curtains simply tied or looped onto the pole, rings sewn directly onto the curtain, and café curtain headings (illustrated on pages 36 and 37).

There are different types of brackets available to enable poles to be fitted into a recess or to a ceiling or sloping wall as well as in the conventional manner.

Poles are a sensible option for French doors where a pole can be extended beyond the frame, leaving room for the doors to be opened freely without touching the curtains when they are stacked back.

Curtains hung from poles can be enhanced with contrast-bound leading edges which will emphasise the elegant vertical lines and counterbalance the horizontal line of the pole. The tops of the curtains can also be defined with a contrast binding.

Fitting poles
Poles should be fixed either to the height of the window architrave or 10-15cm (4-6in) above the architrave or soffit and should be extended either side of the window so that the curtains stack back over the wall rather than over the window.

If the pole is to be extended either side of the window with a deep architrave and the brackets are to be fixed to the wall, mount the brackets on wooden blocks as deep as the architrave, to allow the rings free movement along the pole.

ILLUSTRATION NOTES

Page 52
Poles and finials, reading from left to right at the top of the page.

Twisted ball gadroon finial
Cup and orb finial
Plain ball finial
Pointed gadroon finial
Button ball end finial
Ribbed ball finial on a reeded pole
Inverted cup and orb finial
Ball gadroon finial
Ball and orb finial on a reeded pole

Reading from left to right at the bottom of the page.

Mediaeval finial
Arrow finial
Flight finial
Pineapple finial
Mediaeval finial
Acanthus finial
Spear finial
Acorn finial
Mediaeval finial

Page 57
Pencil-gathered curtains hung from a pole and held by ombras. If the pencil gathers have been hand-sewn the curtains will not stack back well, but tape pencil gathers will stack back well. A very understated curtain treatment which focuses attention on to the decorative finials and ombras.

Page 58
Curtains with smocked heading dropped 5cm (2in) down from top. 1cm (½in) contrast-bound top and 2cm (¾in) leading edge. Held open by straight contrast-bound smocked tie-backs.

Page 59
Puff-headed curtains hung from a pole and held by ruched tie-backs. The ruched tie-backs combine well with the puff heading. The puff heading does not draw back far so it is better to use tie-backs.

Page 60
French-headed curtains hung from a pole. The curtains have 1cm (½in) contrast-bound tops and 2cms (¾in) contrast-bound leading edges that are held by contrast bound tie-backs. The spaces between the French pleats are dressed back so that the curtains will stack back well. This simple but smart treatment works well in a large range of settings.

Page 61
Goblet-headed curtains hung from a pole. The curtains have 1cm (½in) contrast-bound tops and 2cm (¾in) contrast-bound leading edges and are held by banana-shaped contrast-piped tie-backs. Knotted rope has been sewn at the base of each pleat. The knotted rope adds depth to the treatment and emphasises the goblet heading. Surprisingly perhaps, this treatment works well in most situations.

Page 62
Box-pleat headed curtains hung from a pole and held back by box-pleated tie-backs with bound edges. As they will not draw back very far, it is essential to have tie-backs.

Page 63
Top pinched-pleated headed curtains, hung from a pole and held back by rope tie-backs. Bobble fringe sewn down leading edge. Unusual but classic heading.

Page 64
Single curtain with hand-sewn rings and very little fullness. Attached triangles of fabric sewn between the rings, with tassels sewn at the tip of the triangle. 4cm (1½in) contrast-binding along side edges and

hem. The curtain is held open by a barrier rope tie-back. Size of triangles can be varied. Heading shown to best advantage when drawn across the window.

Page 65

One curtain hung onto the pole with fabric loops and permanently held by rope. This is a purely decorative, non-functional curtain. Here, the French doors would need to open outwards.

Page 66

Simple curtains hung from an iron pole. The rings have been sewn directly on to the curtains, to hold the small pleats. The curtains are permanently held by high rope tie-backs.

Page 67

A French-headed door curtain hung from a portiere rod and held by a double tassel tie-back. When the door is opened, the curtain will move with the door.

Page 68

A channel-headed curtain pushed onto a pole, with a small stand-up frill. It is held by a brass curtain band. The pole has been finished with dramatic arrow and flight finials. As the pole is not visible it can be inexpensive wood dowelling.

Page 69

Sill length curtains with a short attached gathered valance. The curtains are hung on an iron pole and held back by small tie-backs. Tie-backs are a sensible idea for curtains which hang over a sink.

Page 70

French-headed curtains hung from a pole with an attached valance trimmed with bullion fringe. The curtains are held by plain tie-backs trimmed with bullion fringe. This is a useful treatment where a valance is required but there is no dead wall space above the window to accommodate it. A minimal amount of light is lost with this valance treatment.

Page 71

French-headed curtains hung from a pole with swags and balloon tails attached at the base of the heading and finished with choux rosettes. This is one possible method of using sumptuous swags and tails where there is no dead wall space above the window.

Page 72

Goblet-headed curtains hung from a pole with an attached valance trimmed with a knife-pleated frill. The curtains are held by piped banana-shaped tie-backs. This is another useful treatment where a valance is required but there is no dead wall space above the window to accommodate it. A minimal amount of light is lost with this valance treatment. As an alternative heading the valance could have been pencil gathered.

Page 73

Curtains hung from a pole with a small pleated attached valance with a 1cm ($\frac{1}{2}$in) contrast binding at the base of the valance and on the leading edges. They are held by contrast bound tie-backs. These curtains are smart but informal.

Page 74

Curtains tied onto a pole and held open by simple ties. These are purely decorative curtains, as they would not draw backwards or forwards well. They give an informal, light look.

Page 75

Curtains lashed onto a metal pole with rope which is threaded through eyelets. The curtains are held open by a rope tie. Another informal look that is decorative rather than functional.

Page 76
Dramatic curtains with very little fullness in them, hung from a metal pole. The rings have been sewn onto the curtains. The curtains are joined in the middle and then held open by high rope tie-backs.

Page 77
Tab-headed curtains hung from a metal pole with a 10cm (4in) contrast set in (between first and second tabs) from the leading edges and hems. Curtains held open by metal curtain bands. Tab headings are more suitable for curtains that are occasionally opened and closed. Should not be over full.

Page 78
Tab-headed curtains hung from a metal pole. Webbing has been sewn along the top and leading edges and hems. Tabs have also been made out of webbing. Tab headings are more suitable for curtains that are occasionally opened and closed. Should not be over full.

Page 79
Tab-headed curtains hung from a metal pole. Eyelets have been punched on all four edges, and rope inserted. Tab headings are more suitable for curtains that are occasionally opened and closed. Should not be over full.

Page 80
Tape-headed curtains hung from a pole. The curtains have 1cm (½in) check contrast-bound tops, wide contrast-bound leading edges continue round into lining. Held by check fabric ties.

Page 81
Check goblet-headed curtains hung from a pole. The curtains also have wide check contrast-bound leading edges and hems. Held by check fabric ties.

Page 82
Tape-headed curtains hung from a pole. The curtains have 1cm (½in) contrast-bound tops, fan-edge fringe sewn onto leading edges.

Page 83
Curtains with rings sewn onto them and hand-sewn rope along the top and the leading edge. They are held by ombras. These curtains have a simple, traditional look and should not be over full.

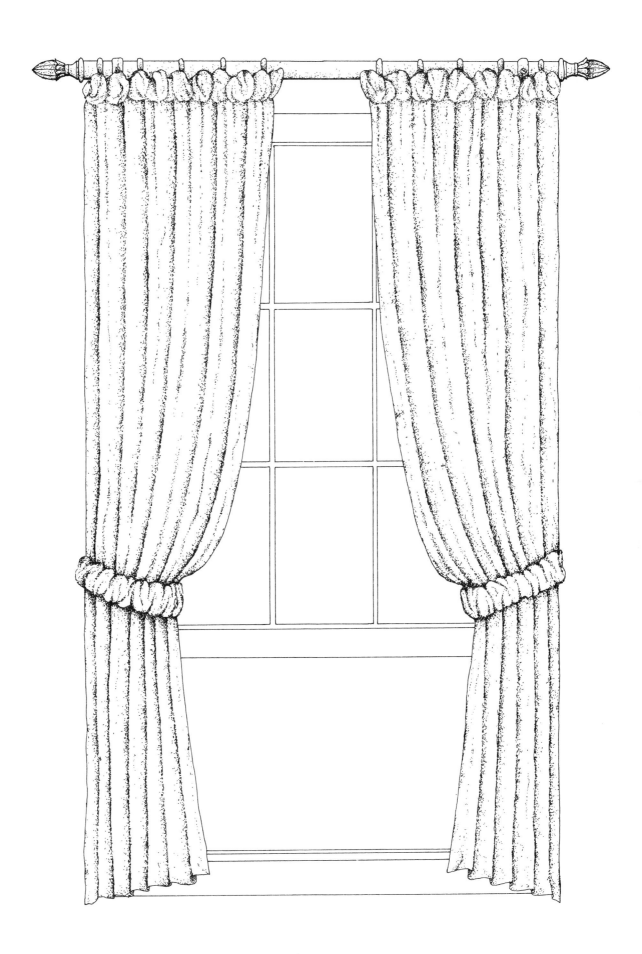

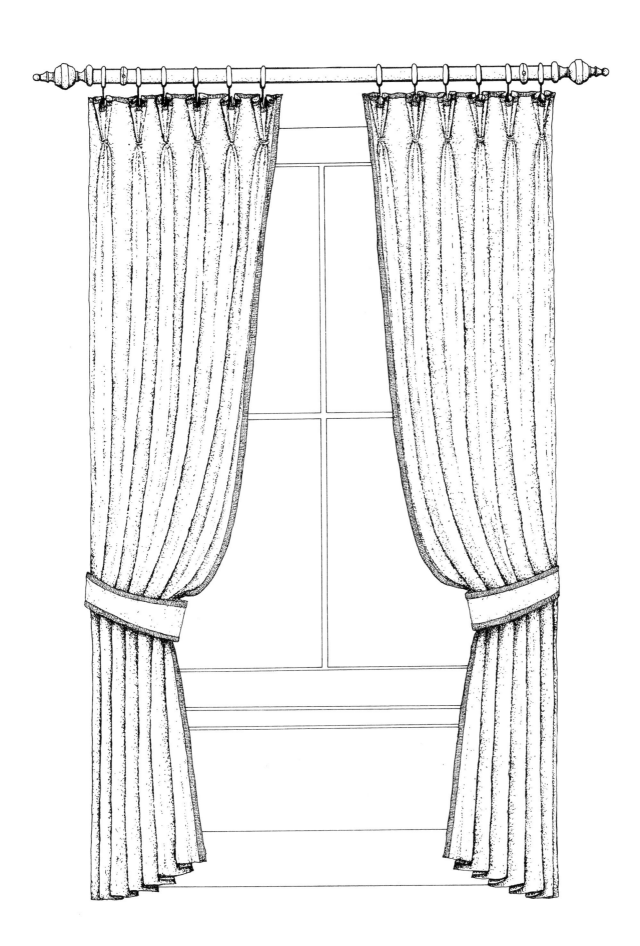

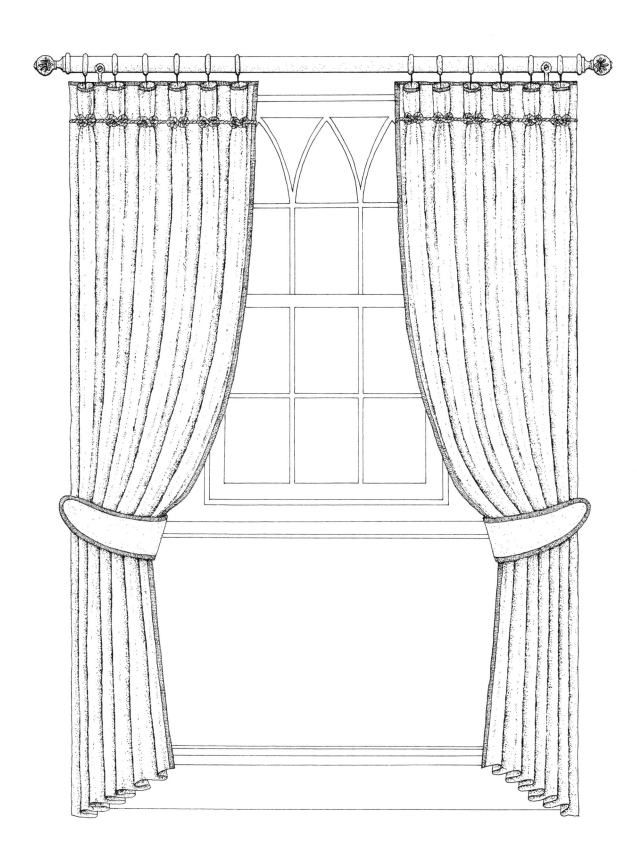

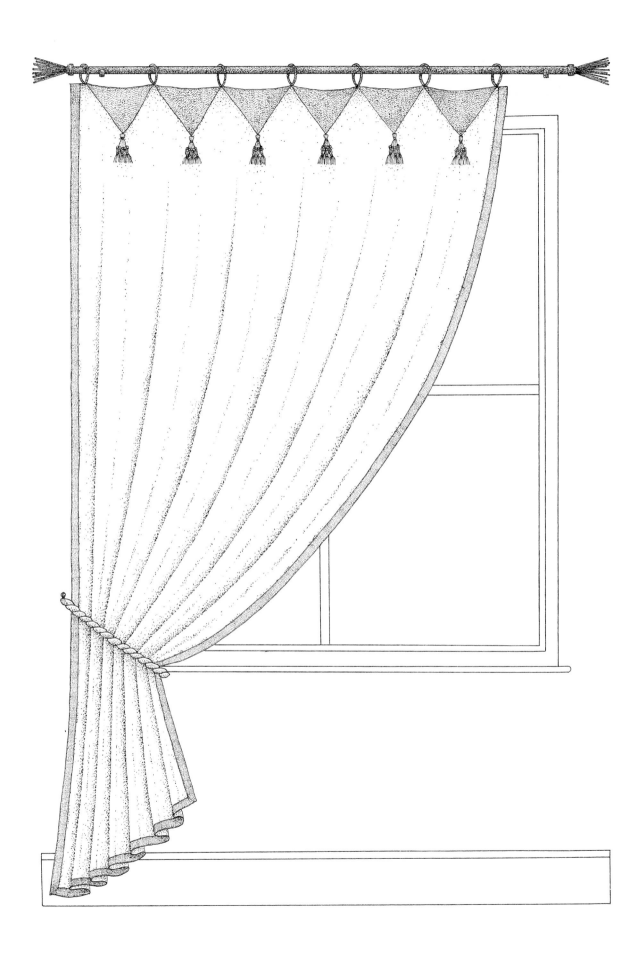

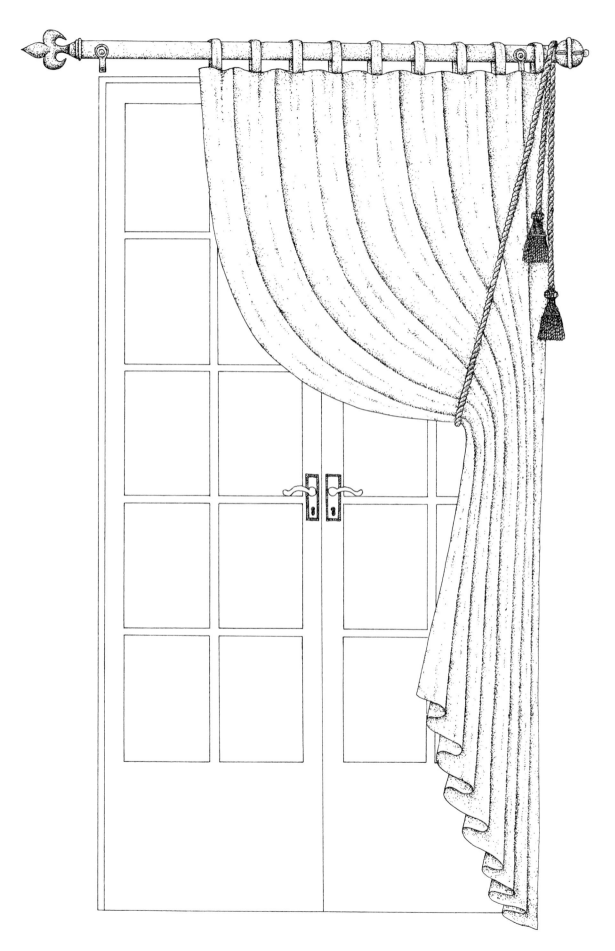

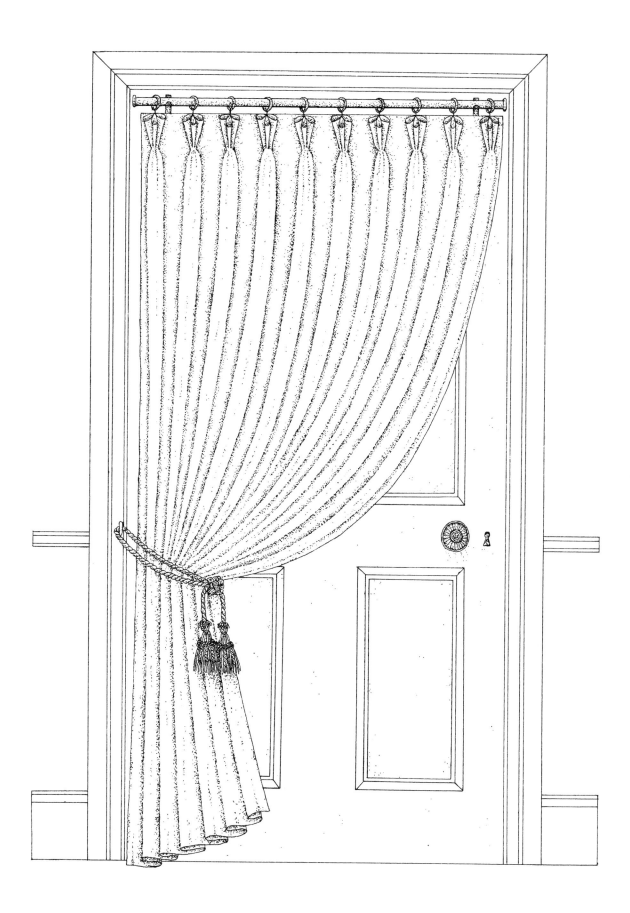

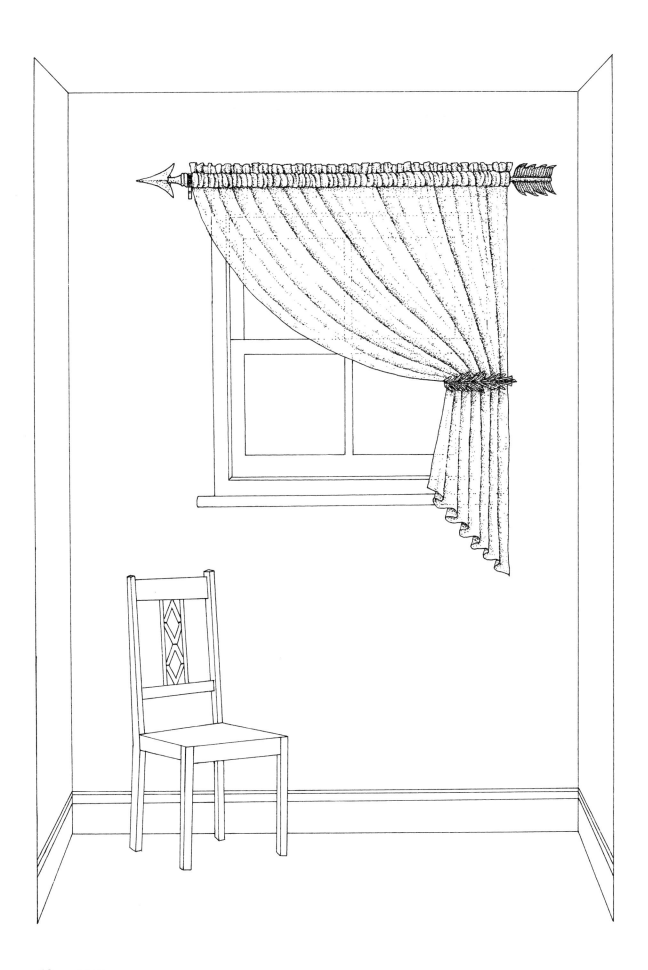

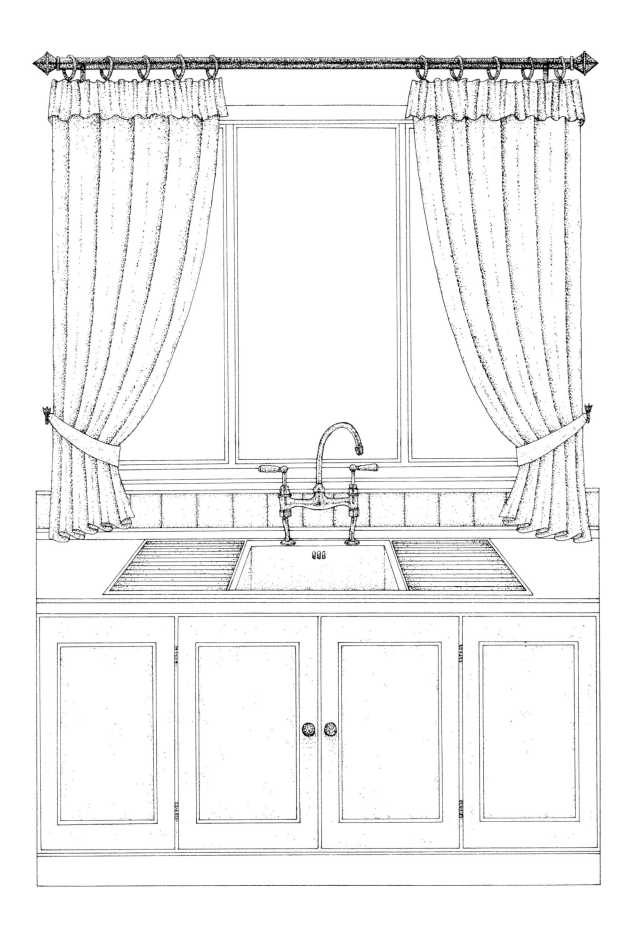

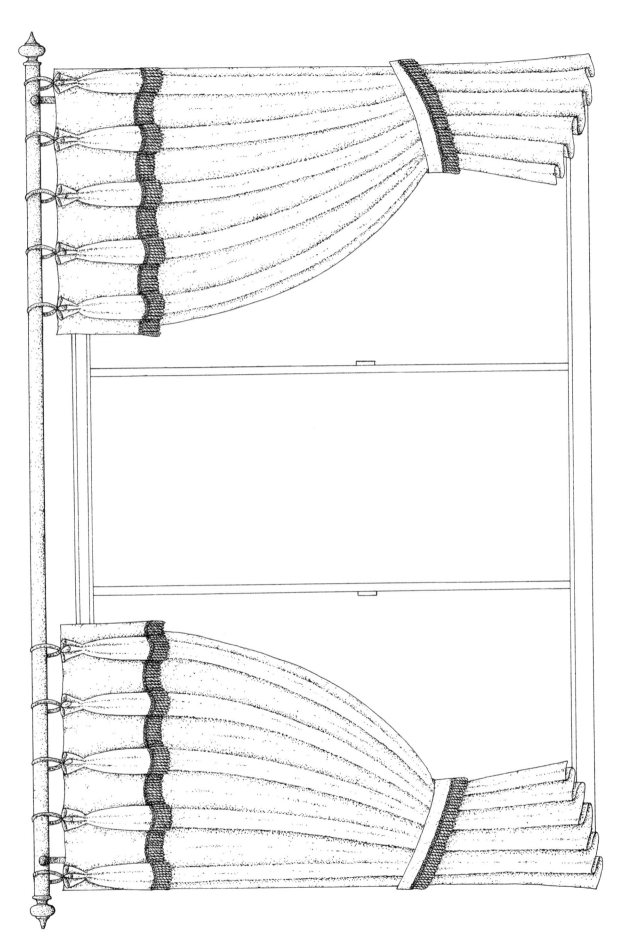

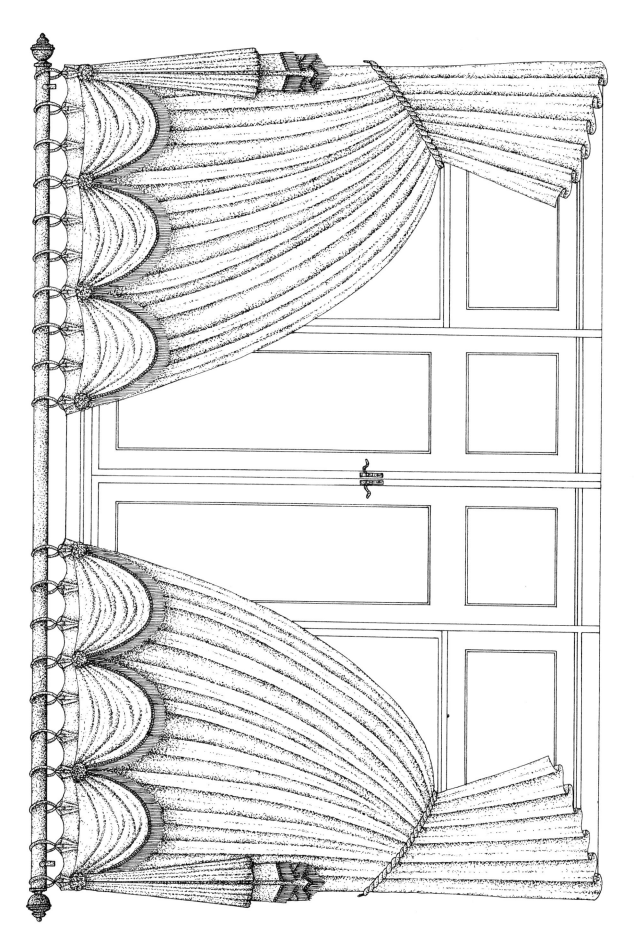

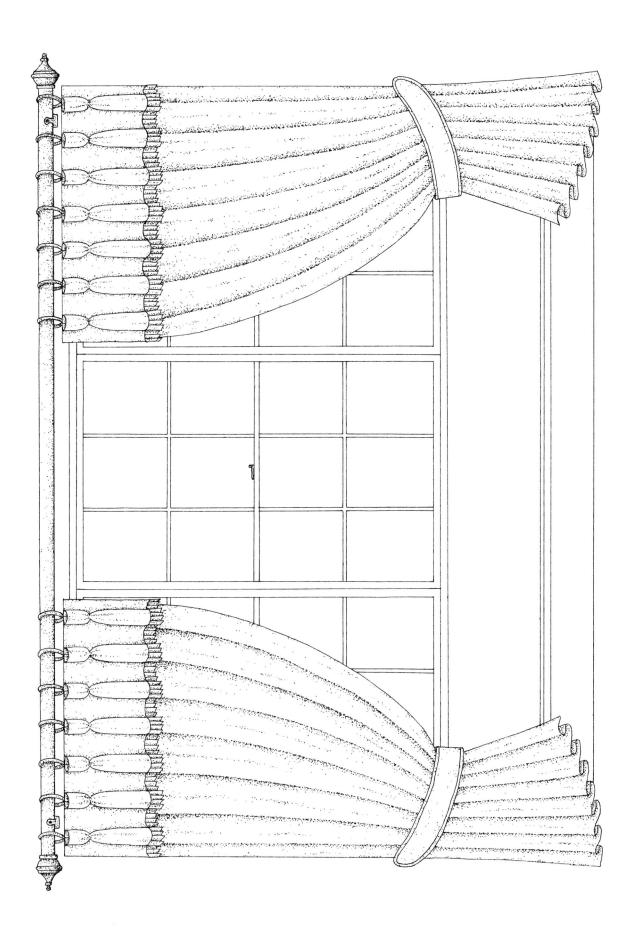

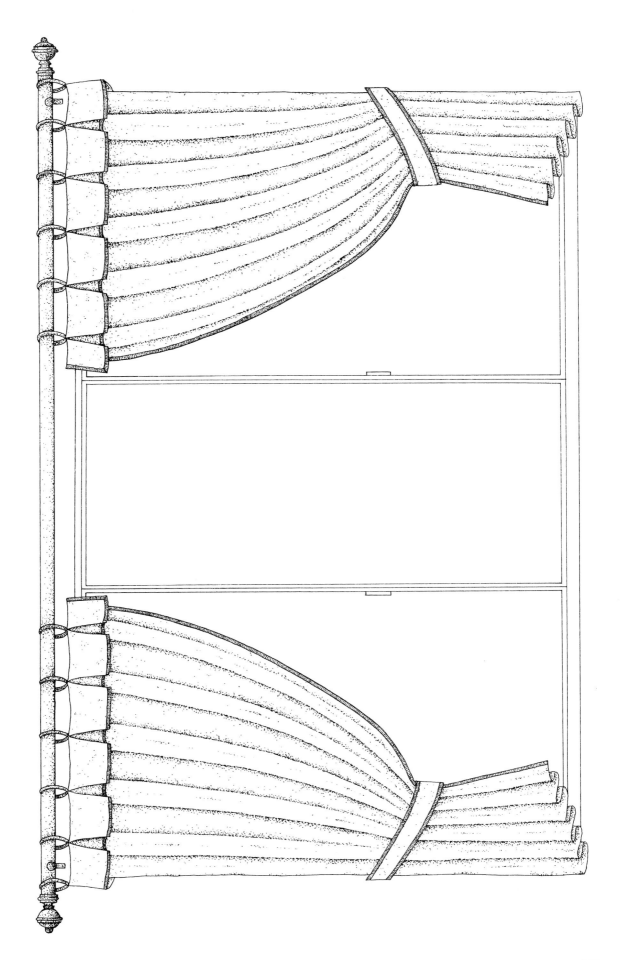

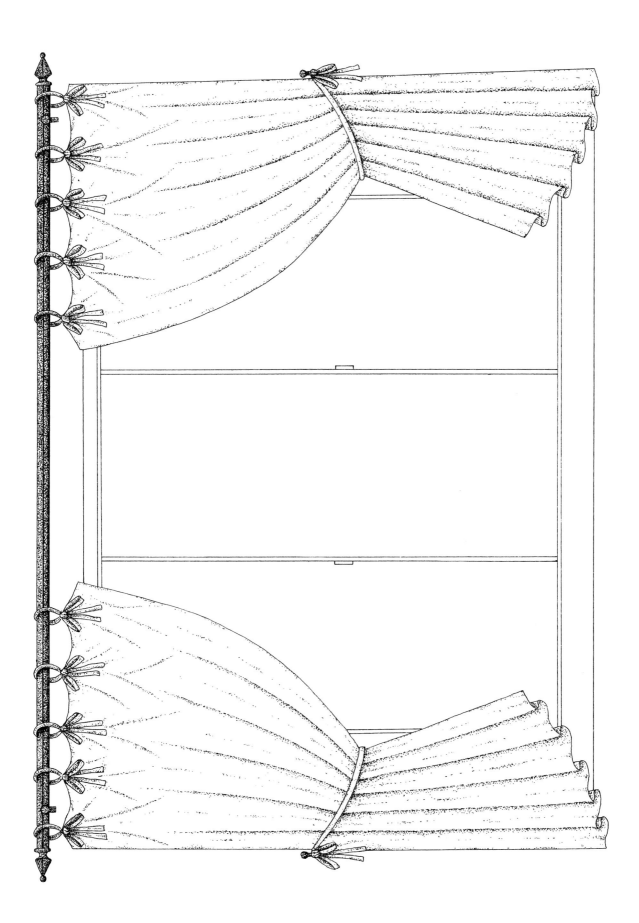

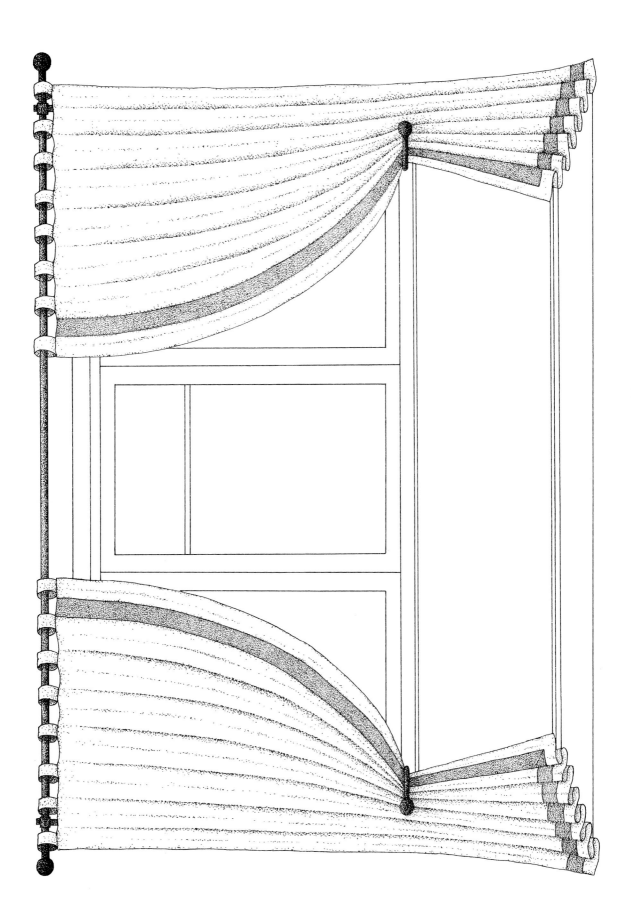

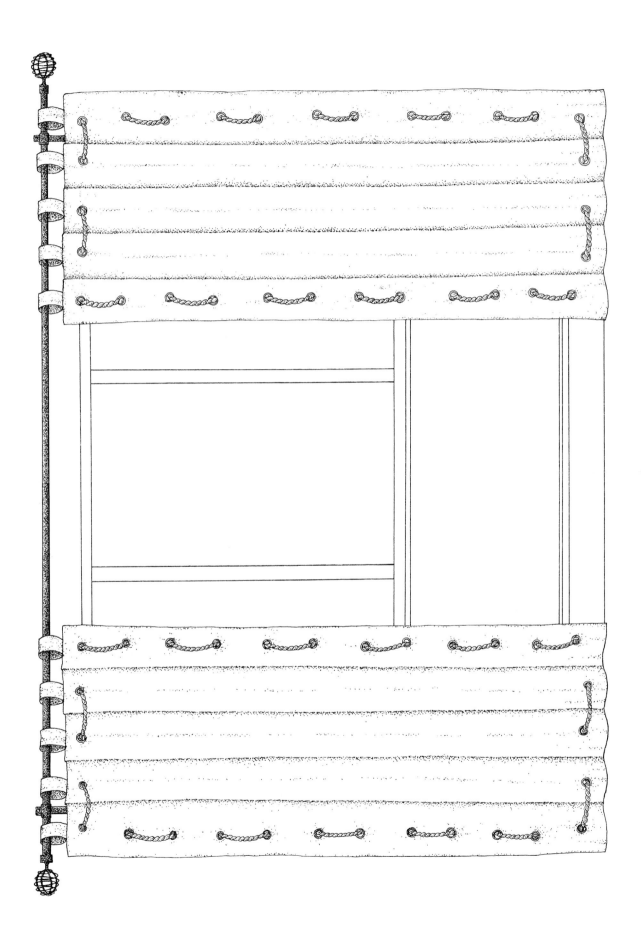

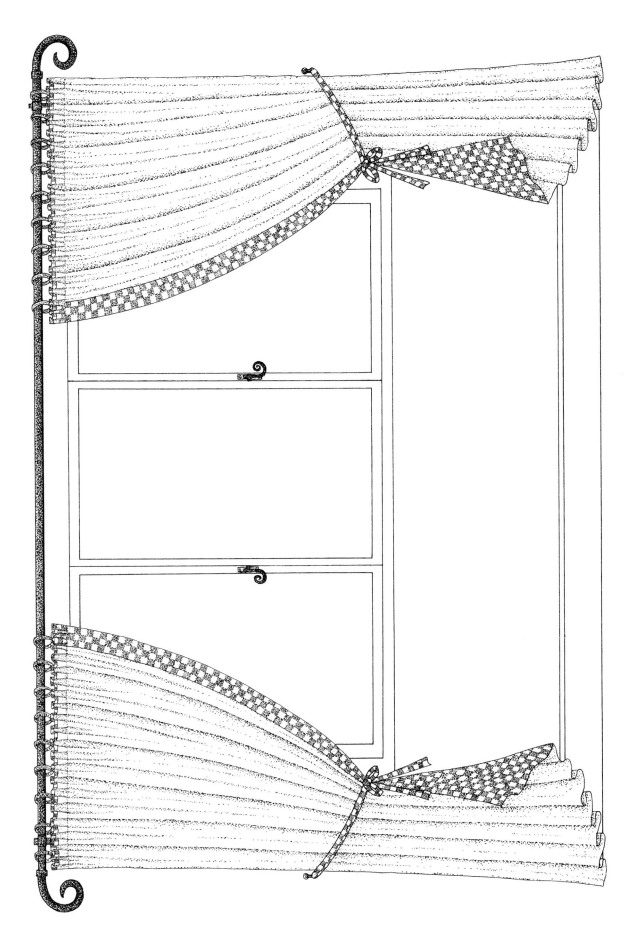

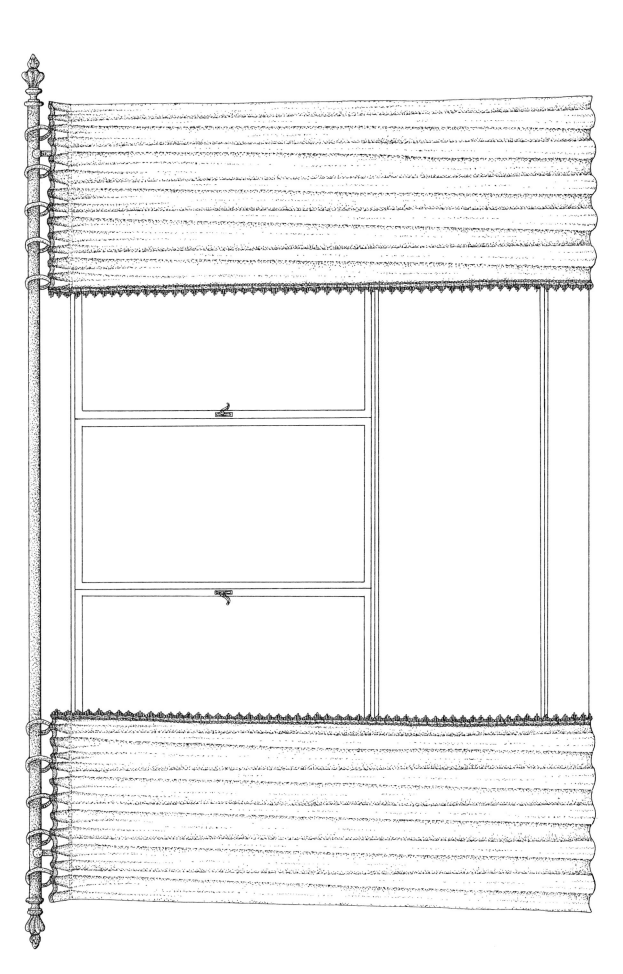

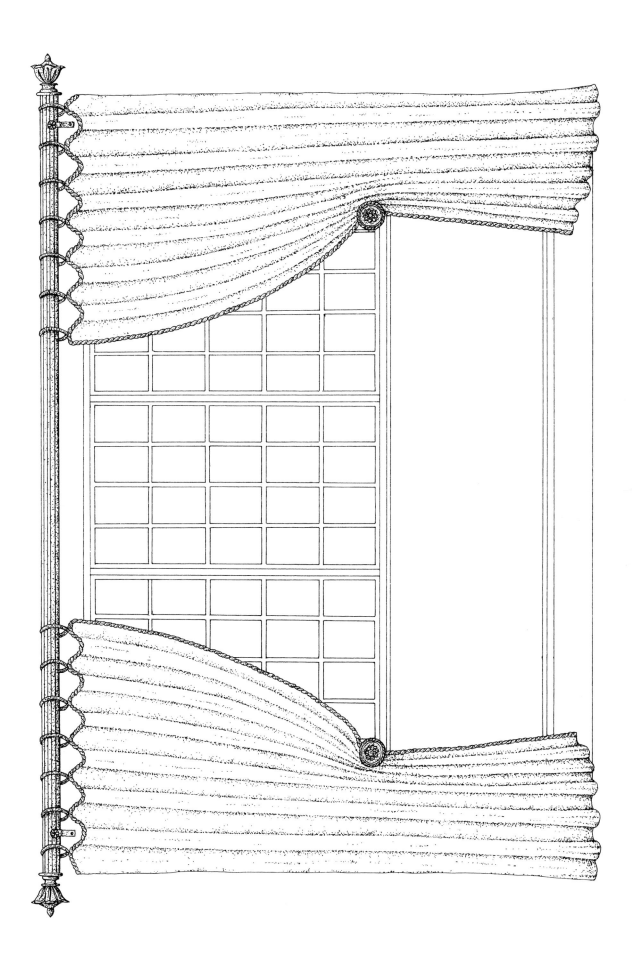

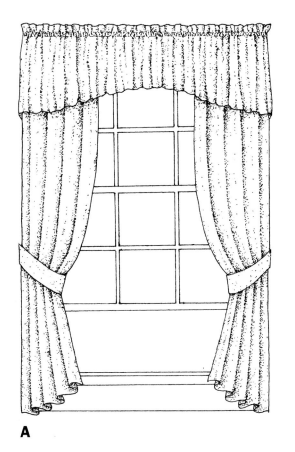

A

B

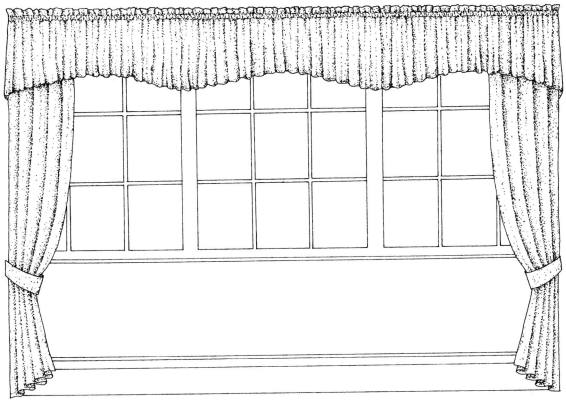

C

VALANCES

- Soft treatment
- The lower edge of the valance can be serpentined
- Can utilise the dead wall space above a window
- Headings that do not draw back can be used

Valances give a soft finish to a window treatment and, depending on the choice of headings and trims used, are suitable for all types of room. A valance is a gathered or pleated pelmet which is hung from the front edge of the pelmet board. It conceals the track and curtain heading.

If there is dead wall space above the window, the pelmet board can be placed above the window frame to make the window appear taller and therefore more elegant. This will also allow more light into the room.

Arched-shaped valances look attractive on tall windows. As the deepest part of the valance falls over the curtain stack-back area, there should be no extra loss of light. For wide windows such as patio windows, the lower edge of the valance can be serpentined. This has the effect of softening the horizontal line of the window and adds extra interest to the design.

Valances offer a splendid opportunity to use the hand-sewn headings that do not draw back and so are often considered unsuitable for curtains. Gathered and smocked headings give a light pretty look, while French- and goblet-pleated headings give a smart tailored appearance.

The base of the pleats can be trimmed with knotted rope or button tufts. The design of the heading and the hem of the valance can be further defined with narrow contrast binding which is most effective, especially on arched and serpentined hem lines. An alternative treatment for the hem is a fringe. Bullion fringe will add visual weight to the hem line, while a block fringe has a lighter appearance and a fan edging creates a soft, subtle finish.

Fringe detailing is an opportunity to use a plain fabric for the window treatment and to incorporate the colours within the room in the fringe.

For a design variation, sew gathered or box-pleated valances onto a flat yoke.

For an elegant finish, valances can be hung from curved or scallop-shaped pelmet boards which give the curtain treatment an interesting three-dimensional look.

Proportions
The proportions of a valance are vital to the success of the design. In a room with a low ceiling the finished length of a valance should be $\frac{1}{6}$ th of the curtain length. However, in a room with a high ceiling, the finished length of a valance should be $\frac{1}{5}$ th of the curtain length. A valance that is too short will look unbalanced in relation to the size of the window.

For an arched or serpentined valance, the shortest point should be no less than $\frac{1}{6}$ th of the curtain length. For tall windows the shortest point can be up to $\frac{1}{5}$ th of the curtain length.

For a soft serpentined shape, the difference between the longest and shortest points can be 10-15cm (4-6in). For a dramatic arched valance, the sides can be twice the length of the centre point.

For box-pleated and gathered valances which are attached to flat yokes at the top, the yokes should be ¼ to ⅓ of the total finished length of the valance.

Fitting valances

The pelmet board from which the curtains and valance is hung, is cut from planed timber 19-22mm (¾in) thick. It should be either painted or covered in lining or curtain fabric.

If possible the pelmet boards should be placed up to the coving or cornice in order to heighten the window treatment and to avoid an unattractive gap between the top of the valance and the coving.

Check that the proposed depth of the valance will cover the soffit or architrave at the top of the window and adjust the height of the pelmet board down if necessary.

Pelmet boards are usually 13-15cm (5-6in) wide with the track set 5-8cm (2-3in) back from the front edge of the board to allow the curtains free movement behind the valance. Pelmet boards can be up to 25cm (10in) wide in order to enable the curtains to clear radiators, for example, but if they are any wider they will look heavy and intrusive.

The pelmet board is secured to the wall using angle brackets, just like a shelf. For pelmet boards over 170cm (67in) in length, a centre bracket is required. This will prevent the wood from bowing and support the weight of the curtains and the valance.

The curtain track is then fitted to the underside of the pelmet board. If necessary use plastic or wood spacers between track and board to create a gap for angle brackets to be slotted through.

There are two methods of attaching valances to a pelmet board. Netting staples (into which the valance hooks can be placed) can be fixed every 10cm (4in) along the front edge of the board. Alternatively the teasel/hook side of a strip of Velcro can be attached to the front edge of the board with a staple gun, and the opposite side of the Velcro strip can be sewn onto the valance heading. (Some heading tapes have a brushed surface that will adhere directly onto the teasel side of the Velcro). This method ensures that the valance is taut against the front edge of board to give a clean finish.

A curved or scallop-shaped pelmet board is a simple and effective way of enhancing the design of a valance, as on pages 102-5. Also see serpentine-shaped pelmet boards, pages 123-4. These pelmet boards can be cut from either planed timber or medium density fibreboard. The depth of the curve should be proportionate to the height of the window, for example, 25-30cm (10-12in) deep for an average window and up to 35cm (14in) deep for tall windows. As the pelmet board is quite deep in the centre it is a useful device to enable full length curtains to be hung in front of a deep radiator.

ILLUSTRATION NOTES

Page 84
Three types of shaped valances.

A A gently shaped arch that gives a soft subtle effect.

B A deeply shaped arched valance which is more dramatic and needs a slightly taller window. The deepest part of the valance falls over the stack-back area and so incurs no extra loss of light.

C A serpentined valance on a wide window, shaped to correspond with the layout of the window glass. The shaped hem of the valance softens the harsh horizontal lines of the window.

Page 91

Set-down gathered-headed valance with a 1cm (½in) contrast-bound top. The lower edge of the valance and the leading edges of the curtains have been trimmed with inset fan edging. Contrast binding is an effective alternative to the fan edging.

Page 92

Smocked-headed arch-shaped valance with 2.5cm (1in) contrast-bound lower edge. The curtains have 2cm (¾in) contrast-bound leading edges and held by contrast-piped, scalloped tie-backs.

Page 93

Pencil-gathered valance with a frill which is contrast bound on both edges. The curtains are held back by contrast-piped, scalloped tie-backs. A very pretty treatment, particularly for bedrooms.

Page 94

Puff-headed, arch-shaped valance with a 2.5cm (1in) contrast-bound lower edge. The curtains have contrast-bound leading edges and are held by ruched tie-backs made up in the contrasting fabric.

Page 95

Set-down gathered-headed valance with a 1cm (½in) contrast-bound top. The lower edge of the valance has been serpentined and trimmed with inset fan edging. The scalloped tie-backs are trimmed with inset fan edging. This valance could be adapted for wide windows.

Page 96

Gathered valance hung behind a shallow wooden cornice box. The lower edge of the valance and the leading and lower edges of the curtains are finished with a fabric border. The box could be covered in the fabric border or painted to match it.

Page 97

Box-pleated valance with check lower edge and hung from gothic-style wooden cornice box. The curtains have wide, check contrast-bound leading edges. They are hung from track which can either be top-fixed to the underside of the cornice box or face-fixed to the wall.

Page 98

Box-pleated tab-headed valance with vertical-striped, wide contrast-bound lower edge and top, tabs and ties. Curtains have horizontal-striped, wide contrast-bound leading edges. To allow the curtains to move freely, the valance pole is mounted on extended brackets, and the curtain track is face-fixed to the wall behind and below the pole. The track must be slightly narrower than the pole.

Page 99

Goblet-headed valance hung from a pole. 1cm (½in) contrast-bound top, 2cm (¾in) contrast-bound lower edge with fringe. Panels between the goblets are check fabric. Curtains have inset wide check border along the leading edges and hems with a narrower contrast border on leading edges and hems. Fringe along the leading edges. To allow the curtains to move freely, the valance pole is mounted on extended brackets, and the curtain track is face-fixed to the wall behind and below the pole. The track must be slightly narrower than the pole.

Page 100
Arch-shaped valance with dropped-down gathered heading, 1cm (½in) contrast-bound top, rope hand-sewn over the gather line. Rope clovers and tassels at either end. Lattice fringe along the lower edge. Curtains have 2cm (¾in) contrast-bound leading edge.

Page 101
Set-down gathered valance with a 1cm (½in) contrast-bound top. Knotted rope has been sewn over the gathers and the lower edge has been trimmed with bullion fringe. The curtains are held by tassel tie-backs. The gathered heading combined with the rope and deep fringe give a soft but formal effect.

Page 102
Smocked-headed valance with a contrast-piped frill, hung from a curved track and curved pelmet board. Curved boards give a pretty and elegant finish to a window treatment.

Page 103
Goblet-headed valance with a 1cm (½in) top and 2.5cm (1in) contrast-bound lower edge and rope knotted at the base of each pleat. The valance and curtains are hung from a curved pelmet board. This valance would work equally well on a straight pelmet board.

Page 104
Set-down trellis headed valance with a 1cm (½in) contrast top and fan-topped block fringe along the lower edge. The valance has been hung from a scallop-shaped pelmet board. Scallop-shaped boards give a soft elegant finish to a window treatment.

Page 105
Arched valance with a set-down gathered heading and a 1cm (½in) contrast-bound top. Rope has been sewn over the gathers and the lower edge has been trimmed with a bullion fringe. The curtains are held by barrier rope tie-backs and are hung from a curved pelmet board. The dramatic arch shaping and the curved board give a striking effect.

Page 106
Arch-shaped trumpet valance hung from a pole with a 2.5cm (1in) contrast- bound lower edge. The curtains have 2cm (¾in) contrast-bound leading edges and are held back by brass ombras. A sheer curtain is held by a tassel tie-back. The curtain tracks are hidden since they are fixed behind and below the pole.

Page 107
Arch-shaped trumpet valance hung from a pole and trimmed with rope along the top edge and bullion fringe along the lower edge. The curtains are held by tassel rope tie-backs and the track is fixed behind and below the pole. A very smart, grand treatment, suitable for classically shaped windows.

Page 108
Trumpet-pleated arch-shaped valance hung from a pole. The lower edge of the valance is trimmed with bullion fringe and a flat braid is sewn about 2.5cm (1in) above the top of the bullion fringe. The curtains have the flat braid set in from the leading edges and are held by double tassel tie-backs. The curtain track is fixed behind and below the pole. A very smart, grand treatment, suitable for classic shaped windows.

Page 109
Box-pleated valance with contrast-binding of 2cm (¾in) depth on lower edge. Sewn onto a contrast-piped yoke. The curtains have 2cm (⅔in) contrast-bound leading edges.

Page 110
Serpentined gathered valance with fringe along lower edge sewn onto a flat buckram yoke with contrast-bound 1cm (½in) top. Rope with central loop is sewn along bottom of the yoke. Rope clovers and tassels at either end of valance. The curtains have 2cm (¾in) contrast-bound leading edges.

Page 111
Arch-shaped gathered valance with fringe along the lower edge; sewn onto a buckram yoke which is covered with knife pleated fabric with 1cm (½in) contrast-bound top. Tails with coronets and fringe are set on the valance at each end. Central trumpet with fringe set on to valance. Valance is finished with knotted and looped rope.

Page 112
Double goblet-pleated valance with a 1cm (½in) contrast-bound top and rope knotted at the base of each pleat. Lower edge trimmed with bullion fringe. The curtains have 2cm (¾in) contrast-bound leading edges and are held by barrier rope tie-backs. For double goblet pleats, you usually get two pleats per width of fabric.

Page 113
Double goblet-pleated valance with a 1cm (½in) contrast-bound top and rope knotted at the base of each pleat. The lower edge of the valance is scallop-shaped in the spaces between the pleats and trimmed with bullion fringe. The benefit of this valance design is that the fabric can be pleated to show patterned fabrics to their full advantage. For double goblet pleats, you usually get two pleats per width of fabric.

Page 114
French-pleated valance with a 1cm (½in) contrast-bound top and bullion fringe sewn along the lower edge. This valance is hung at a wide window and could easily also be used at a narrower window in the same room.

Page 115
Goblet-headed valance with a knife-pleated frill sewn into the lower edge. The curtains are held by scallop-shaped tie-backs. The knife-pleated frill combines well with the goblet heading. This valance is hung at a wide window and could easily also be used at a narrower window in the same room.

Page 116
Goblet-pleated valance with a 1cm (½in) contrast-bound top and rope knotted at the base of each pleat. The lower edge of the valance is arch-shaped and trimmed with bullion fringe. The benefit of this striking design is that no more light is lost than with a straight valance because the arched shaping only starts to deepen over the curtains. The curtains are held by double tassel tie-backs.

Page 117
Goblet-headed valance with two lengths of thin rope knotted at the base of each pleat. The rope falls in arcs between the pleats. The lower edge of the valance has a 2.5cm (1in) contrast binding and is also scallop-shaped in the spaces between the pleats.

Page 118
Pencil-headed valance with a frilled hem. The valance is drawn up with tape at regular intervals to create the scoops.

Page 119
Serpentined valance with a set-down gathered heading and a 1cm (½in) top and 2.5cm (1in) contrast-bound lower edge. The serpentined shaping softens the horizontal line on a wide window.

Page 120
Set-down smock-headed valance with 1cm (½in) contrast-bound top. The lower edge of the valance is serpentined and is further softened by an in-set frill.

Page 121
Serpentined valance with a set-down gathered heading and a 1cm (½in) contrast-bound top. Rope has been sewn over the gathers and the lower edge has been trimmed with a bullion fringe.

Page 122
Gently arched valance which is also arched at the top edge. The arches are formed by hanging a straight valance from a shaped pelmet board. The valance has a set-down gathered heading and a 1cm (½in) contrast-bound top. Rope has been sewn over the gathers and the lower edge has been finished with a contrast-piped frill.

Page 123
Arch-shaped gathered valance with 2cm (¾in) contrast-bound lower edge and set-on goblet coronet-topped trumpets (contrast-bound top and bottom), sewn onto a yoke with 1cm (½in) contrast binding, hand-sewn rope knotted at base of each goblet coronet. Valance is hung from a serpentine-shaped pelmet board.

Page 124
Arch-shaped dropped-down gathered valance fringed on lower edge and 1cm (½in) contrast-bound top. Set-on goblet coronet-topped trumpets and tails (contrast-bound top and fringed lower edge) with hand-sewn rope knotted at the base of each goblet coronet. Valance is hung from a serpentine-shaped pelmet board.

Page 125
Arch-shaped gathered valance with a set-down gathered heading. Rope has been sewn over the gathers and knotted over each of the four individually attached goblet coronet-topped trumpets. The lower edge of the valance has been trimmed with bullion fringe. This is an unusual treatment for a wide window.

Page 126
Gathered valance set onto a flat yoke. The yoke has been piped top and bottom and there is a small frill at the top of the yoke. The curtains are held by tie-backs with a piped frill on the top and lower edges.

Page 127
Box-pleated valance set onto a flat yoke. Rope has been sewn onto the top and lower edges of the yoke. The lower edge of the valance is trimmed with fringe. The tie-backs have been trimmed with rope top and lower edges.

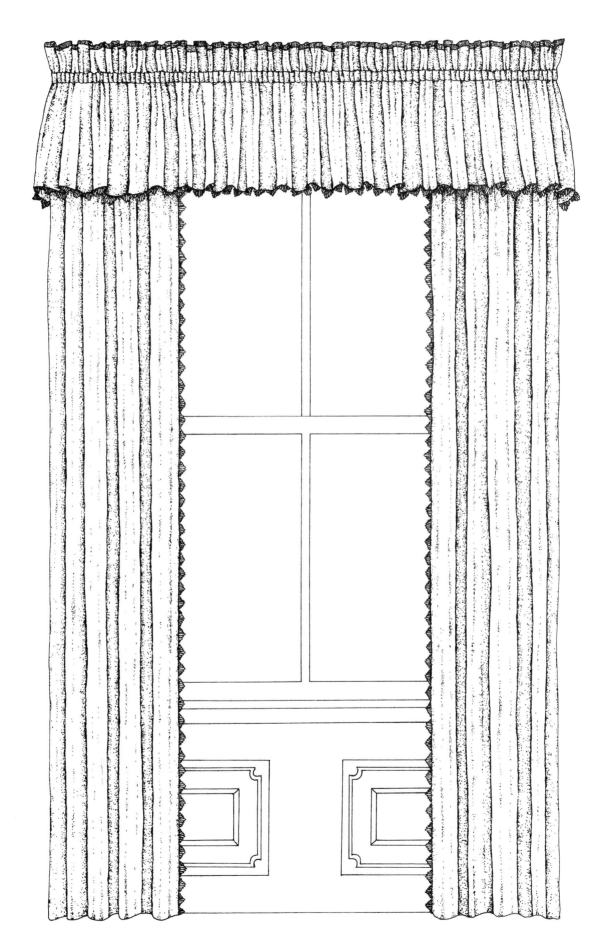

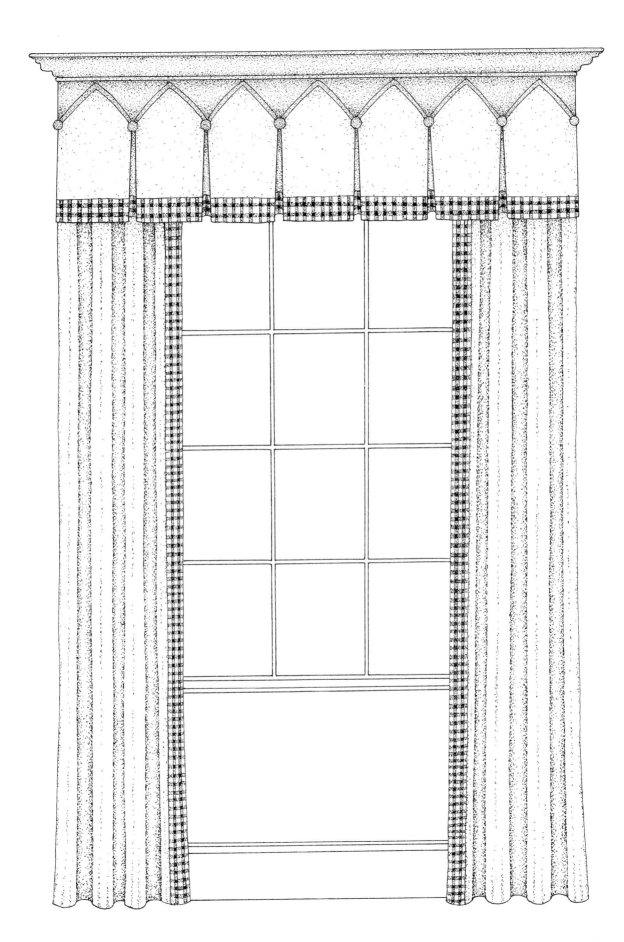

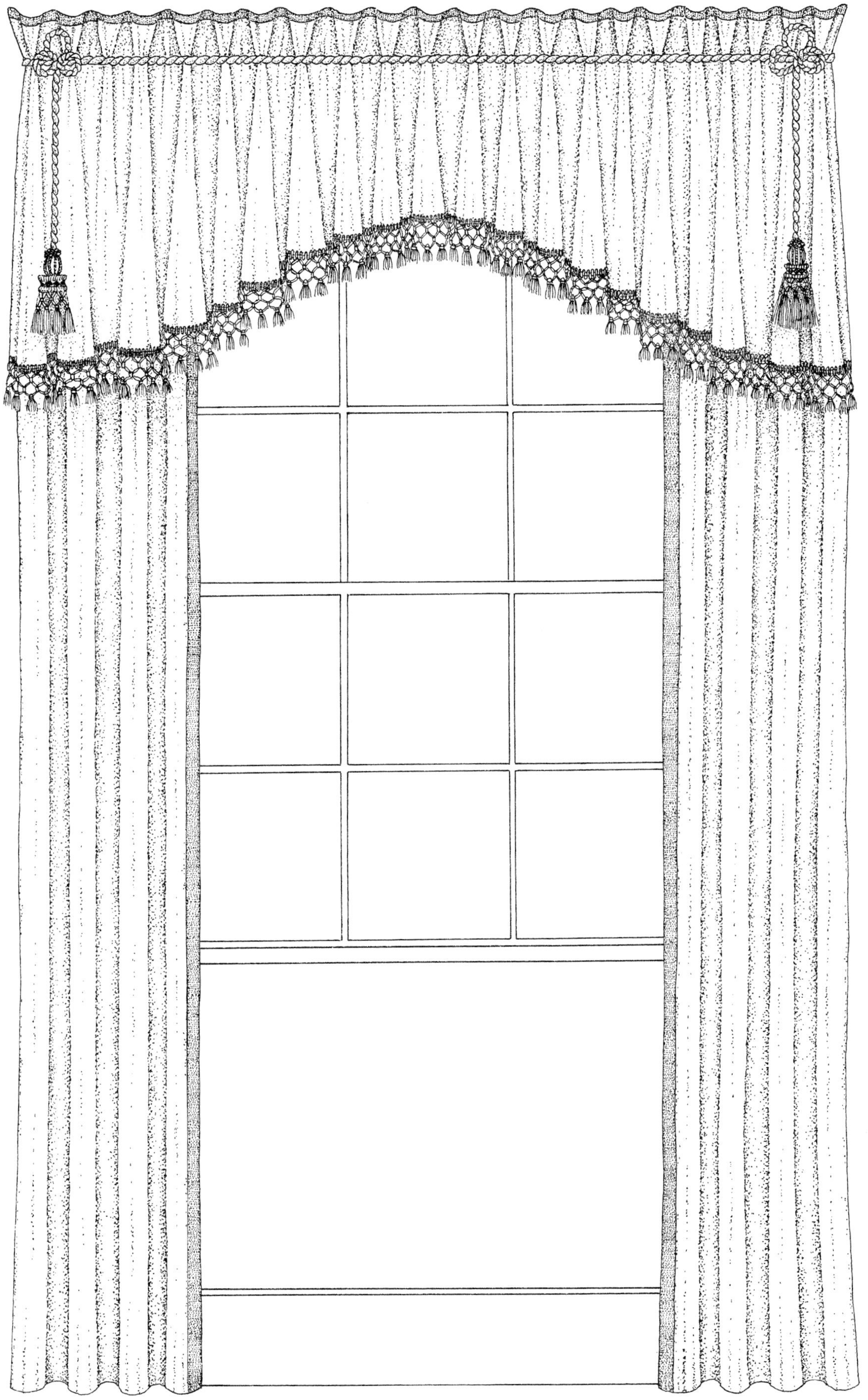

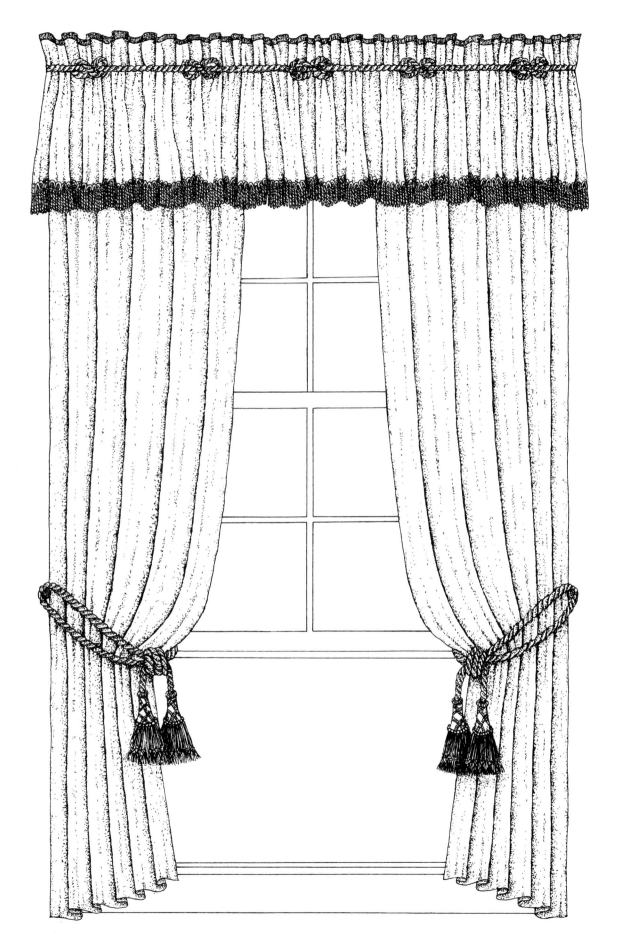

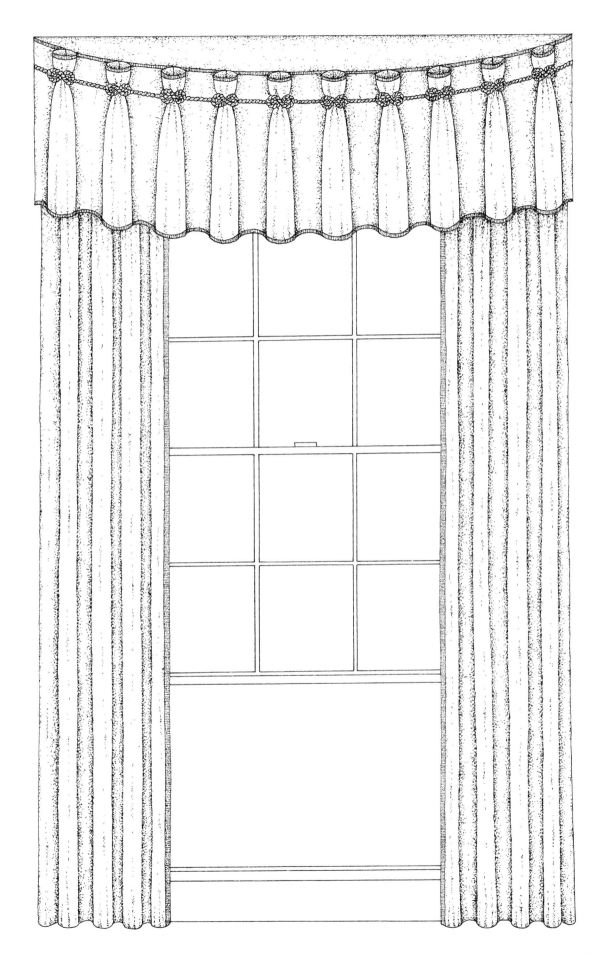

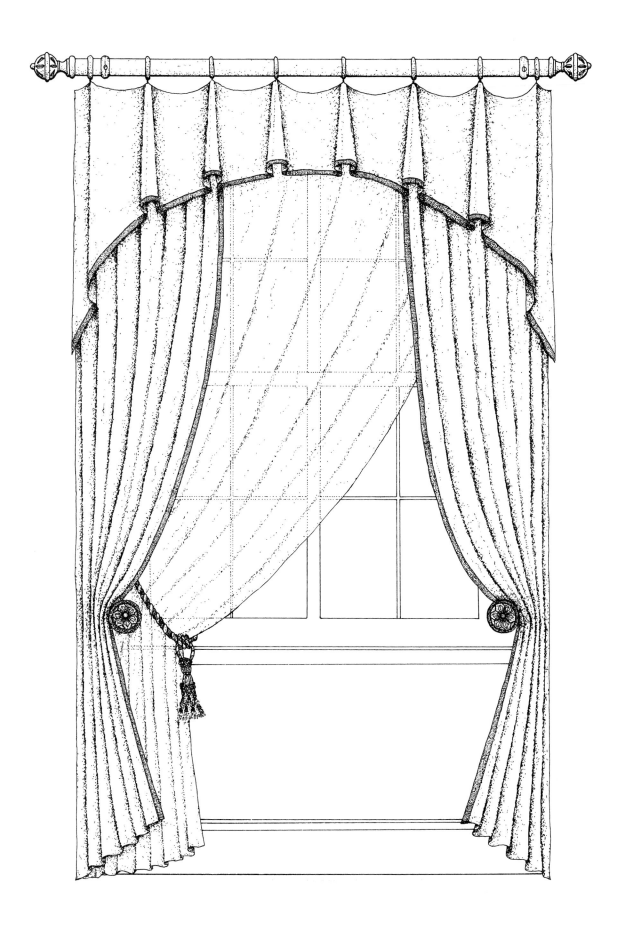

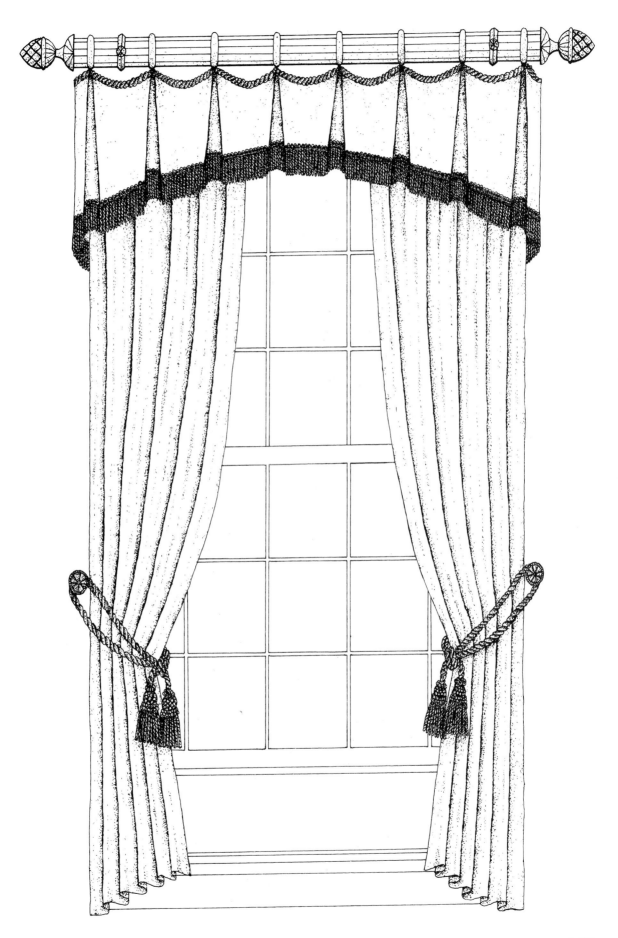

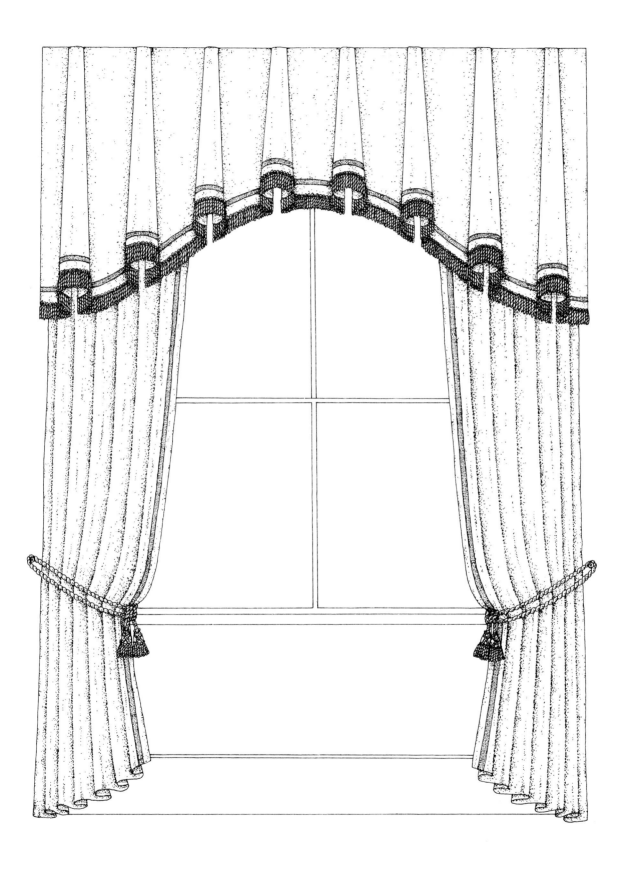

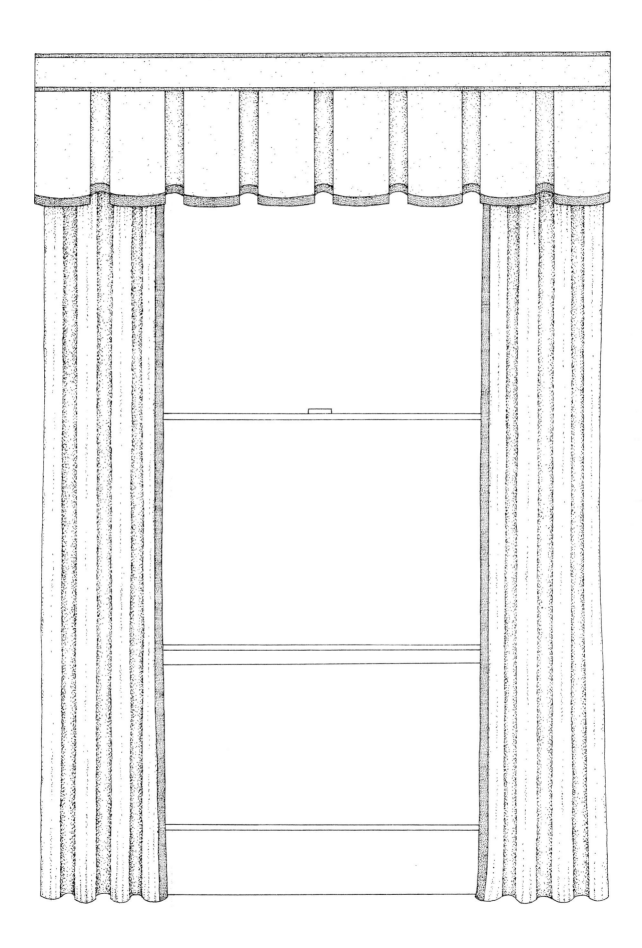

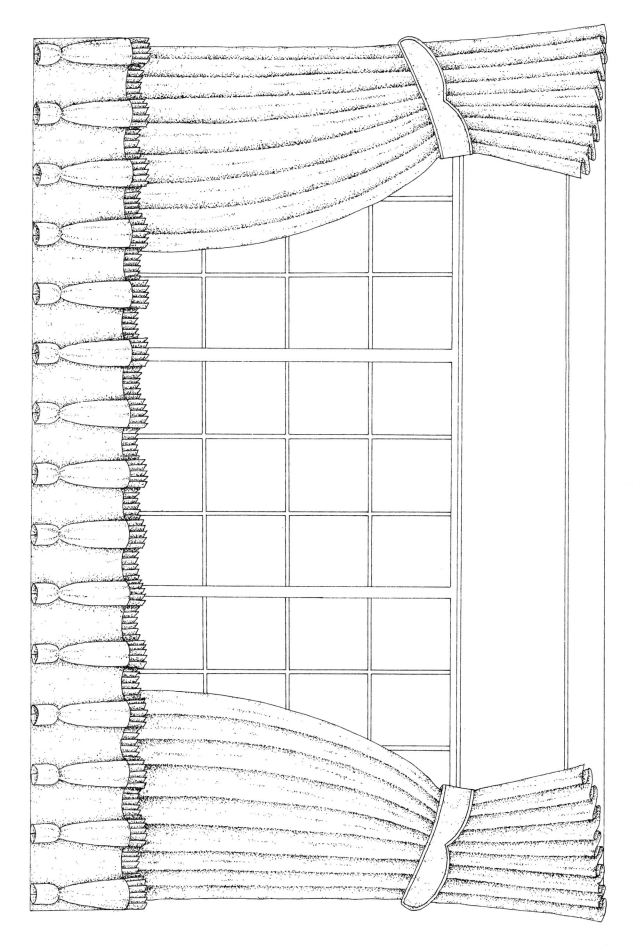

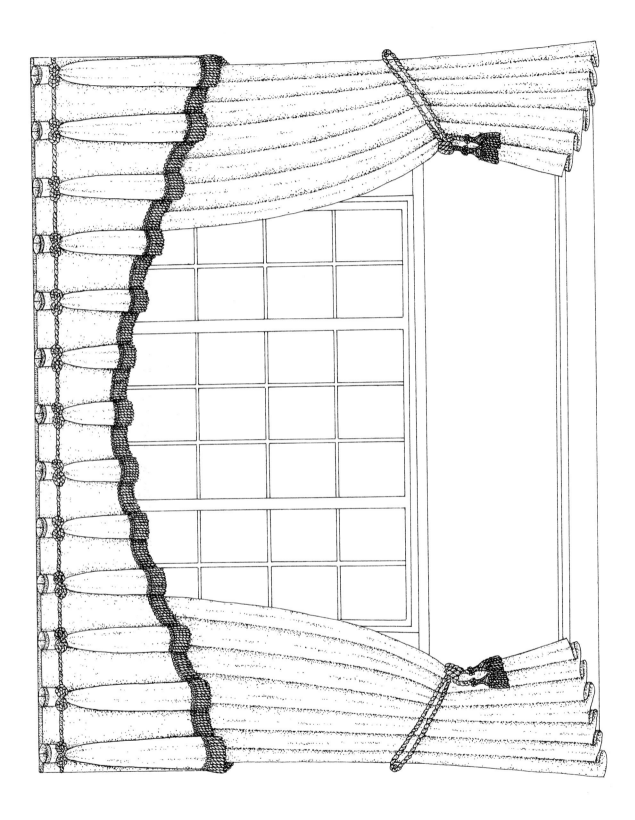

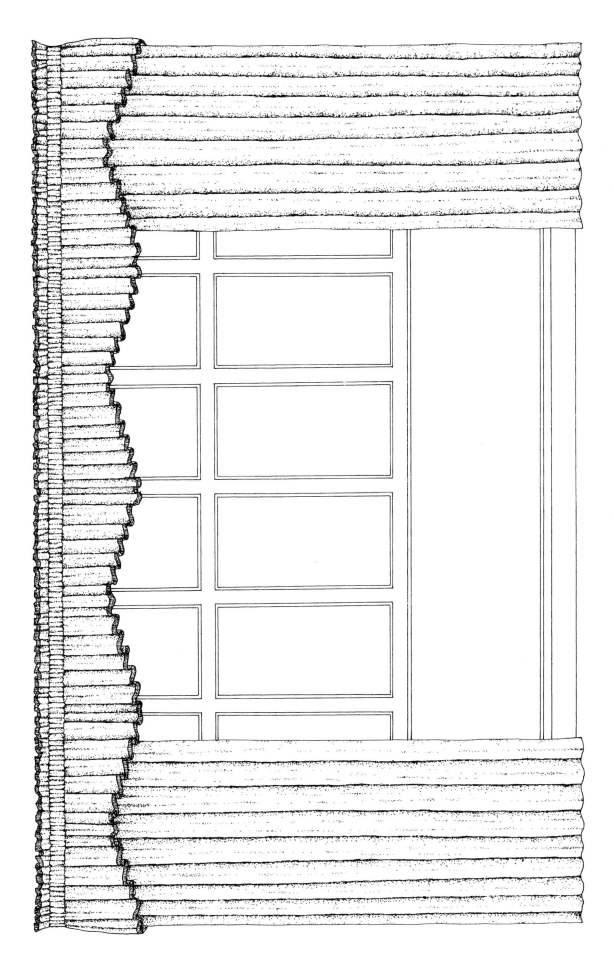

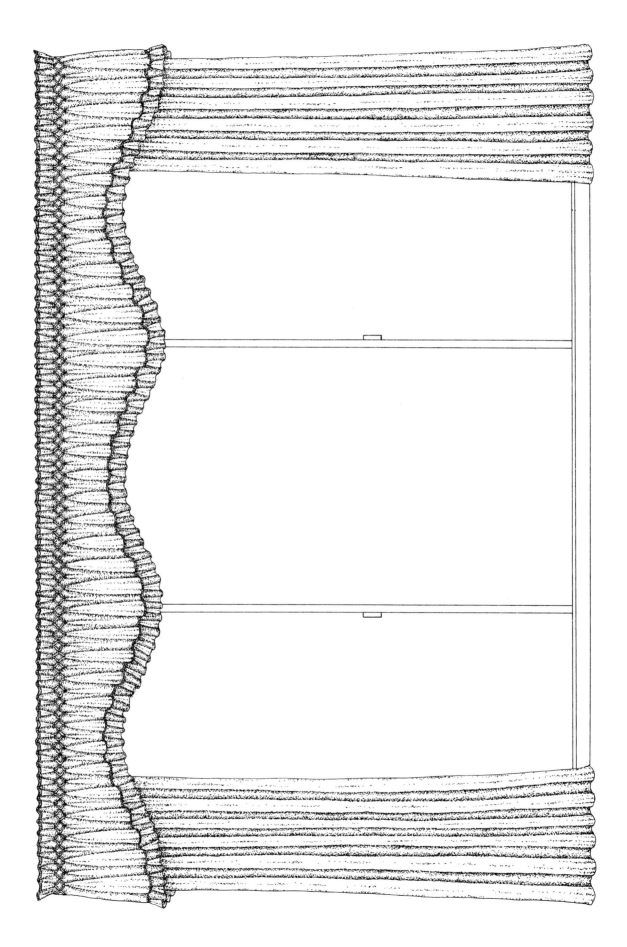

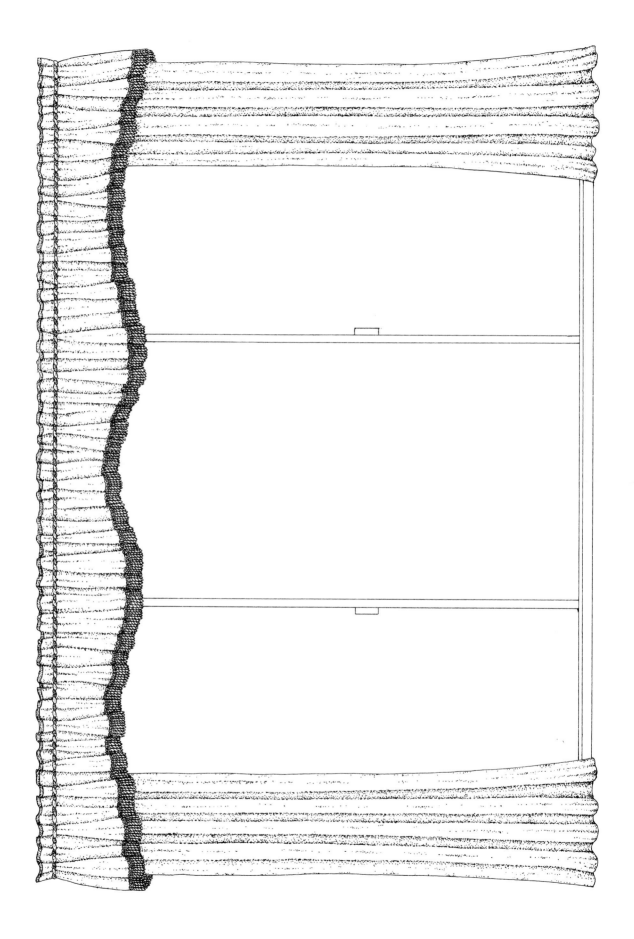

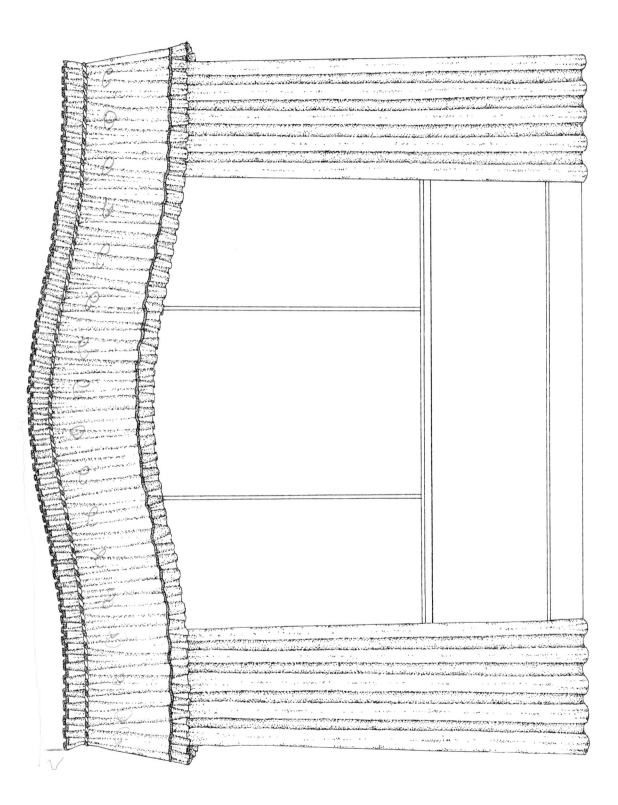

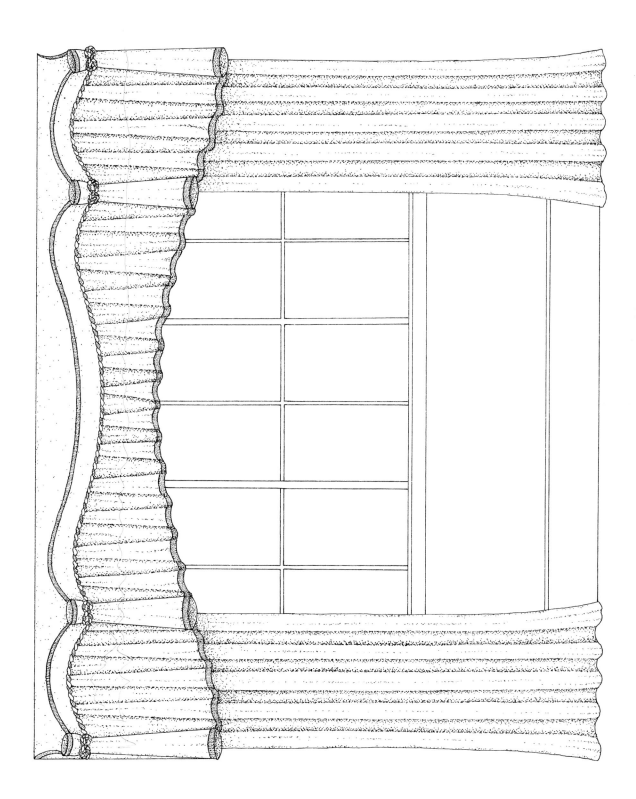

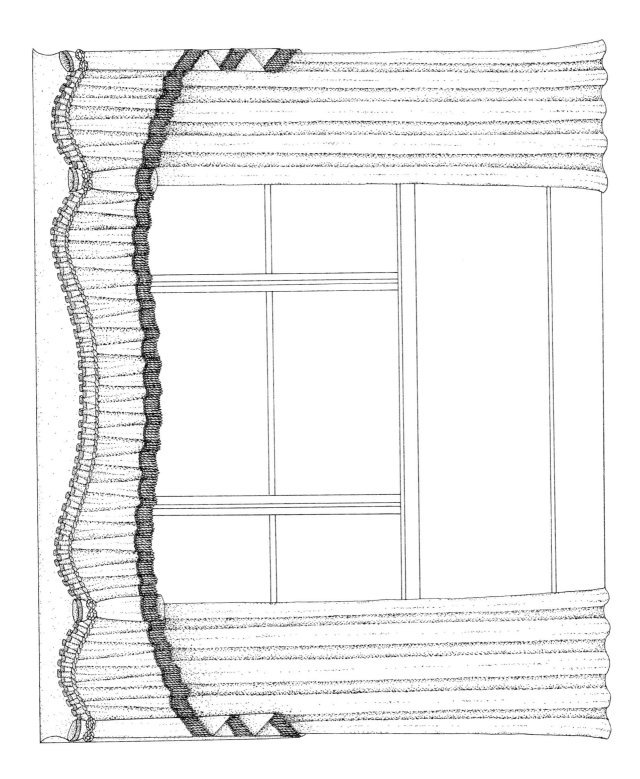

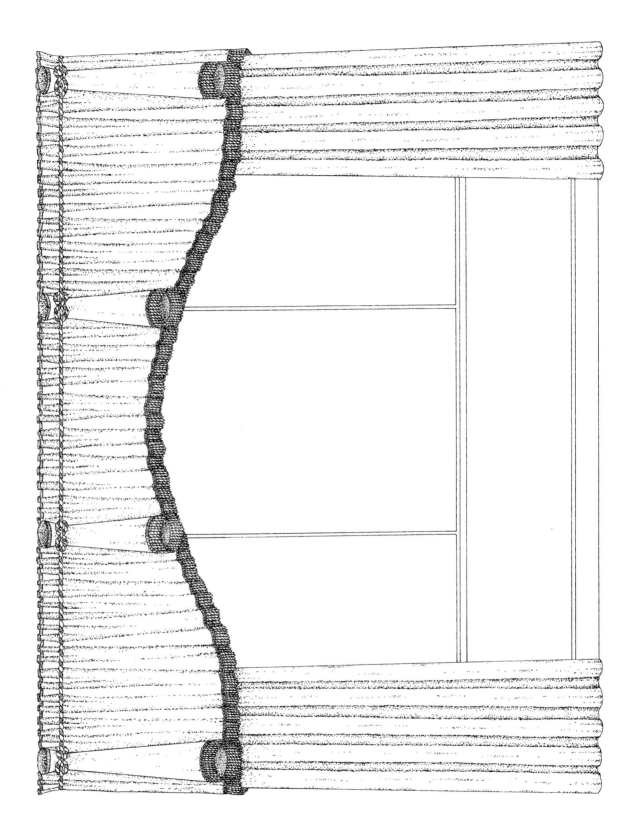

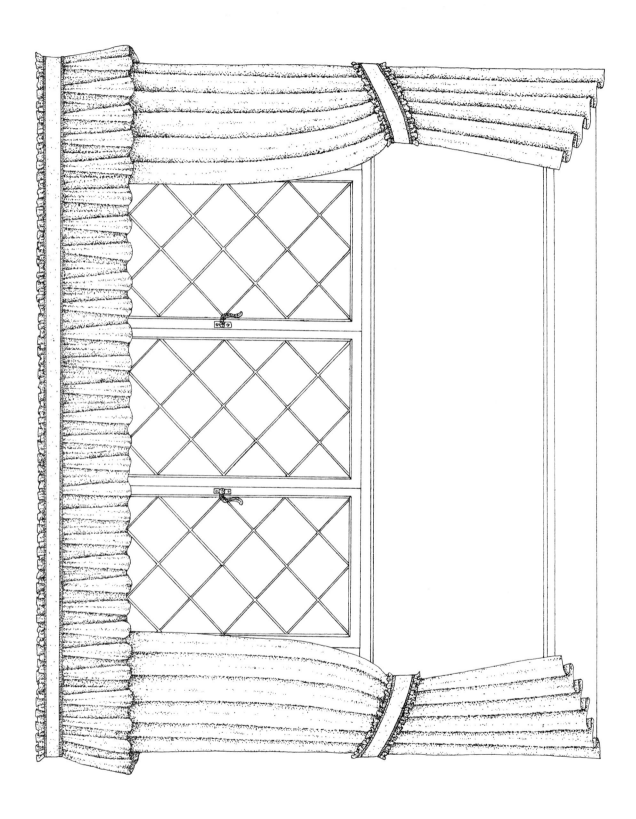

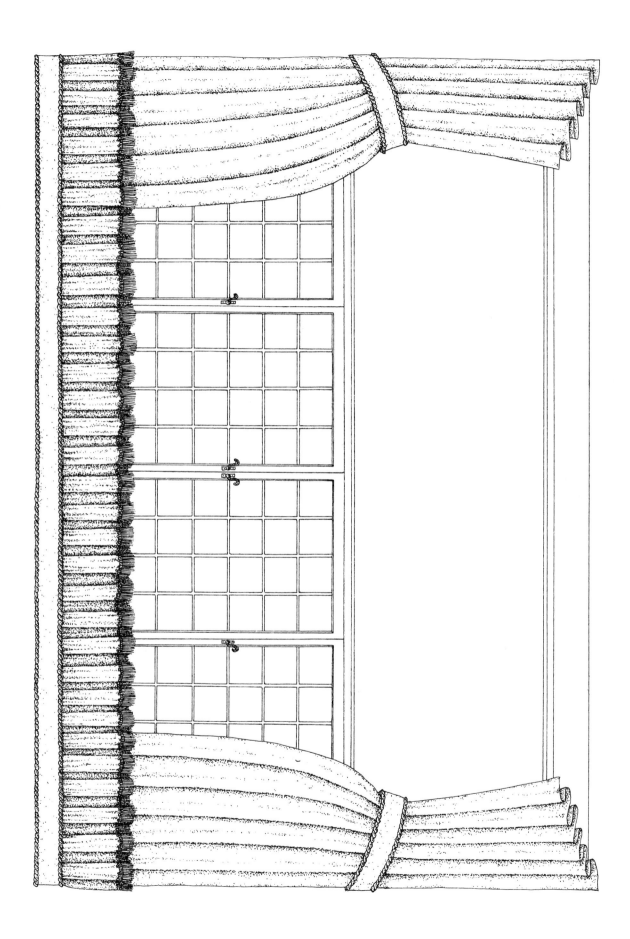

PELMETS

- The lower edge of the pelmet can be cut to any shape
- The pattern of the fabric is shown to best effect
- Can utilise the dead wall space above a window
- Economical on fabric

A pelmet is a fabric-covered band of buckram, canvas or plywood which is fixed onto the front edge of a pelmet board. It conceals the track and curtain heading. Pelmets can be fitted to any shape of window and the design can easily be adapted to suit different sizes of windows within the same room. They can be fitted on the dead wall space above the window so that less light will be lost and the window will appear more elegant.

Pelmets are suitable for a full range of window treatments from the simple to the dramatic. Depending on the shapes, fabric and trims chosen, they can be austere, classic, pretty or even amusing.

The shape can be a straight band, or the lower edge can be gently curved. Curves can be shaped to emulate architectural details in the room or to emphasise the design of the fabric.

Fabrics with distinctive prints such as damasks or toiles de jouy are shown off to best advantage on pelmets because they are viewed flat rather than their design being lost in the folds of curtains, valances or swags.

The lower edges of pelmets benefit from being defined with braid or rope trims. Braid or rope in a striking contrast colour will accentuate the shape of the pelmet even more. Fabric contrast-binding works well for straight shapes, but is not practical for intricate shapes. The flat lines of the pelmets can straightforwardly be softened by placing individually-made trumpets or swags on top of them. The trumpets or swags can also be connected with rope.

Proportions

The usual proportions for pelmets are $\frac{1}{6}$th to $\frac{1}{5}$th of curtain length. However, for cottage windows with low ceilings the depth of the pelmet can be as little as $\frac{1}{8}$th of the curtain length. At the other extreme are lambrequins, which are shaped to come down the sides of the windows. The shortest point of the lambrequin should be $\frac{1}{6}$th of the curtain length but the sides can be very long and dramatic.

Fitting pelmets

There are two types of pelmets, soft and hard. A pelmet is constructed in the same way as a tie-back where fabric is laid over a pelmet buckram or thin ply-board and lining is slip-stitched to the reverse side. Webbing tape or Velcro is stitched to the top of the pelmet which can then be secured to the pelmet board.

The pelmet board from which the curtains and pelmet are hung is cut from planed timber 19-22mm ($\frac{3}{4}$in) thick which should be either painted or covered in lining or curtain fabric. If possible the pelmet board should be placed up to the coving or cornice in order to heighten the window treatment and to avoid an unattractive gap between the top of the pelmet and the coving. Check that the proposed depth of the pelmet will cover the soffit or architrave at the top of the window and if necessary adjust the height of the pelmet board.

Pelmet boards are usually 13-15cm (5-6in) wide, with the track set 5-8cm (2-3in) back from the front edge of the board to allow the curtains free movement behind the pelmet.

The board can be up to 25cm (10in) wide in order to enable the curtains to clear radiators, for example. If they are any wider they will look heavy and intrusive.

The pelmet board is secured to the wall using angle brackets. For pelmet boards over 170cm (67in) in length a centre bracket is required to prevent the wood from bowing and to support the weight of the curtains and the pelmet.

The curtain track is then fitted to the underside of the pelmet board. If necessary use plastic or wood spacers between the track and the board to create a gap for angle brackets to be slotted through.

ILLUSTRATION NOTES

Page 128
A Chinese-shaped pelmet with a scalloped hem trimmed with tassels. Braid has been hand-sewn to the surface of the pelmet in a looped design.

Page 133
Pelmet with braid along the top edge and architectural-shaped lower edge (also with braid) with central tassel. The curtains have braid set in from the leading edges, there is a roller blind behind.

Page 134
A-D Four pelmets with gentle curves along the lower edges. The lower edges have been trimmed with narrow braid. These are classic pelmet shapes.

Page 135
A-D Four pelmets with repeated scallop shaping along the lower edges. The lower edges have been trimmed with narrow braid. A scalloped edge gives a pelmet a pretty look.

Page 136
Four geometric-shaped pelmets which can look very dramatic in formal situations but equally can look fun on a small kitchen window.

A A straight pelmet with a deep contrast-bound top and lower edge.

B A pelmet with zigzag shaping along the lower edge. The top and lower edge have been trimmed with a flat braid.

C A pelmet with castellated shaping along the lower edge. The shape has been accentuated by a braid trim inset from the top and lower edge.

D A straight pelmet that has been stepped at the corners of the lower edge. The top and lower edge have been trimmed with a narrow braid.

Page 137
A-D Four pelmets with Gothic shaping along the lower edges. The tops and lower edges have been trimmed with a narrow braid, except for pelmet C which has been trimmed with rope. The points of pelmet D have been finished with tassels.

Page 138
A pelmet with an enlarged scalloped shaping along the lower edge. The lower edge has been trimmed with narrow braid

and finished with two tassels. The curtains have 2cm (¾in) contrast-bound leading edges and are held by contrast-bound tie-backs which have been finished with tassels.

Page 139
A pelmet which is straight in the middle with shaped sides. The pelmet has been trimmed with braid on all edges. Knotted rope and tassels have been sewn at the centre of the pelmet. The curtains have contrast-bound leading edges and hems and are held by tassel tie-backs which are hung from ombras.

Page 140
An embroidered or stencilled pelmet with a curved lower edge. Inset narrow braid accentuates the top and lower edge. The curtains have braid in-set from the leading edges. The tie-backs are also embroidered.

Page 141
A lambrequin pelmet with a curved lower edge and very deep dramatic sides. It has been trimmed with fringe, decorated with braid and fixed into a pelmet box at the top. The curtains are held by double tassel tie-backs. This is a very sumptuous and rich pelmet.

Page 142
A pelmet with an arch-shaped lower edge and three set-on trumpets and coronets. The trumpets have been contrast-lined and rope has been knotted at the point where the trumpets and coronets meet. The tie-backs have also been trimmed with knotted rope.

Page 143
A pelmet with an arch-shaped lower edge and two set-on trumpets with coronets. Rope has been knotted at the point where the trumpets and coronets meet, and has then been tied into a rope clover at the centre with rope and tassels hanging down. The curtains are held by double tassel tie-backs.

Page 144
A pelmet with small scallops along the lower edge and on-set swags and short tails. The lower edge of the pelmet has been trimmed with narrow braid. The swags and tails have been contrast-bound and are finished with two Maltese crosses. The swags and tails soften the pelmet. The curtains have 2cm (¾in) contrast-bound leading edges and are held by scallop-shaped contrast-bound tie-backs.

Page 145
A pelmet with three scallops along the lower edge and on-set swags and decorative tails finished with two bows and a chou rosette. The lower edge of the pelmet has been trimmed with narrow braid. The swags and tails soften the flat pelmet. The curtains are held by banana-shaped tie-backs also trimmed with braid.

Page 146
A straight pelmet with a curve in the centre and shaped sides which has been fitted at a wide window. Flat braid set in from the lower edge accentuates the shape. The tie-backs are also trimmed with flat braid.

Page 147
Diamond-quilted pelmet with fringed serpentined lower edge, hung from decorative wooden cornice box. Rope and tassel at either end. Curtains have diamond quilted leading edges.

Page 148
Pelmet with fringed serpentined lower edge and 1cm (½in) contrast-bound top. On-set goblet-headed trumpets with rope trim level with bottom of goblet, and knotted at base of each goblet. Curtains

have wide contrast-bound leading edges. Rope is sewn at the seam between the curtain.

Page 149
Scalloped pelmet, slightly deeper at either side. Trimmed with rope on all four edges and rope and tassel dividng each scallop.

Page 150
Fringed swag-shaped pelmet with set-on fringed side tails and decorative tails. Rope along the top. Gives illusion of swags and tails, but more economical with fabric.

Page 151
A pelmet with a repeated scallop-shaped lower edge which has been fitted at a wide window. The top edge is trimmed with rope and the lower edge with fringe and tassels.

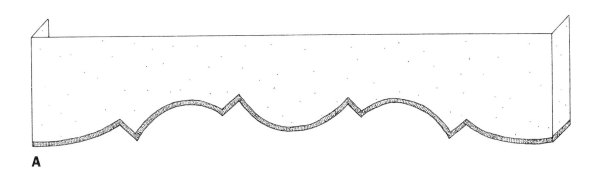

A

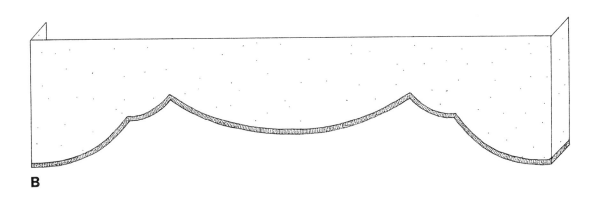

B

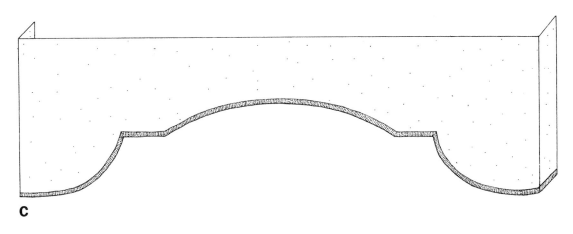

C

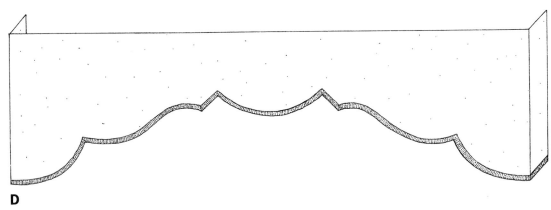

D

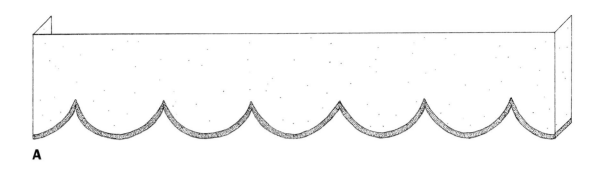

A

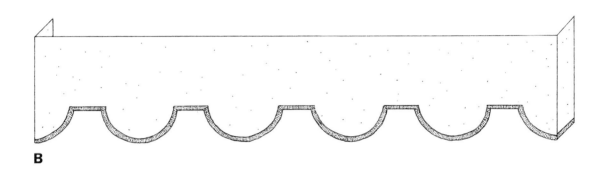

B

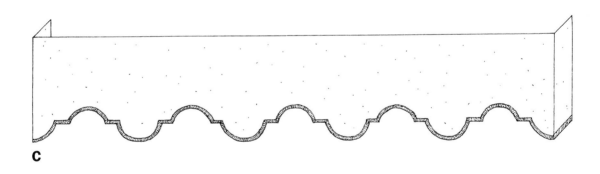

C

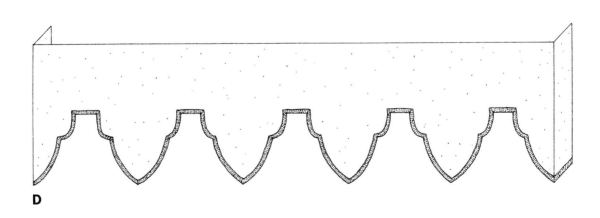

D

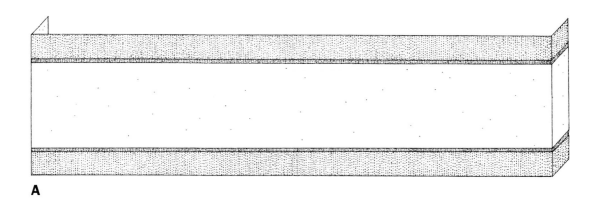

A

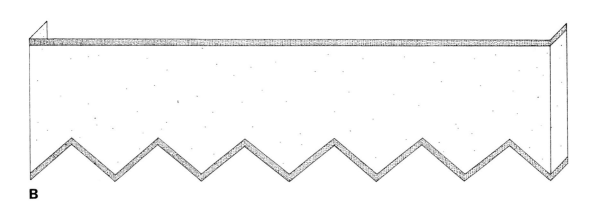

B

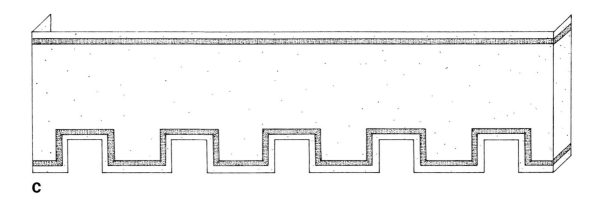

C

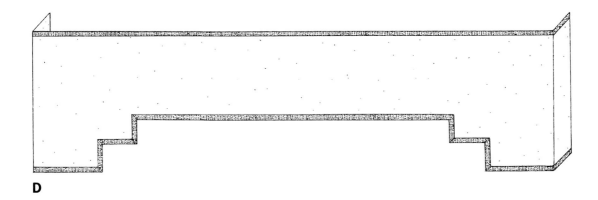

D

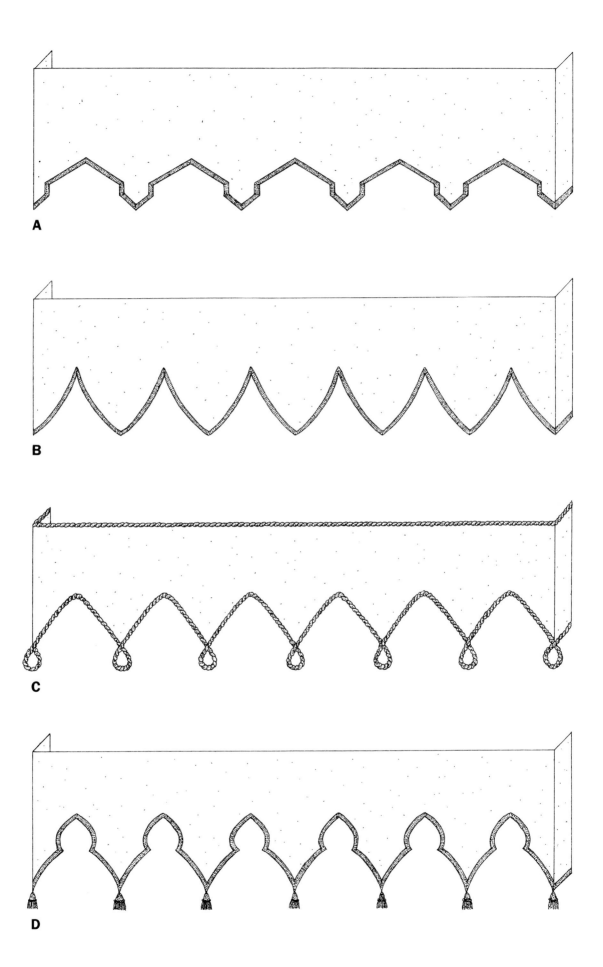

A

B

C

D

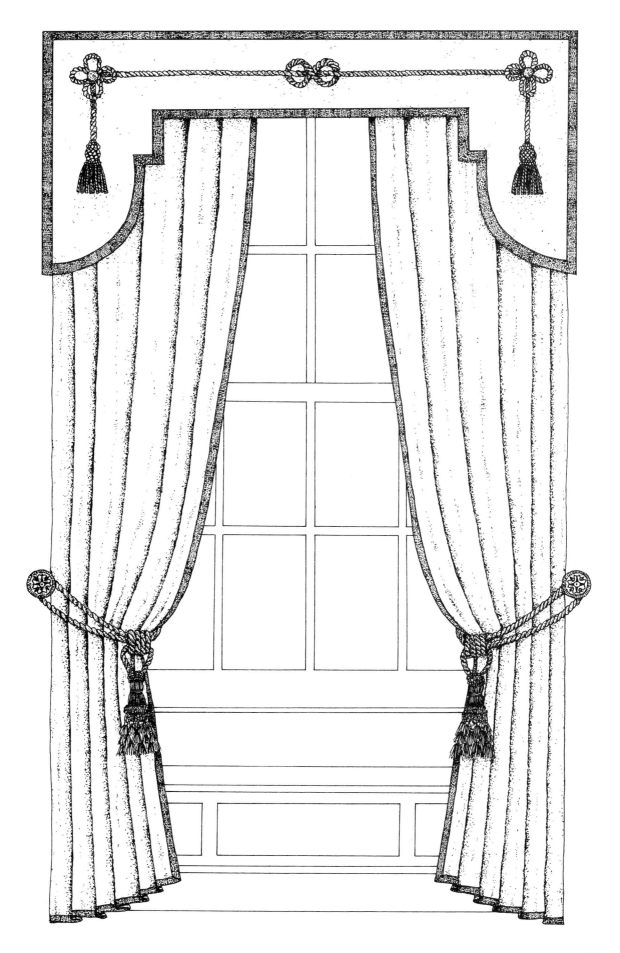

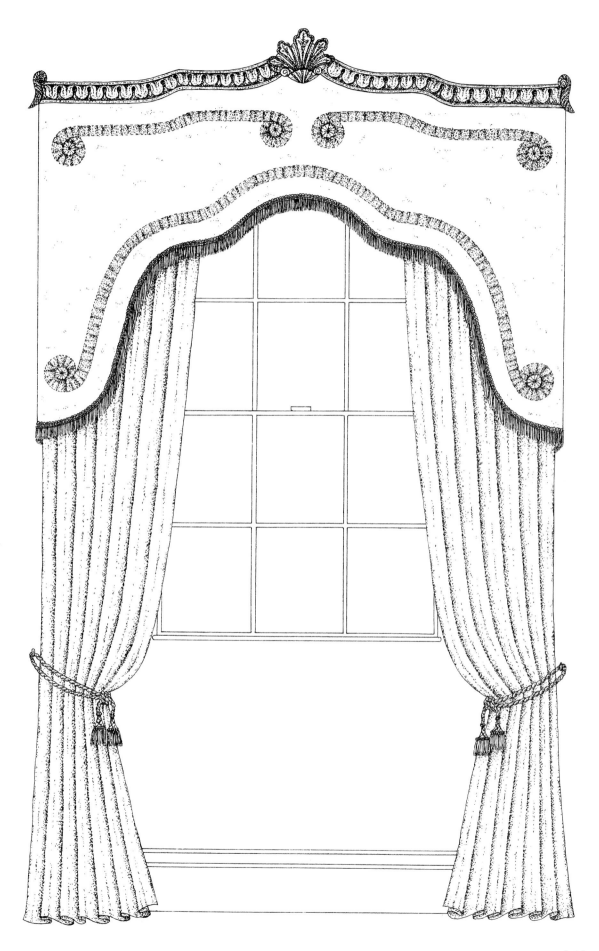

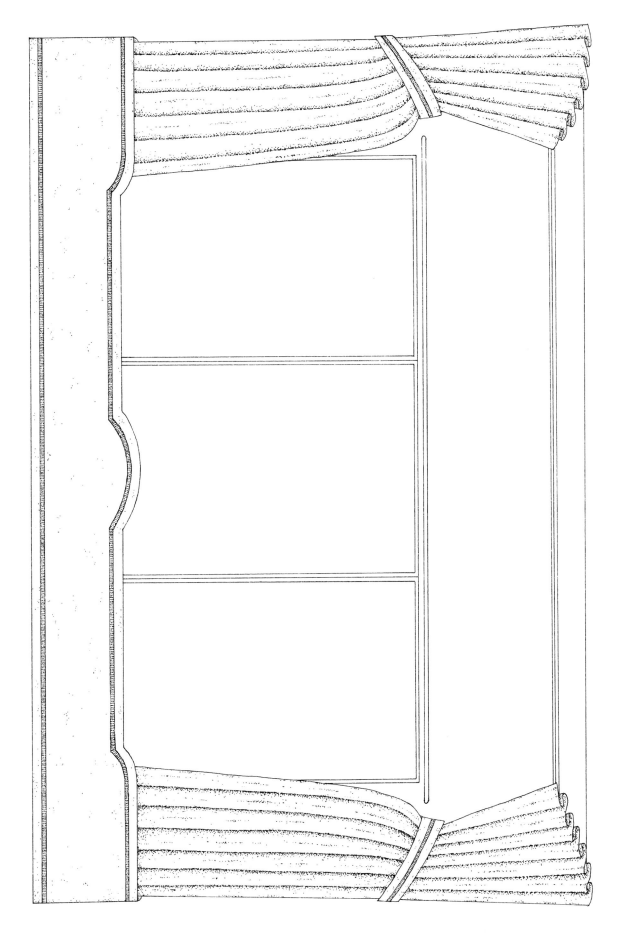

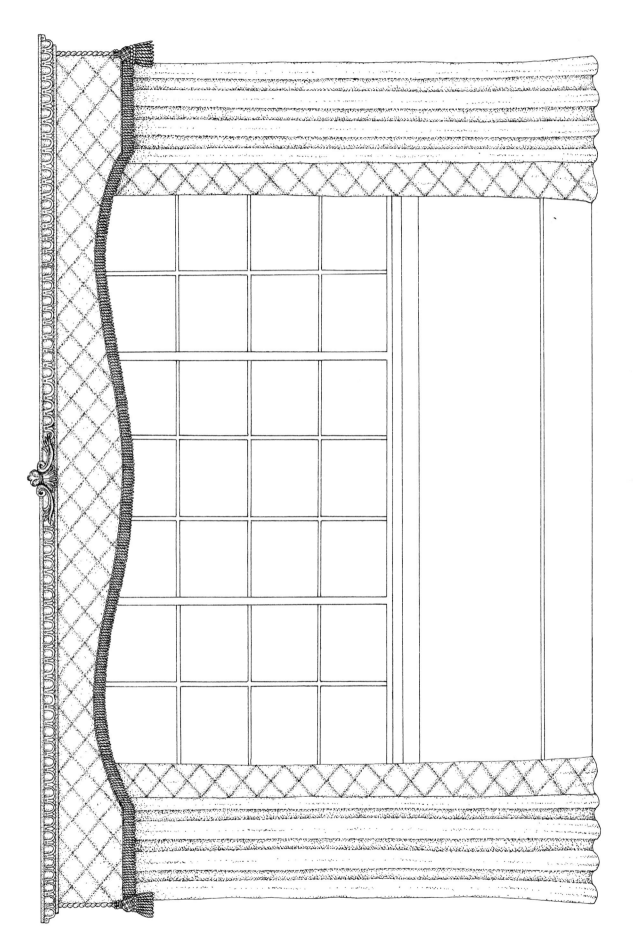

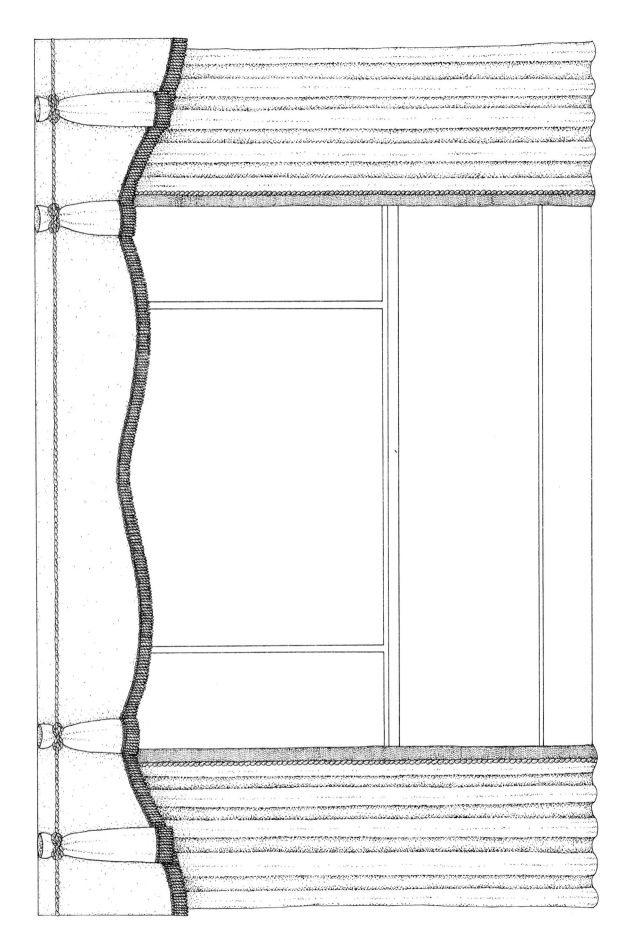

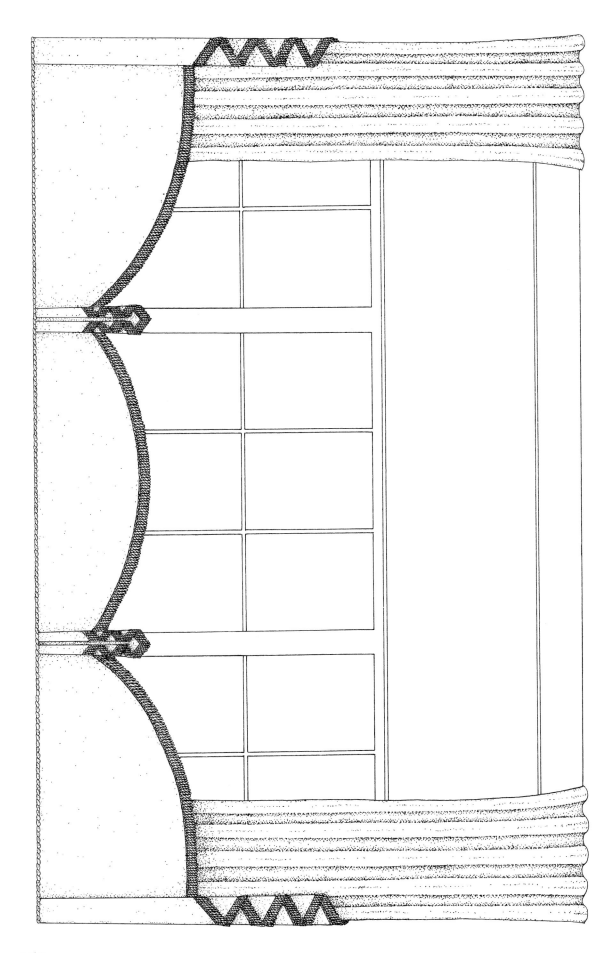

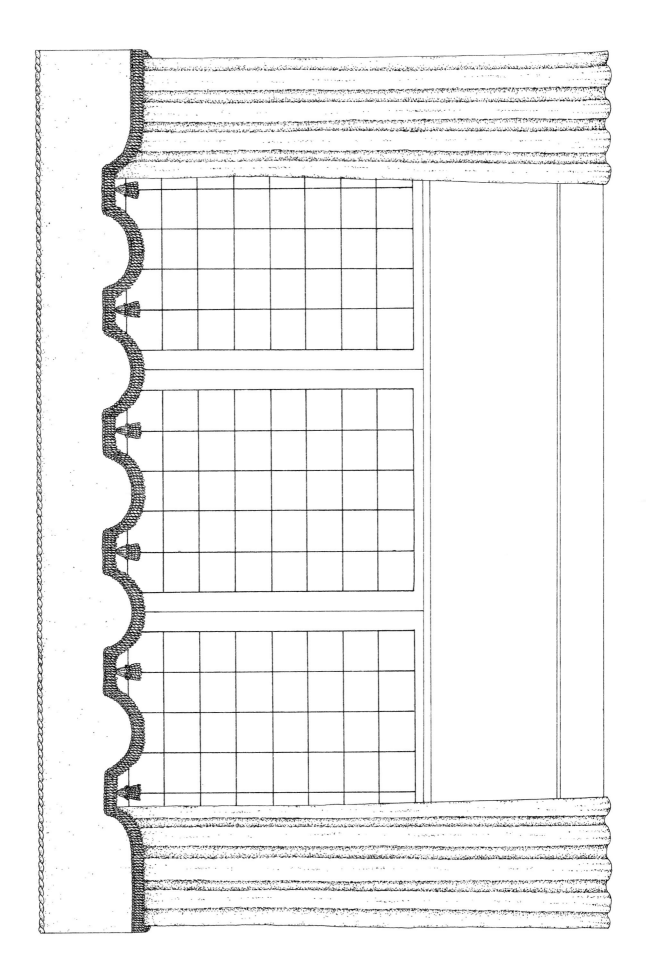

SWAGS AND TAILS
INCLUDING VENETIAN WINDOWS

DESIGN BENEFITS
- A sumptuous and impressive window treatment
- Can be formal or deliberately casual
- Surprisingly versatile
- Easily adapted for different widths of windows in the same room

Swags and tails are the ultimate way to dress a window, creating a grand treatment that is suitable for formal rooms. They look sophisticated when made up in rich fabrics and trimmed with fringe. However, untrimmed swags and tails look much simpler and can be used for informal settings, even kitchens and bathrooms.

Generally speaking, the wider the window the more swags there are in a design. Where there are windows of dissimilar widths in the same room, a narrow window could have one swag design and a wide window could have a three-swag design.

Most swags and tails are fitted onto a pelmet board. They are arranged to give the illusion of continuous drapery although each element is made up and fitted separately. On a pelmet board swags can either be overlapped or butted together. Good pattern cutting is the key in a swag treatment, as even swags draped over a pole require the fabric to be formally shaped with all the components fitted individually. When curtains are hung behind swags and tails draped over a pole, the curtains are hung from a track which is fitted behind and below the pole.

For informal drapery where swags and tails are casually wrapped around a pole, the swags and tails are made up from individually-cut basic shapes which are seamed together into a length of fabric and then draped over the pole in situ.

The side tails finish off swags and add length and elegance to the window treatment. As the reverse sides of the tails are visible they should be lined, either in the main fabric or in a contrasting fabric. The diagonal hemlines of the tails usually start level with the base of the swag, but in a few cases these diagonal hemlines start well below the swag. Tails can either be straight, tapered or cone-shaped.

Swagged valances are a pretty soft swag treatment which can be trimmed with frills or fringes along the lower edge. The swags are made up into a continuous valance with trumpets at the intersections of the swags and at the end of the valance. The trumpets can be contrast-lined to draw attention to the pretty scalloped lower edge.

Proportions
The success of the swag treatment lies in the use of pleasing proportions. To achieve a balanced look, swags and swagged valances should be $\frac{1}{5}$th of the top of the pelmet board to floor measurement at their deepest point. The tails should be either two or three times the length of the swags. To mock-up the position and depth of swags put a length of chain against the

window to form arcs of the swags and outline the proposed design. On a historic note, 18th century proportions would be shallower than above. 19th century proportions would be deeper.

Fitting swags and tails

Swags and tails and swagged valances are usually finished at the top with a fabric binding. The binding can either be tacked or stapled onto the pelmet board or pole or can be attached with Velcro.

If possible, the pelmet board or pole should be placed up to the coving in order to heighten the window treatment and to avoid an unattractive gap between the top of the swag treatment and the coving.

Check that the proposed depth of the swags will cover the soffit or architrave at the top of the window and if necessary adjust the height of the pelmet board or pole.

For swags draped over a pole with curtains set behind, the pole brackets are mounted onto 8cm (3in) wood blocks and the curtain track is fixed to the wall. Alternatively, the pole is fixed with small brackets to the front of an 8cm (3in) pelmet board leaving a gap between the pole and the board. The curtain track is then secured to the underside of the pelmet board in the usual manner (see Fitting valances on page 86).

ILLUSTRATION NOTES

Page 152
A single swag draped over a pair of tails. They are trimmed with in-set braid and bullion fringe. The curtains also have braid set in from the leading edges and the hem. This is a simple but striking way of trimming a swag treatment, especially when the colour of the braid contrasts with the fabric colour.

Page 159
Fabric informally draped over three ombras to form swags and tails. This effect is achieved by seaming together shaped pieces and then draping the length of fabric over the ombras in situ.

Page 160
Two fringed overlapped swags hung from a pole with soft fringed side tails falling forwards.

Page 161
Fabric informally wrapped over a pole with arrow and flight finials. This effect is achieved by seaming together shaped pieces and then draping the length of fabric over the pole in situ. A casual treatment that dresses around the window.

Page 162
A swag-shaped pleated valance with double-pleated straight tails with staggered pleats at the top. The valance and the tails are contrast-bound along the lower edges. The curtains are held by tie-backs with contrast-bound lower edges. An unusual dramatic window treatment not suitable for wide windows.

Page 163
A swag-shaped soft pelmet set over a pair of tails with a central trumpet. The double-pleated straight tails have staggered pleats and are relatively short. Braid is set in from the lower edges of the pelmet and tails. The curtains are held by braid-trimmed tie-backs. Again, an unusual dramatic window treatment not suitable for wide windows.

Page 164
A large single swag trimmed with bullion fringe. The triple-pleated straight tails

have also been trimmed with bullion fringe and finished with contrast-bound Maltese crosses.

Page 165
A swag-shaped valance with a set-down gathered heading and a contrast-bound top. The swag-shaped valance and tails are trimmed with fringe. Rope is sewn over the gathered heading of the valance and knotted over each coronet-topped tail.

Page 166
Two swags trimmed with bullion fringe with rope and tassels at the centre. The double-pleated cone shaped tails are trimmed with fringe. A classic swag and tail treatment.

Page 167
Two fringed swags sewn onto a yoke. Goblet coronet-topped fringed tails. Yoke and goblets 1cm (½in) contrast-bound tops, rope trim level with bottom of yoke, knotted at base of each goblet. Rope clover with tassels at centre.

Page 168
Two fringed swags sewn onto a yoke. Goblet coronet-topped fringed tails. Yoke and goblets 1cm (½in) contrast-bound tops, rope trim level with bottom of goblet, knotted at base of each goblet. Fringed decorative tail with central chou.

Page 169
Two swags and an underswag set onto a band with double trumpets at the end. Coronets are set above the double trumpets and the underswag. Rope is placed along the top of the swags with knots at the base of the two outside coronets. There is a central tassel. Curtains are held open by rope-trimmed tie-backs.

Page 170
Swags and triple-pleated cone-shaped tails

fixed onto a shaped pelmet board and finished with choux rosettes. The two outside swags are asymmetrical and meet at a high point in the centre. The centre swag is shaped at the top and a small double tail finishes the treatment. The curtains are held open by ombras. An unusual and elegant swag treatment.

Page 171
A single swag taken up to a chou rosette in the centre. The swag and tails are trimmed with fringe. The diagonal hemline of the double-pleated cone-shaped tails starts well below the swag. An extremely elegant swag and tail treatment.

Page 172
Two swags draped over a pole and taken up into a central ring. Two strands of rope with tassels on each end follow the line of swags. This is an amusing swag and tail treatment. For the curtains to be functional, they would need to be hung from a curtain track that had been set behind and below the pole.

Page 173
A swag with asymmetrical tails informally wrapped over a pole. The tails are scooped up with rope. This effect is achieved by seaming together shaped pieces and then draping the length of fabric over the pole in situ. The single sheer curtain is trimmed with braid on the leading edge. It is held by a tassel tie-back attached to an ombra. This is a decorative rather than functional curtain treatment.

Page 174
A single sheer swag with a channel heading pushed onto a pole with finials on the end. The staggered pleated tails are set behind the pole. Sheer curtains which cross over in the middle are set behind the swag and tails and are held by tassel tie-backs.

Page 175
A swag and asymmetrical tails informally wrapped over a pole. The long tail is held back by a brass ombra. This effect is achieved by seaming together shaped pieces and then draping the length of fabric over the pole. The sheer curtain is set behind the swag and tails and is gathered up permanently, sewn back and secured by a brass ombra and tassel. This is a decorative rather than a functional curtain treatment.

Page 176
A ruched valance trimmed with fringe and also with tassels at the gathers. The curtains are held by tie-backs trimmed with fringe. This is a pretty swag effect, unusual because there are no tails.

Page 177
A ruched valance with double-pleated straight tails. Rope and tassels are sewn at the gathers. The curtains are held open by double tassel tie-backs.

Page 178
Three swags trimmed with fringe and set onto a band. The band has been trimmed on the top and lower edges with rope. Trefoils with tassels have been placed on the band over the swags and tails. The triple-pleated cone-shaped tails are trimmed with fringe.

Page 179
Three fringed swags sewn onto a shallow gathered valance with goblet coronet-topped decorative tails at intersection. The swags have been hung loosely between goblets to show off the valance behind. Side tails also have coronets and fringe, rosettes sewn at the base of each goblet.

Page 180
Three fringed swags sewn onto a yoke covered with pleated fabric and a 1cm (½in) contrast top. The centre swag is wider and shallower than the outer swags. Tasselled rope is tied into a bow at the intersection of the swags. Fringed side tails with goblet coronet tops (with 1cm/½in contrast binding). Rope is knotted at the base of each goblet and sewn on the line where the swags are joined to the yoke.

Page 181
Three swags trimmed with fringe and set onto a band, with two underswags in contrasting fabric. Coronets are set above the tails and underswags. Rope is knotted at the base of each coronet with a tassel hanging down from the centre of each knot. The cone-shaped triple-pleated tails are trimmed with fringe and contrast lined. A formal swag and tail treatment adaptable for different widths of window.

Page 182
Three swags with triple-pleated cone-shaped tails trimmed with frills. The swags and tails are set onto a deep flat band of pleated fabric and finished with choux rosettes.

Page 183
Three swags and two trumpets with triple pleated cone shaped tails. The swags, tails and trumpets have all been trimmed with a piped frill for a pretty soft look.

Page 184
Three swags, two cones and a pair of tails with 2.5cm (1in) contrast-bound lower edges. The cones are fixed at the point where the swags are butted together. The tails and the cones are tapered (starting narrow at the top, widening in the middle and ending in a point). They are contrast-lined with a tassel at the bottom. The tapered tails give a light, slightly quirky look. This treatment is suitable for modern as well as traditional rooms.

Page 185

A swagged valance which has been draped over the pole at the ends and held with rings at each trumpet. The triple-pleated cone-shaped tails have been set behind the pole. The tails are made up separately and are contrast-lined. An unusual swag treatment which looks very light. It would take on a more sophisticated look if it were trimmed with fringe.

Page 186

Two swags trimmed with fringe which have been draped over a pole. The triple-pleated cone-shaped tails are trimmed with fringe and contrast-lined in a striped fabric. The diagonal hemline of the tails starts below the swags. The striped fabric has been used to cover the pole. This is a stunning sophisticated treatment.

Page 187

Three swags trimmed with fringe and draped over a pole. The central swag is set in front of the two outside swags. The triple-pleated cone-shaped tails are contrast lined and trimmed with fringe. A very elegant treatment, but one which could look informal without the fringe and made up in a simple fabric.

Page 188

Three swags trimmed with fringe and draped over a pole. The central swag is set in front of the two outside swags. The side tails are triple-pleated double tails trimmed with fringe and finished with a rope clover and tassels at the top. This is a very sophisticated treatment.

Page 189

Three swags trimmed with fringe and draped over a pole. A decorative tail trimmed with fringe is fixed behind the pole at the point where the swags are butted together. The triple-pleated cone-shaped tails are contrast-lined and

trimmed with fringe. The pole has been painted with lines and stars. A very sophisticated treatment.

Page 190

A swagged valance with a 2.5cm (1in) contrast binding along the lower edge. The tops of the trumpets are finished with choux rosettes. The curtains are held by contrast-bound tie-backs. The design is pretty and sophisticated.

Page 191

A swagged valance trimmed with bullion fringe which gives a sophisticated look. The outer trumpets cascade into elegant tails.

Page 192

A swagged valance trimmed with fringe and set onto a flat band. Rope has been placed along the top and lower edge of the band with rope clovers above the trumpets. There are five swags and seven trumpets in this valance. But it would work equally well with as few as two swags and three trumpets. A rather formal window treatment.

Page 193

A swagged valance trimmed with a piped frill which would work just as well with as few as two swags. A very pretty treatment suitable for bedrooms.

Page 194

A Venetian window with swags and tails fitted to the shape of the window. The outside swags are ruched with a rope and tassel, and the centre swag is set over the outside swags. The double-pleated cone-shaped tails are trimmed with fringe and finish in line with the window-sill. The diagonal hemlines of the tails start well below the swag. There are no curtains, so the window frame detail is clearly visible.

Page 195
A Venetian window with straight pelmet board placed across the top. Three fringed swags with rope clovers and tassels at the intersection of the swags. The centre swag is narrower and shallower than the outer swags, to emphasise the shape of the window. Fringed side tails and rope runs across the top of the pelmet board.

Page 196
A Venetian window with a straight pelmet board across the top. Three fringed swags with goblet coronet-topped-headed decorative tails at the intersections. They are sewn onto a shallow gathered valance, and hung loosely between the goblets to show off the valance behind. The centre swag is narrower and shallower than the outer swags to emphasise the shape of the window. Fringed and goblet coronet-topped side-tails. Two rows of rope are looped across the swags from knots beneath the goblets.

Page 197
A Venetian window with swags and tails trimmed with fringe and fixed to a pelmet board which has been placed across the top of the window. The central swag is shallower than the outside swags to echo the window shape. The double pleated tails are straight. The curtains are held by rope tassel tie-backs.

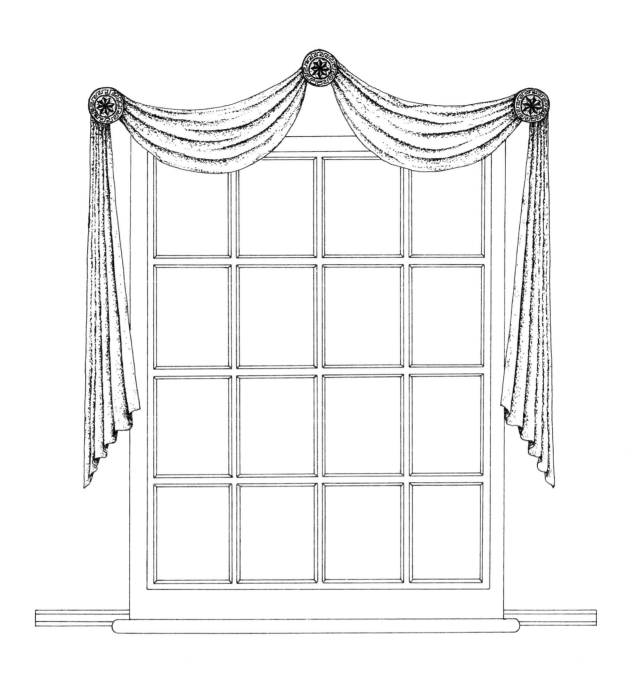

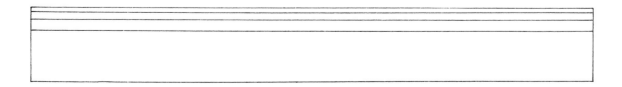

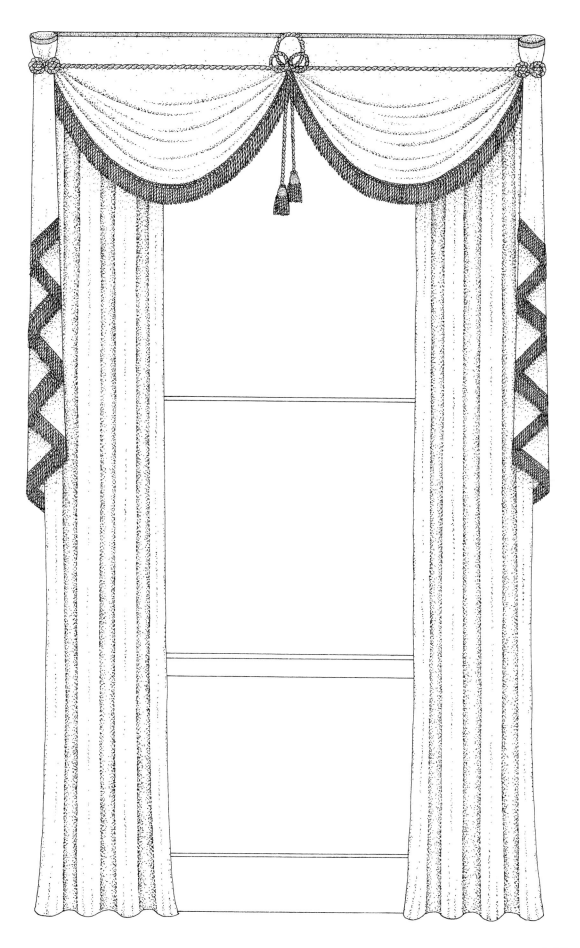

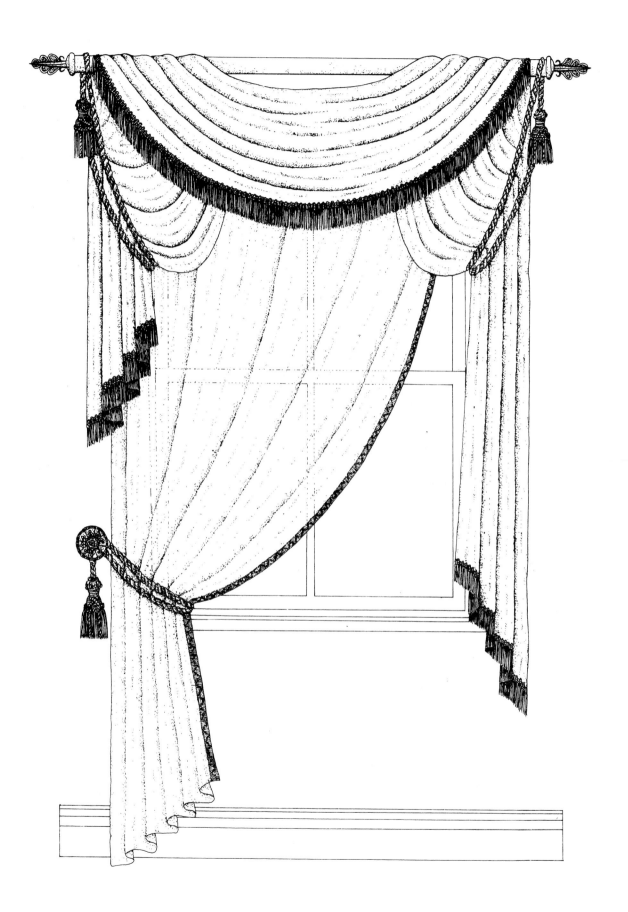

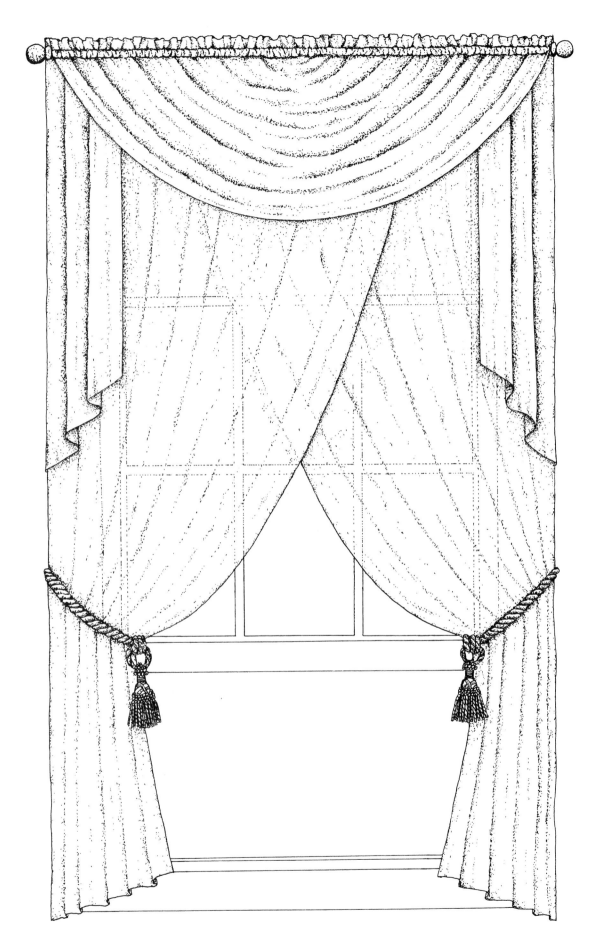

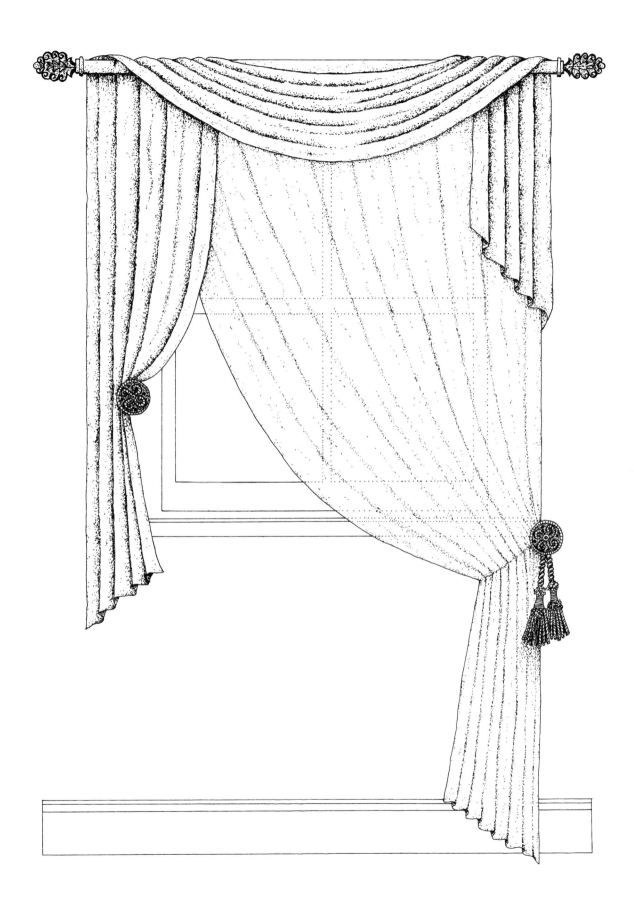

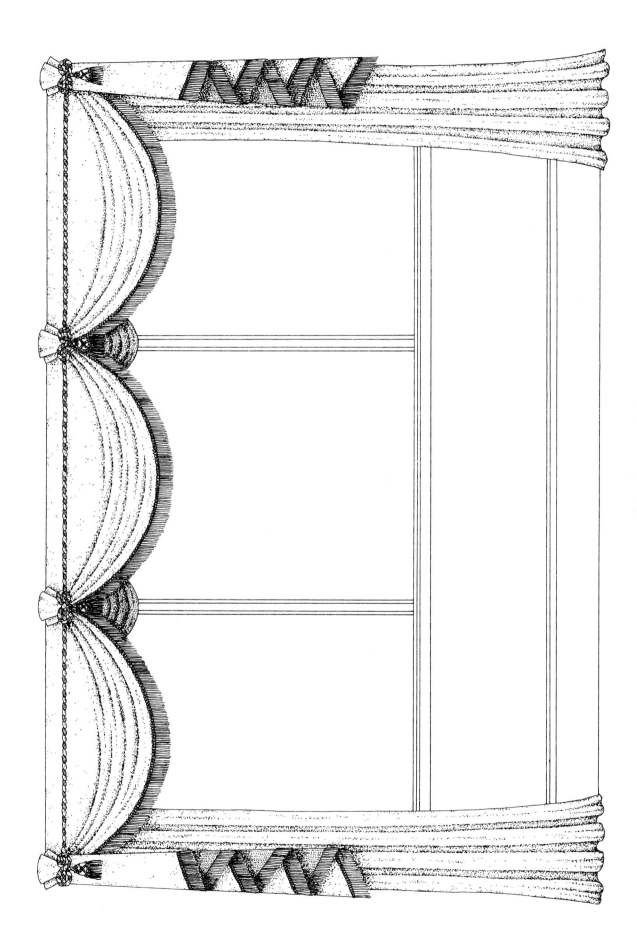

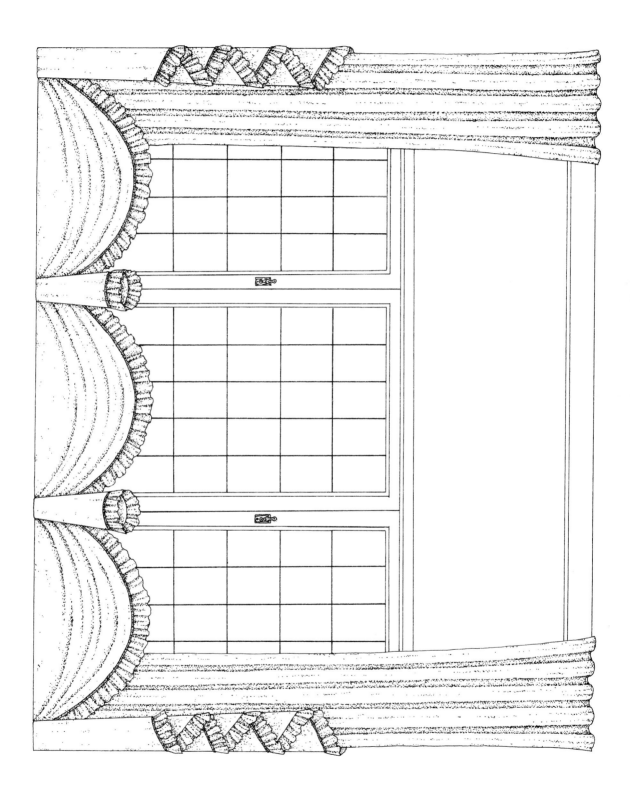

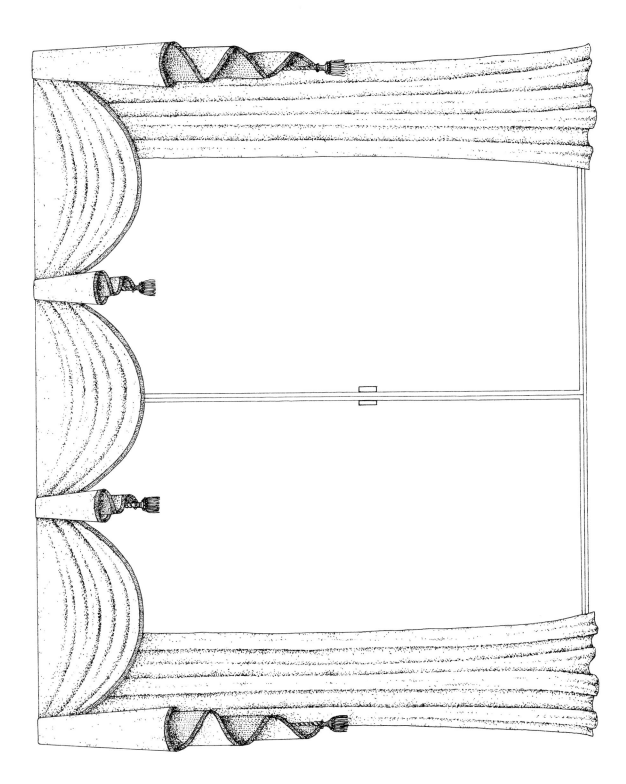

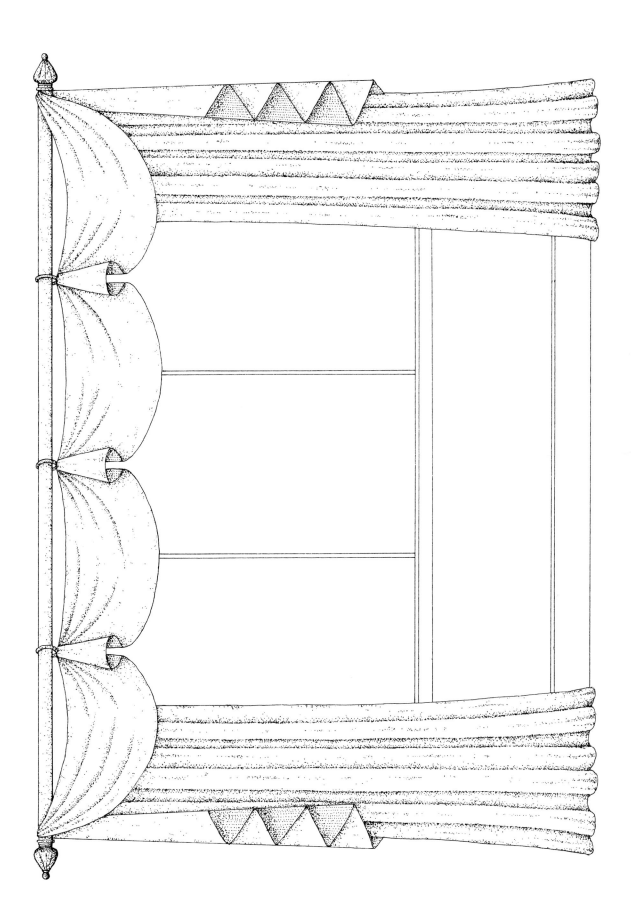

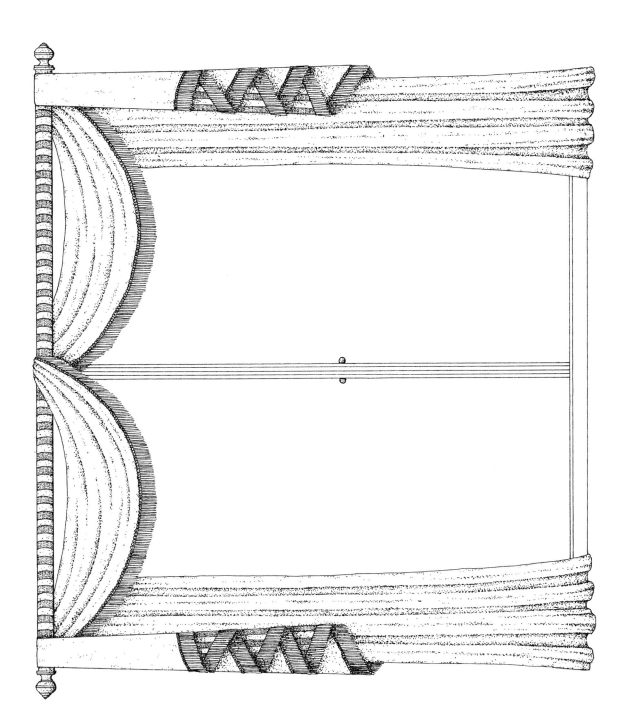

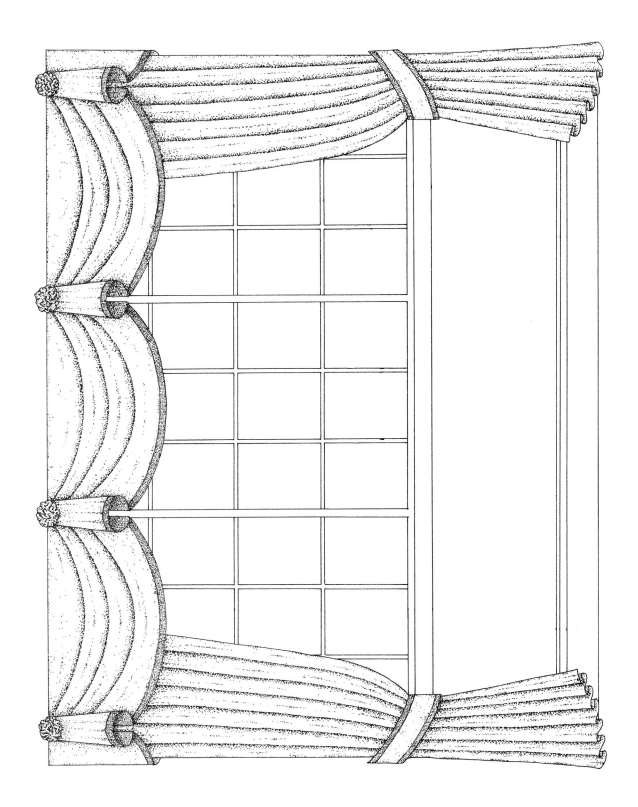

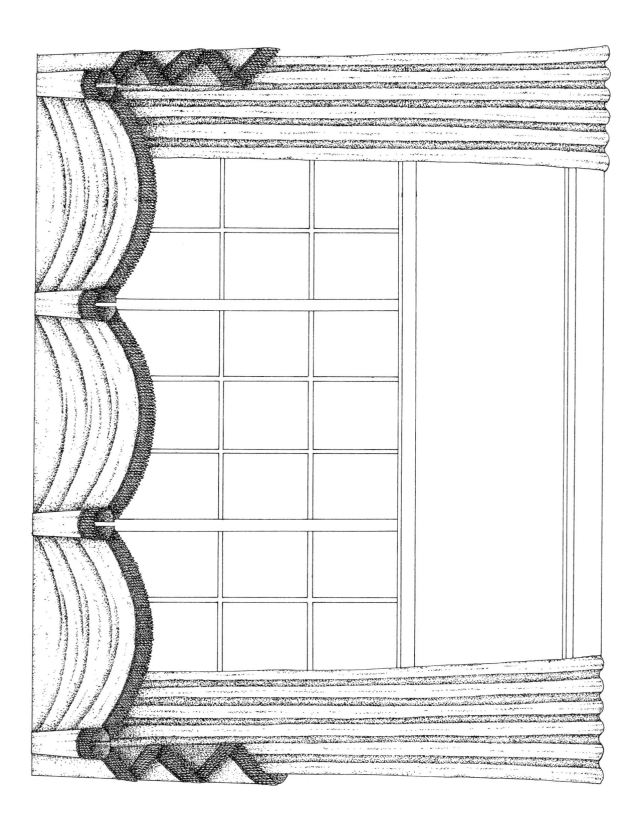

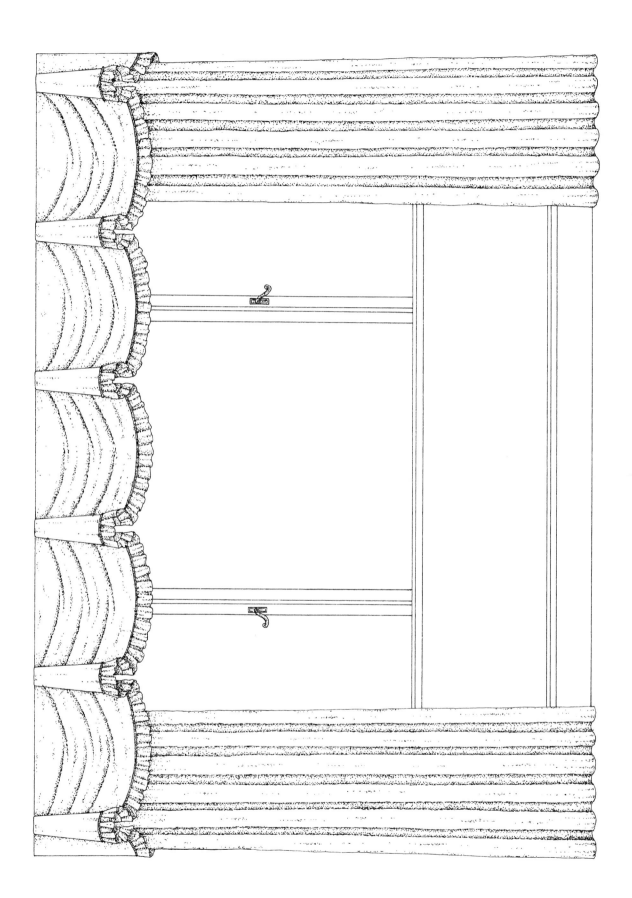

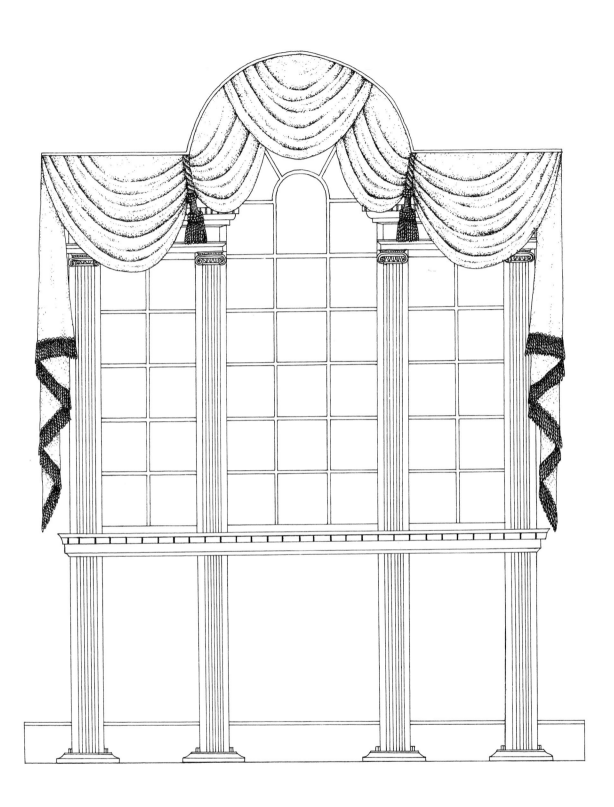

BLINDS

DESIGN BENEFITS
- No space required at sides of window
- Can be used with curtains
- Ideal for small windows
- Economical on fabric

Blinds can either be used on their own as a simple treatment or in conjunction with curtains in a multi-layered treatment. They are a useful treatment for small windows or for windows where there is no space at the side for a curtain (for example, where a cupboard butts up to the window). Blinds can be fitted either inside or outside the window recess or architrave.

The three main types of blinds are roller, Roman and Austrian. Roller and Roman blinds are simple flat blinds; Austrian blinds are gathered and more elaborate. A roller blind is pulled up and down by a spring mechanism, whereas Roman and Austrian blinds are pulled by cords.

A blind can often solve the problem of which window treatment to use when there are dissimilar windows in the same room. It is possible to have an elaborate window treatment on a large window, and then use a roller or Roman blind, made up in the curtain fabric, on a small window in the same room. An Austrian blind would be an alternative option: continuity could be provided by using the same heading as the curtains or valance on the blind, as well as matching the fabric and other design details such as contrast binding, fringes or frills.

ROLLER BLINDS

These are simple functional blinds made out of a flat piece of stiffened fabric which is wound round a wooden or metal roller with a spring fixed onto the end. A wooden lath is inserted in the hem at the lower edge to keep the blind flat and straight. For added design detail the lower edge, below the lath, can be shaped and trimmed with braid or fringe. Where the top of the roller blind will be visible, it can be 'reverse rolled' so that the fabric falls in front of the roller. In this case the blind will stand 5cm (2in) proud of the window.

Roller blinds are a practical solution for kitchen and bathroom windows and can be fitted neatly in the recess of a window. They can be bought ready-made in a standard range of fabrics or instead can be custom-made in laminated fabrics. A useful device for bedroom windows is to combine blackout roller blinds with curtains. Holland blinds are roller blinds made out of plain woven cream cotton fabric. They offer protection from harmful sunlight and are often used in conjunction with curtains.

ROMAN BLINDS

These blinds provide a smart, tailored window dressing, suitable for modern as well as traditional rooms. They pleat up into even horizontal folds. To keep the folds straight and even, metal rods or wooden laths are inserted in pockets in the lining at regular intervals. The top of the blind is fixed onto a narrow wooden batten. The blind is drawn up by cords which are then wrapped around a hook.

Roman blinds can look smart with inset borders or with a simple 2cm (¾in) strip of contrast fabric along the lower edge. Alternatively, block fringe can be sewn along the lower edge for added texture and interest.

Tournament blinds are Roman blinds with two or more vertical bands of braid or ribbon which are attached to each batten. The bands fall loosely when the blind is pulled up. Another stunning variation of a Roman blind is a fantail blind. The lower battens are split up the middle, so that when the blind is pulled up the broken battens form a fan shape.

AUSTRIAN BLINDS

These blinds are thought of as a feminine, frilly, window treatment, but they can take on a smart, formal look when made up in a damask and trimmed with fringe. They can have a gathered or a pleated heading and are corded to pleat up into soft scoops. The top of the blind is fixed onto a narrow wooden batten. It is drawn up by cords which are then wrapped in a figure of eight around a cleat hook.

The wider the window, the more scoops in the Austrian blind. For a design variation the first scoop can be set in from the side edges so that the sides then drop down and form tails. However, the dropped-down sides will stop light coming into the room.

London blinds are corded in the same manner as Austrian blinds. The fabric lies flat with an inverted pleat at each side of the blind.

ILLUSTRATION NOTES

Page 198
An Austrian blind with a set-down gathered heading, with one scoop and dropped-down sides. Knotted rope is sewn over the gathers.

Page 203
Tabbed-headed fringed flat valance hung from a pole with dress curtains. A functional roller blind with fringe along lower edge, central rope and tassel pull.

Page 204
Most roller blinds are finished with a straight edge, but for extra interest the lower edge can be shaped.
A Repeated scalloping.
B Gentle curves.
C Castellated shaping.
D Zigzag shaping.

Page 205
A roller blind with a curved lower edge trimmed with braid. The roller blind is fitted in the recess of the window with a pelmet fitted outside the architrave. The lower edge of the pelmet is contrast-bound and mimics the curved lower edge of the roller blind. The pelmet adds depth and interest.

Page 206
A roller blind fixed onto the architrave of the window with a serpentined contrast-bound smocked valance. The serpentined valance softens the horizontal line of the blind and also dresses the window.

Page 207
A roller blind set behind a swag with asymmetrical tails draped over a pole. The pole has arrow and flight finials. This is a fun treatment for a kitchen window, but would work equally well on a bathroom or a landing window.

Page 208

A Roman blind with braid set in from the edges is a smart treatment suitable for most types of room. The blind has been fixed inside the architrave.

Page 209

A tournament blind fixed inside the architrave. This stunning but simple treatment has ribbon trim looped between each fold of the blind.

Page 210

A Roman blind contrast-bound on three sides.

Page 211

A Roman blind with fringed lower edge. Fringed sill-length tails with goblet coronets, sewn on the side edges. Rope knotted at the base of each goblet and run along the blind. This treatment is suitable for occasional use, as the blind may disturb the tails.

Page 212

A Roman blind with a 2cm (¾in) contrast-bound lower edge. A goblet-headed yoke with 1cm (½in) contrast-bound top has been sewn onto the top of the blind. Rope knotted at the base of each goblet. If necessary to support the weight of the yoke, put stiffening in the first pleat of the blind.

Page 213

Roman blind with puffed heading sewn across the top. Alleviates the possible starkness of a plain Roman blind.

Page 214

Roman blind with a fringed swag sewn onto the top. Rope runs along the top with knots and tassels at either end.

Page 215

A fantail Roman blind, fixed inside the architrave but it would also work well on the outside. An unusual but very effective blind.

Page 216

An Austrian blind with a pencil gathered heading. It has three scoops with a contrast-piped frill on the lower edge. A pretty, soft window treatment suitable for bedrooms and bathrooms. The blind has been set inside the architrave.

Page 217

An Austrian blind with a 1cm (½in) contrast top and smocked heading. It has three scoops with a contrast-piped frill on the side and lower edges. The smocked heading works well with the frill edging. The blind has been fixed onto the outside of the architrave.

Page 218

An Austrian blind with one scoop and dropped-down sides. It has a channel heading with a 5-10cm (2-4in) stand-up frill above the channel. The channel heading can be pushed onto ordinary wooden dowelling with decorative finials on the end. The cords go up to a batten fixed behind the pole.

Page 219

A French-headed Austrian blind with one scoop and dropped-down sides. It has a box-pleated frill around the sides and lower edge. The heading and pleated frill give a tailored look to the blind. Knife pleats can be used instead of box pleats. The blind has been fixed onto the outside of the architrave.

Page 220

A pencil-gathered Austrian blind with a 1cm (½in) contrast top and 2cm (¾in) contrast-bound sides and lower edge, two scoops and dropped-down sides, fixed outside the architrave.

Page 221

An Austrian blind with a set-down gathered heading with a 1cm (½in) contrast-bound top and fringe along the lower edge. A classic style of blind, suitable for formal rooms. The blind has been fixed outside the architrave.

Page 222

A soft pleated London blind with one scoop and dropped-down sides, trimmed with fringe along the lower edge. The tops of the inverted pleats are finished with Maltese crosses. The blind has been fixed outside the architrave.

Page 223

A soft pleated London blind with inverted pleats in contrasting fabric, tassels at the top and bottom of the pleats and flat braid on the outside edges. It has been fixed inside the architrave.

Page 224

A-B A fish-tail blind with contrast edges on three sides. This is an unlined blind often made in a sheer fabric.

C-D A reefed blind that is drawn to one side with Italian stringing.

Page 225

Informal unlined 'sail-cloth' blinds with eyelets hooked onto cup-hooks screwed into a batten fixed to the wall.

A-B Fabric tabs sewn onto the blind are looped up onto the hooks.

C-D The corner of the blind is pulled up diagonally with a cord.

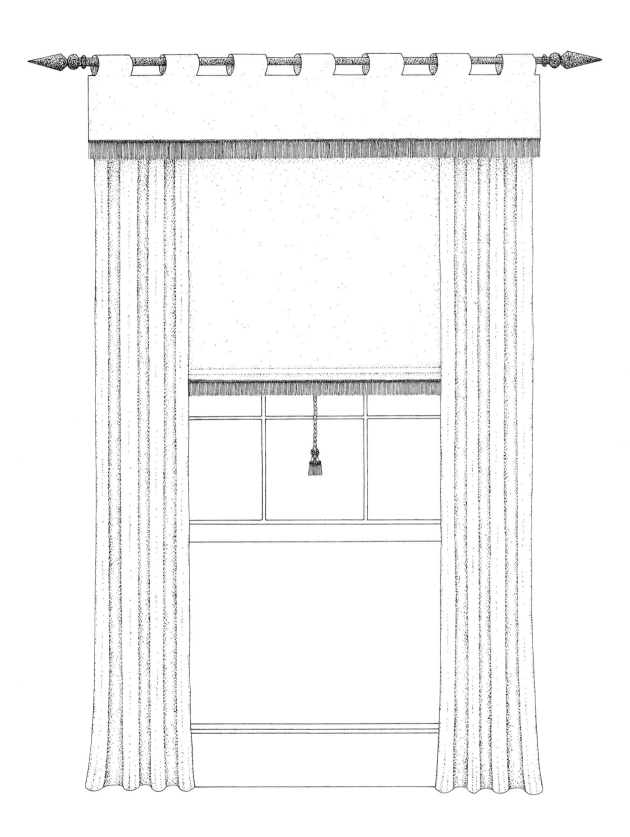

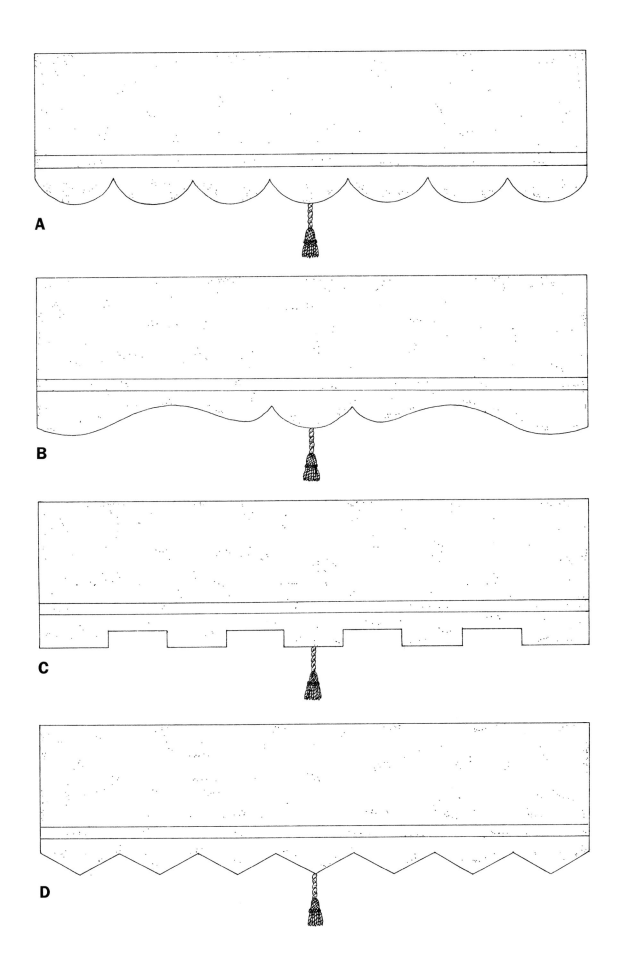

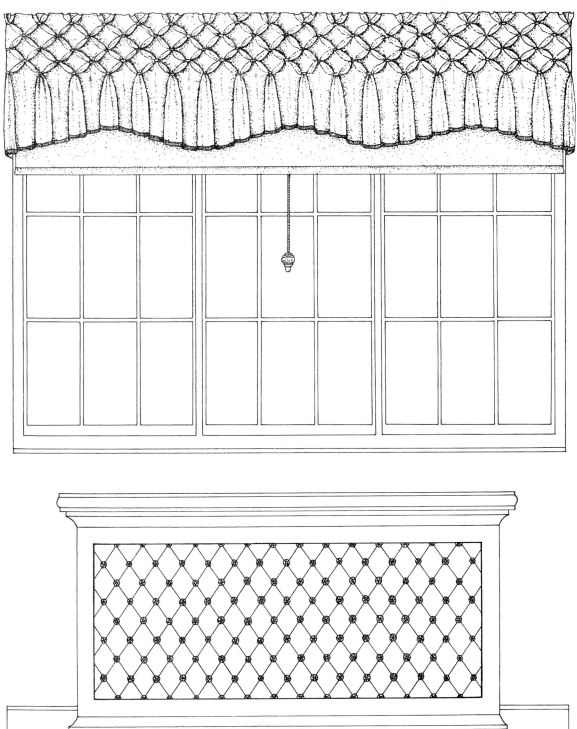

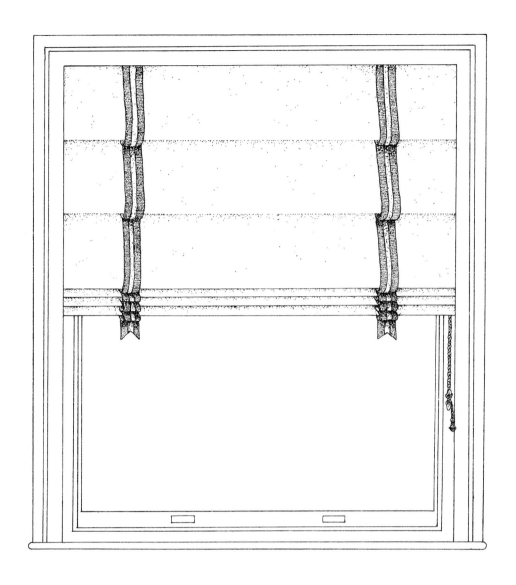

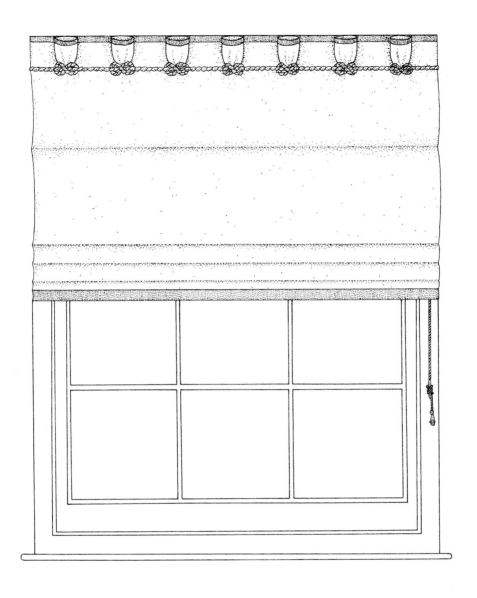

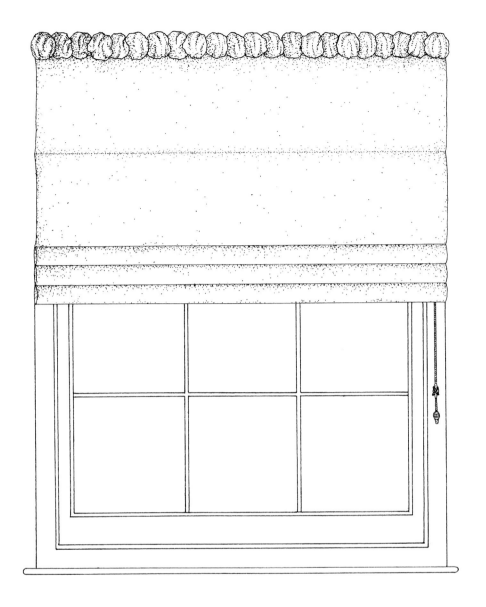

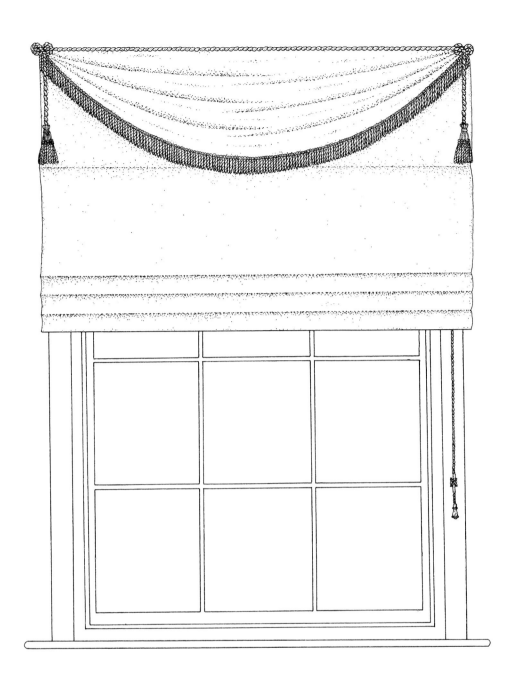

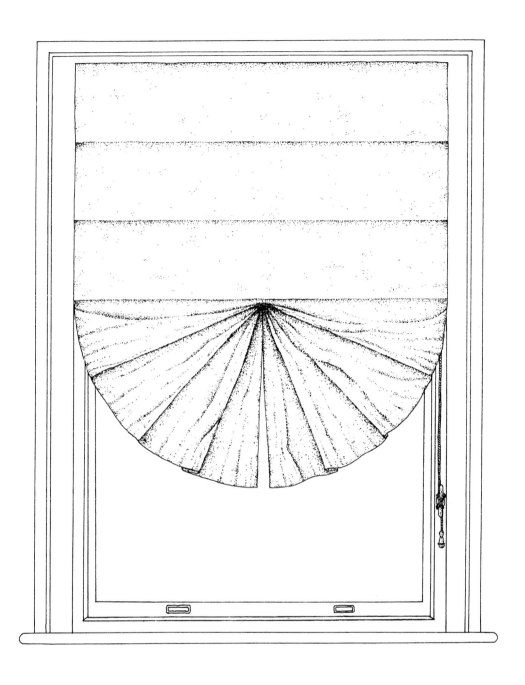

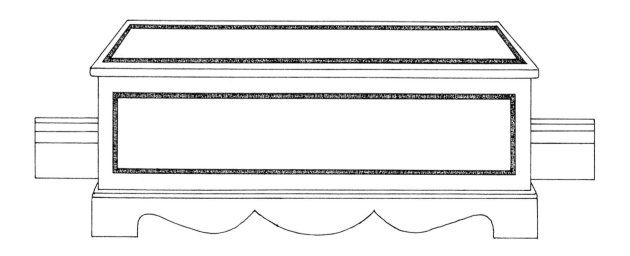

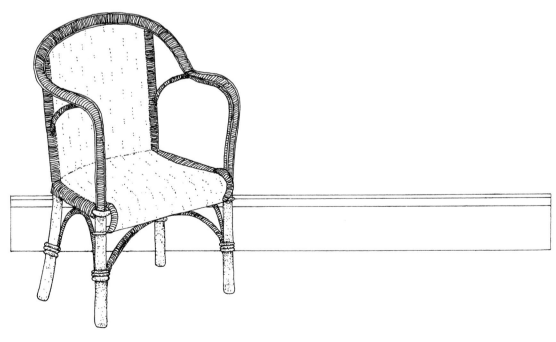

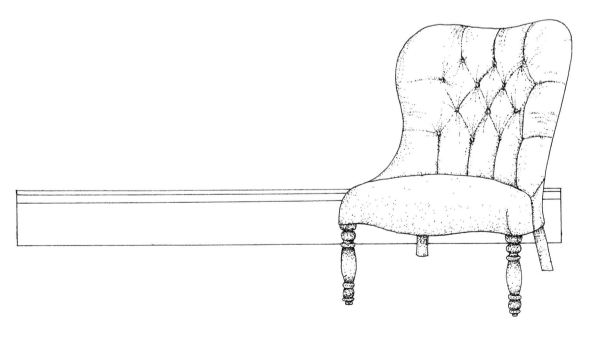

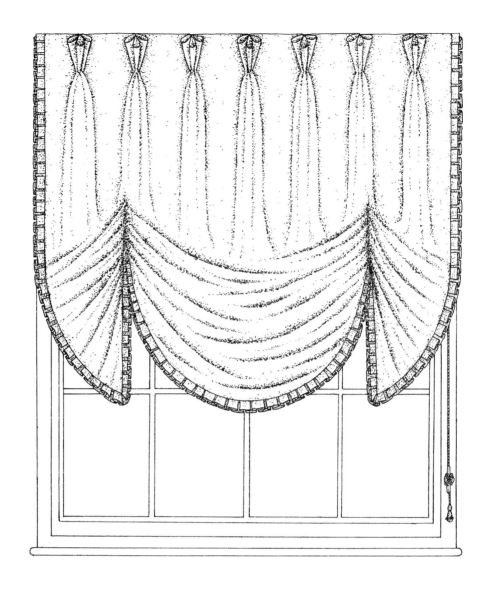

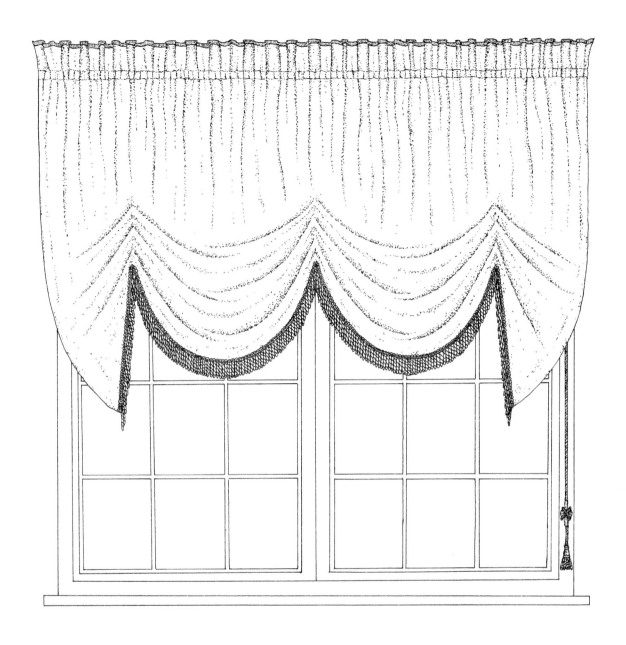

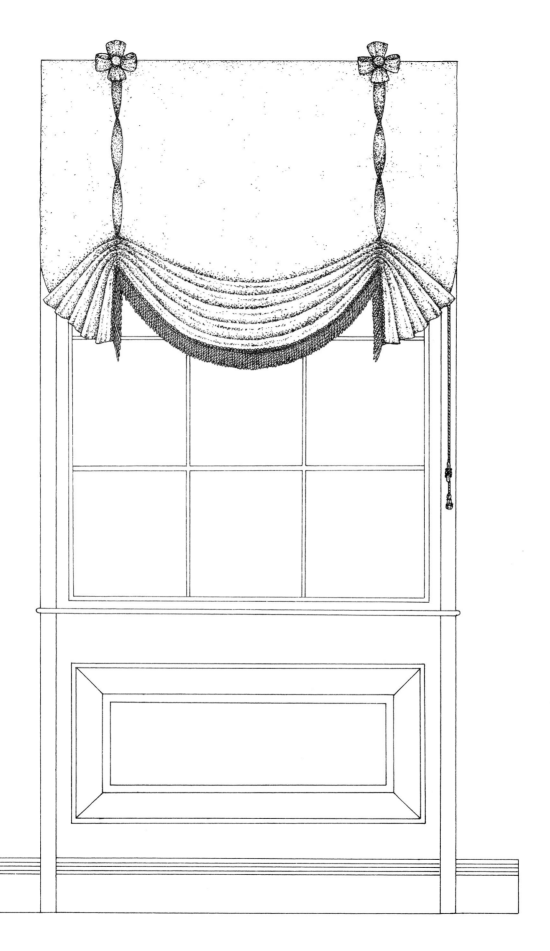

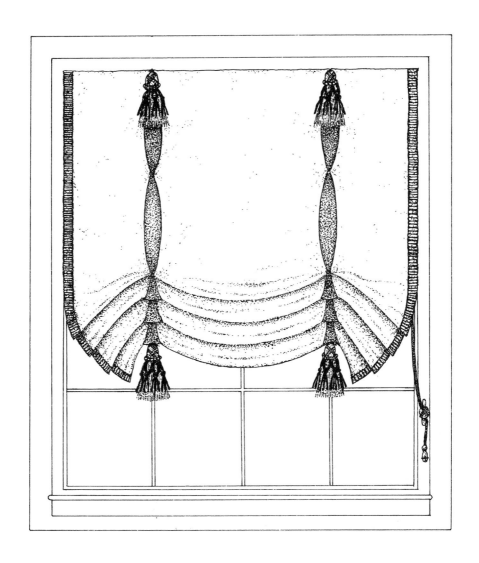

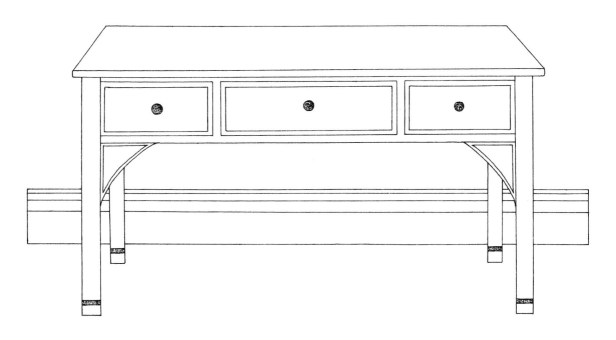

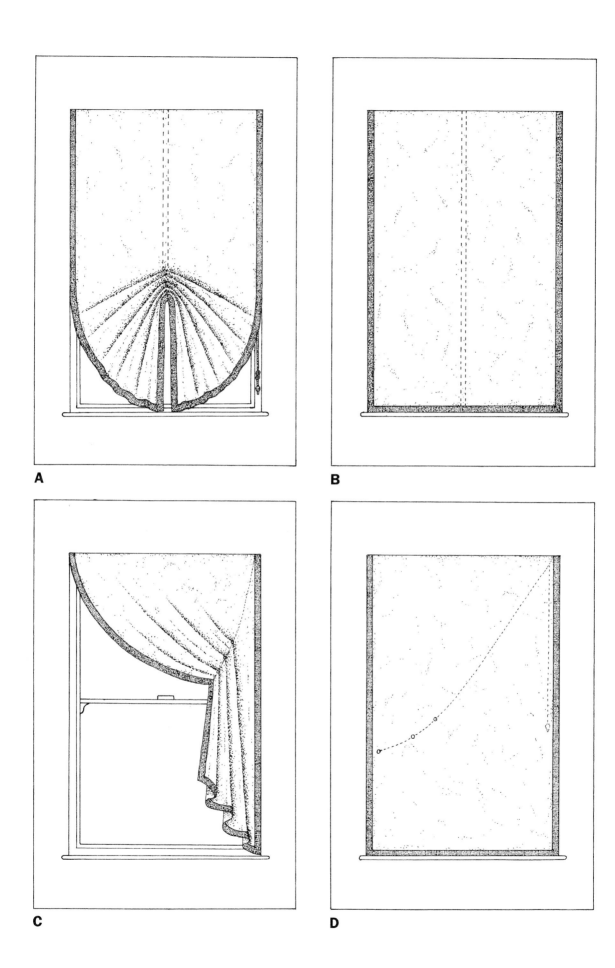

A

B

C

D

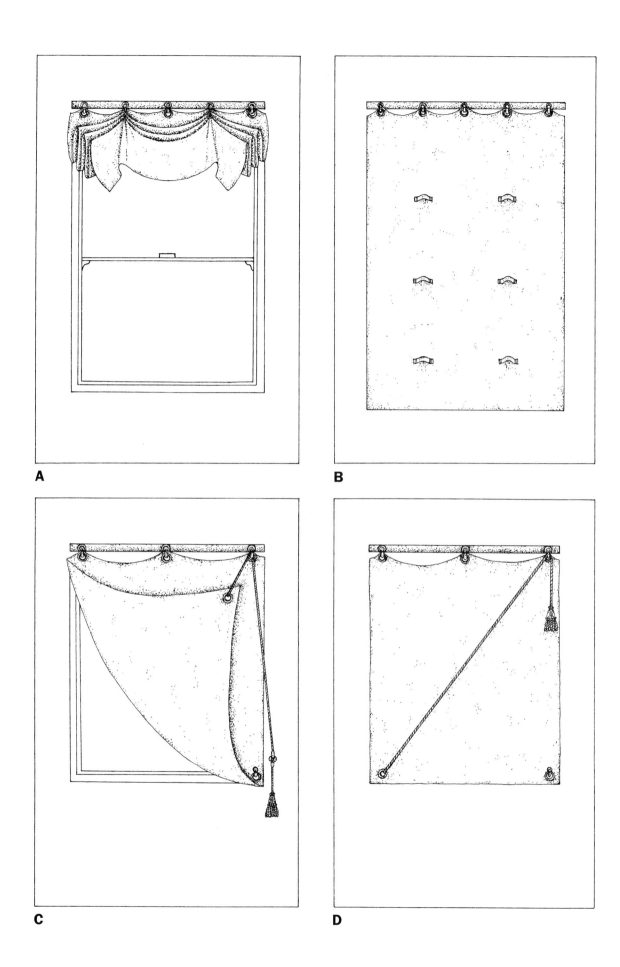

A

B

C

D

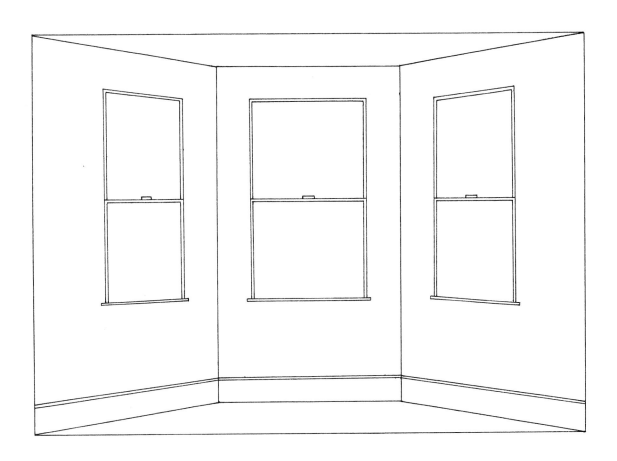

BAY WINDOWS

Bay windows present an exciting and added challenge. The curtain treatment is more successful if the bay is treated as a whole rather than as individual windows. Fabric-covered laths, poles, valances, pelmets, swags and tails, blinds can all be adapted and fitted in a bay window.

Most bay windows are two-angled, but they can have several angles.

The dead wall space at the sides of the bay window can be utilised for the curtain stack-back area. Dead wall space at the angles of the bay can be dressed with intermediate curtains to soften the lines of the window.

Where there is a window seat in a bay window, it is not possible to have full-length curtains going round the bay. One solution is to have full-curtains going across the front of the bay. Other options are to combine such curtains with blinds in the window or simply to dress the window with blinds (see pages 232-236).

A fabric-covered pelmet board with a fascia is an appropriate treatment where there is no wall space above the bay window.

Proportions
Use the same proportions as for a straight window. Where there is a straight window and a bay window in the same room, the curtain treatment that is used on the straight window can usually be adapted for the bay.

For some valances and pelmets, care should be taken to balance the design at the angles of the window. This advice also applies to swags and tails. For example, swags should start and finish at the angles of the pelmet board.

Fittings for bay windows
Plastic tracks can curve round bays quite easily but they will not take the weight of heavy curtains.

Metal tracks can be bent to go round bays. They are normally top-fixed onto pelmet boards, but can be face-fixed.

A 'reverse bend' track needs to be used where corded tracks require both concave bends in the angles of the bay and convex bends at the sides.

A pole can be an appropriate treatment where there is no wall space above the window. You will normally hang a curtain at each angle because of brackets at the corners.

ILLUSTRATION NOTES

Page 226
A bay window with unattractive dead wall space between the windows which is covered by a four-curtain treatment. The dead wall space above the window has been covered with a shaped goblet-headed valance.

Page 230
Four puff-headed curtains held by scallop-shaped tie-backs and hung from a fabric-covered pelmet board with a fascia. Puff-headed curtains do not stack back very tightly so they need to be held by tie-backs.

Page 231

A pair of French-headed curtains with a 1cm (½in) contrast-bound top and 2.5cm (1in) contrast-bound leading edges hung from a fabric-covered pelmet board with a fascia and held by contrast-bound tie-backs. The pelmet board would need to be set well above the French doors if they opened inwards, in order to give easy clearance.

Page 232

A pair of French-headed curtains with 2.5cm (1in) contrast-bound leading edges, hung from a pole. The pole has been fitted across the front of the bay window and Roman blinds with in-set braid have been fitted to the windows. This is a suitable treatment where there are window seats.

Page 233

A pole fixed across the front of the bay with drop-down gathered dress curtains, held with banana-shaped tie-backs. Three functional Austrian blinds placed at each window, so that the window seat can be used when the blinds are down. The blinds have the same drop-down gathered heading as the curtains, a fringed lower edge, and each has one scoop with drop-down sides.

Page 234

Full-length dress curtains with functional window-seat length curtains inside the bay. Flat pelmet, with deep contrast-bound top and bottom, follows the shape of the bay.

Page 235

Window-seat length curtains with a gathered valance, with 2cm (1in) contrast-bound lower edge. Window-seat cushion is piped and has a floor-length gathered valance. This gives the illusion of full-length curtains.

Page 236

Dress curtains with serpentined fringed drop-down gathered valance. Plain roller blinds with central pulls at the windows.

Page 237

Four curtains with set-down tape heading hung from a pole, held by tassel tie-backs.

Page 238

A pair of curtains held by contrast-bound tie-backs. The French-pleated valance has a 2.5cm (1in) contrast-bound lower edge. Four curtains would have worked equally well with the valance.

Page 239

Flat pelmet tied onto a pole with rope through eyelets. The pole is mounted on blocks so that the curtains can move freely on their track behind. This neat treatment does mean that light will be lost as the curtains must remain in the bay, rather than returning onto the wall.

Page 240

Square bay with valance and curtains returned onto the wall — the track runs from the left-hand wall, round the bay, and onto the right-hand wall. Box-pleated valance with 1cm (½in) contrast-bound top and fringe along lower edge. Rope is sewn along the valance, set down 7.5cm (3in) from the top. Note the box pleats should line up with the angles of the bay.

Page 241

Square bay with valance and curtains returned onto the wall — the track runs from the left-hand wall, round the bay, and onto the right-hand wall. A pair of curtains held by contrast-bound tie-backs — the box-pleated valance has a 2.5cm (1in) contrast-bound lower edge and is set onto a contrast-bound yoke. Note that the box pleats should line up with the angles of the bay.

Page 242
A pair of curtains held by smocked tie-backs. The valance has a set-down smocked heading.

Page 243
A pair of curtains hung from a curved track and pelmet board in a bow window. The valance has a set-down tape heading with a rope sewn over it. It has a 1cm (½in) contrast-bound top and a 2.5cm (1in) contrast-bound hem.

Page 244
To permit wall sconces, this bay window has been treated as three separate entities: three pairs of goblet-headed Italian-strung curtains have 1cm (½in) contrast-bound tops, knotted rope at the base of each goblet and fringe down leading edges.

Page 245
Four puff-headed, Italian-strung curtains. They are fitted to the front edge of the pelmet board and are permanently joined in the centre of each window. The Italian stringing is dramatic and the centre curtains cover the unattractive wall area between the windows.

Page 246
A pair of curtains with a graduated shaped pelmet which follows the shape of the bay. The pelmet is trimmed with fringe and finished with trumpets at the sides and in the corners. Shaping the pelmet to fit the bay takes careful planning.

Page 247
Three swags with trumpets in the corners and tails at the sides, all trimmed with fringe. The swags start and finish at the corners and the tails are returned to follow the line of the side walls.

Page 248
Four swags, a central tail and side tails trimmed with fringe and draped over a pole. There are two swags over the centre window and one swag over each side window. The curtains are hung from a track set behind and below the pole and are held by tassel tie-backs.

Page 249
Four swags with three decorative tails at the intersections of the swags and a pair of tails at the sides. Each tail is finished with a Maltese cross. The four curtains are held by scalloped shaped tie-backs.

Page 250
Six swags with three decorative tails at the centre of each window, two long double tails in the corners of the bay and a pair of tails at the side. The swags and tails have all been trimmed with fringe. The four curtains are held by tassel tie-backs. A very sumptuous bay window treatment.

Page 251
Six swags with two long double tails in the corners of the bay and a pair of tails at the side. The swags and tails have all been trimmed with fringe and finished with rope clovers above the tails and at the intersection of the swags. The four curtains are held by tassel tie-backs. Another very sumptuous bay window treatment.

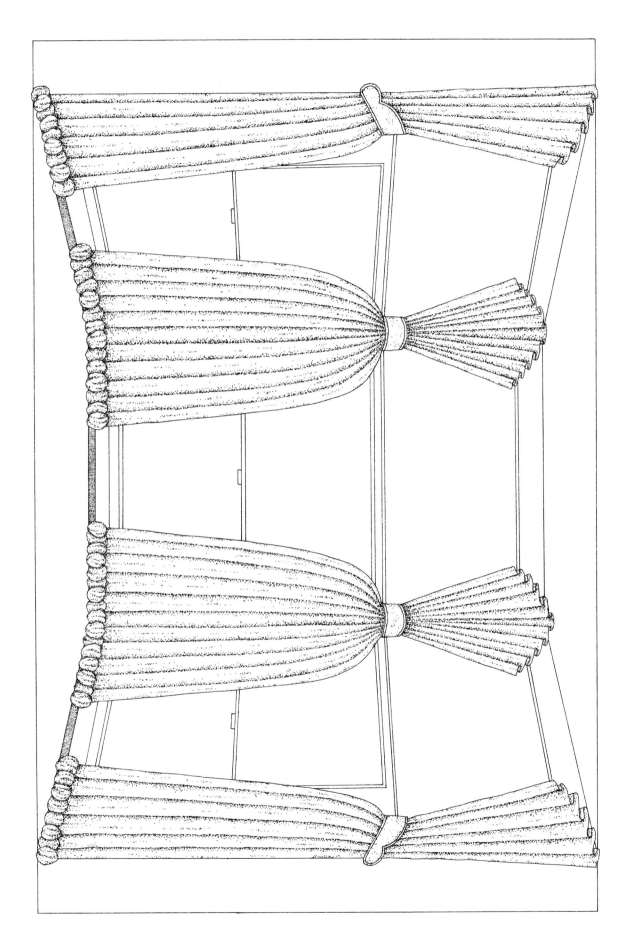

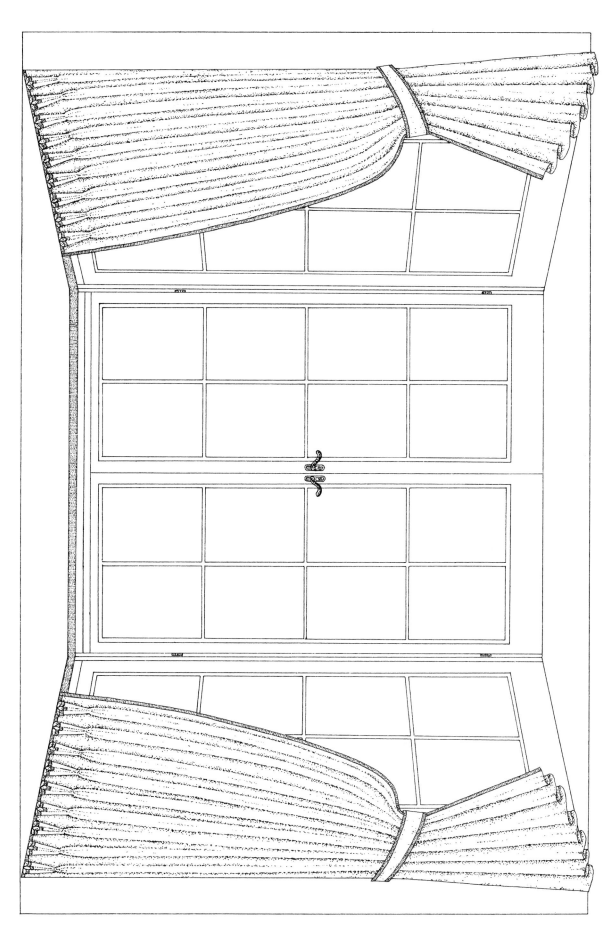

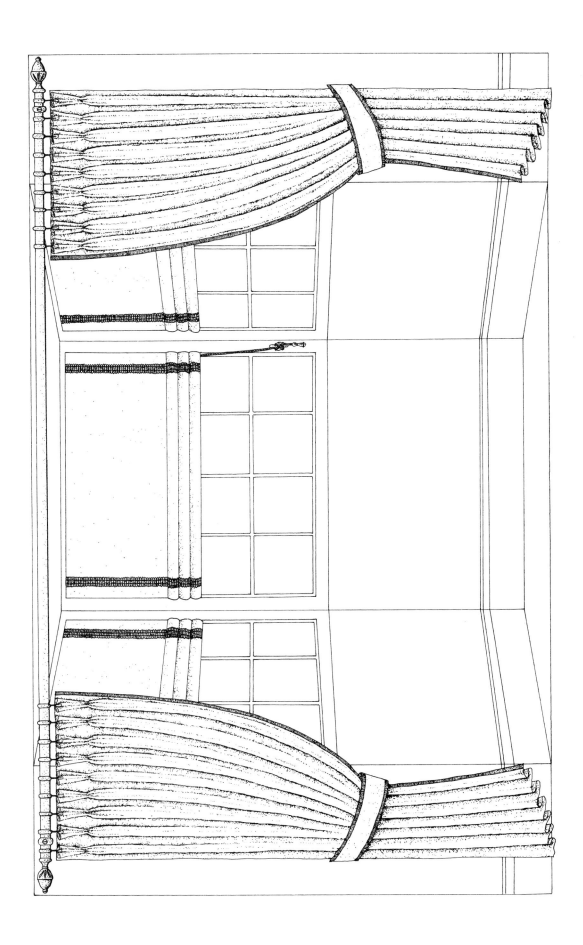

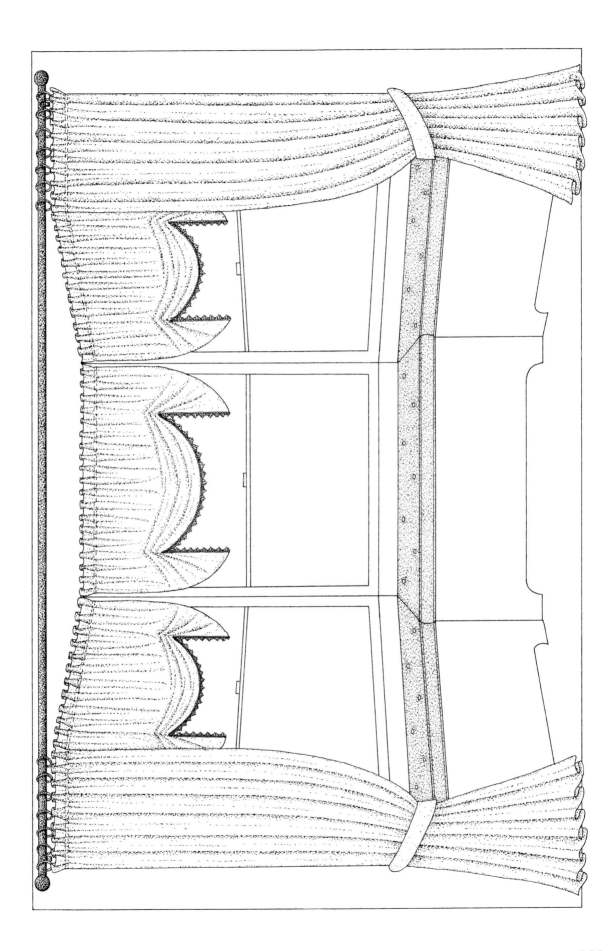

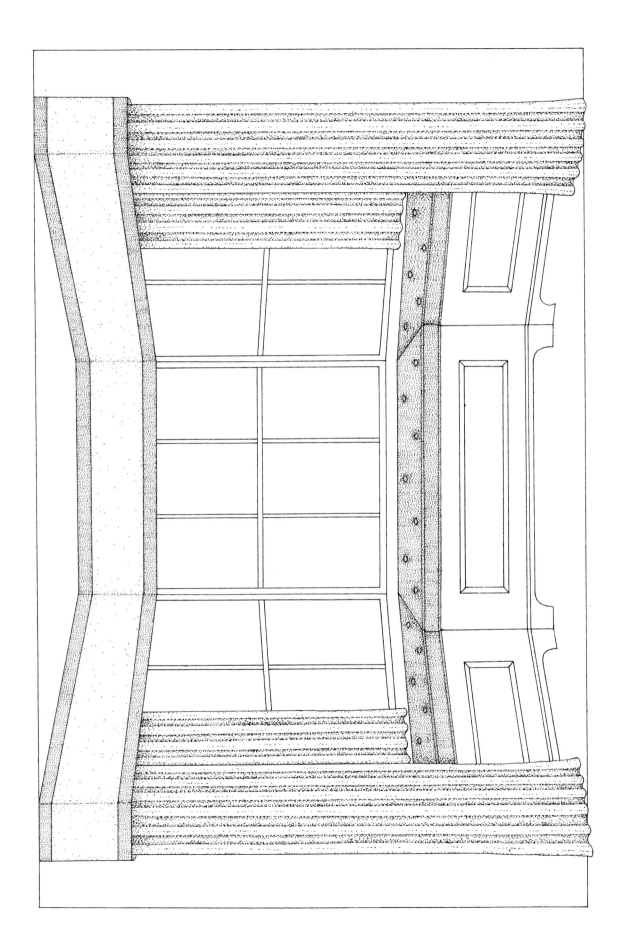

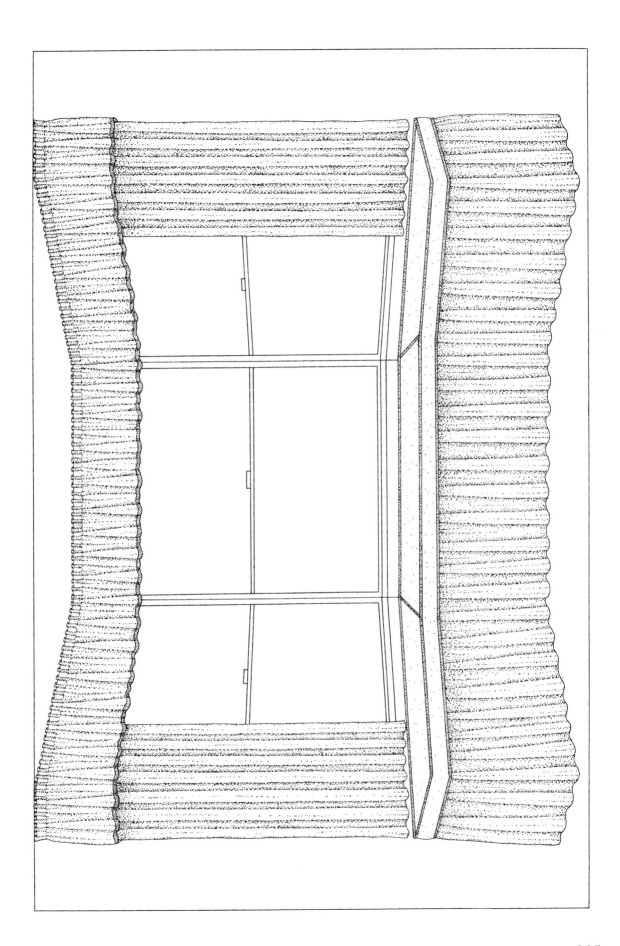

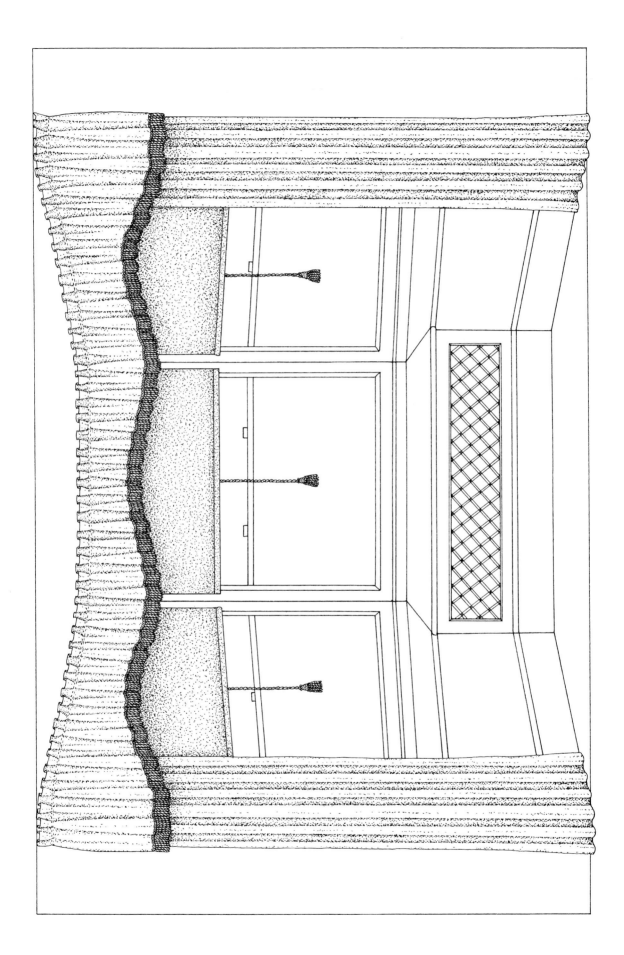

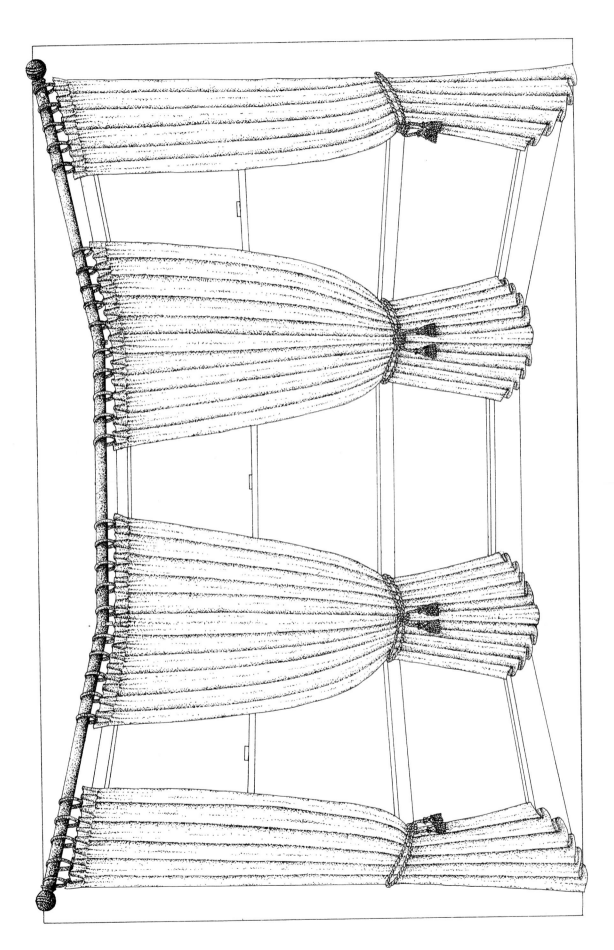

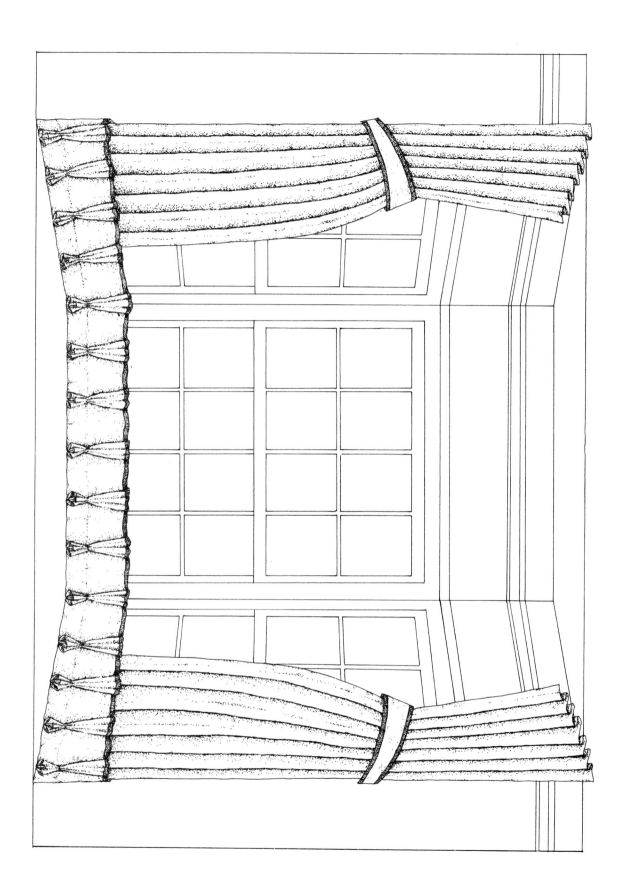

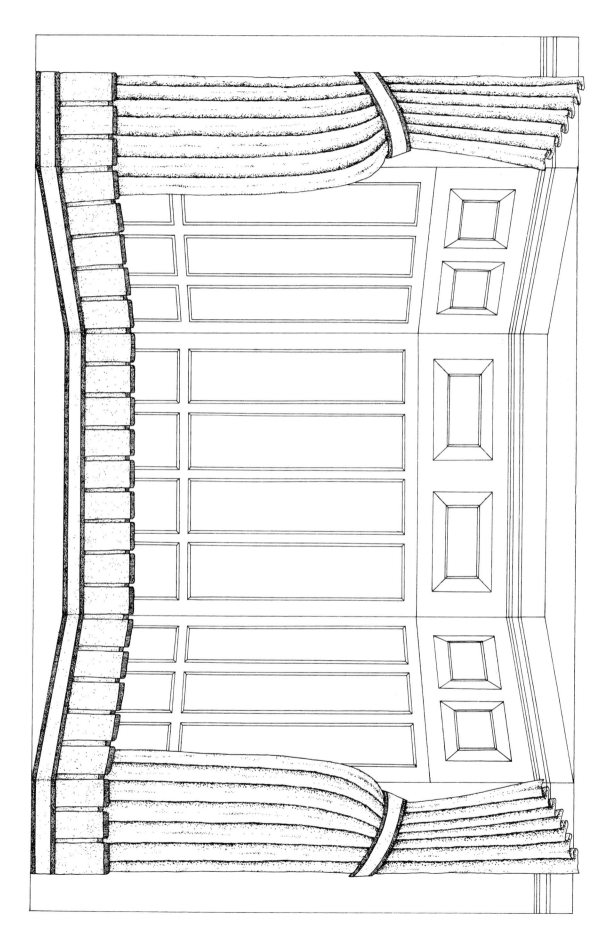

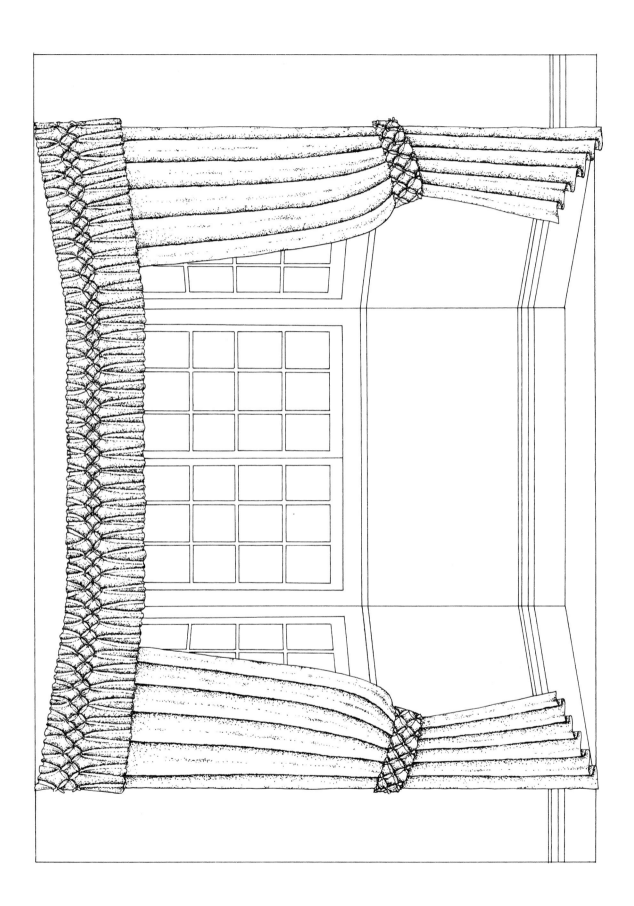

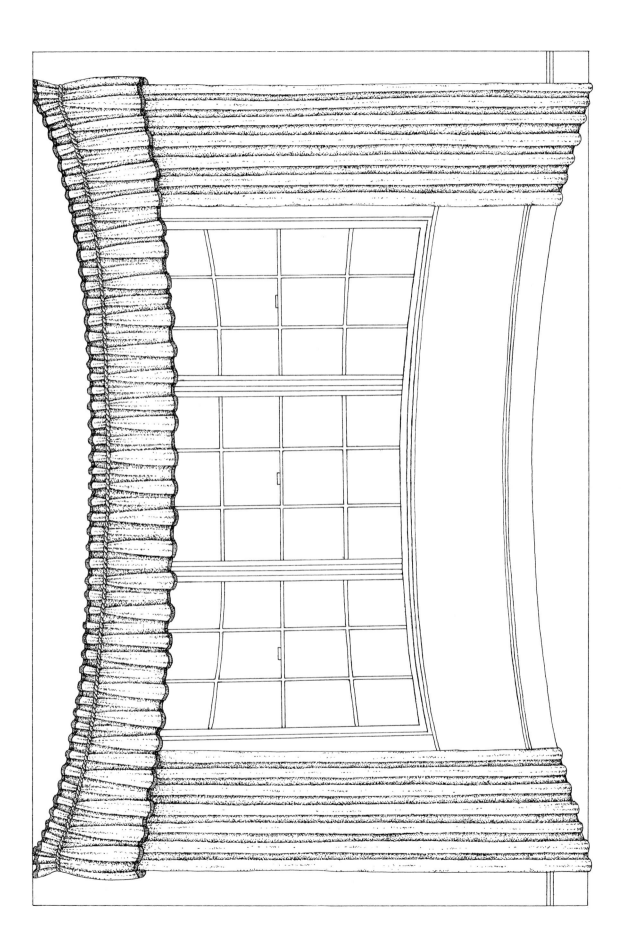

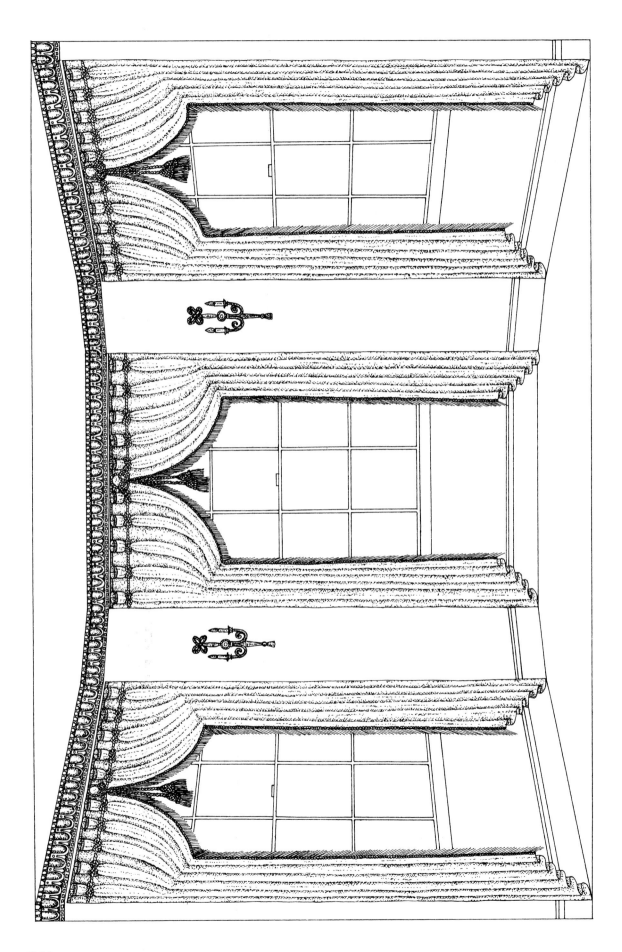

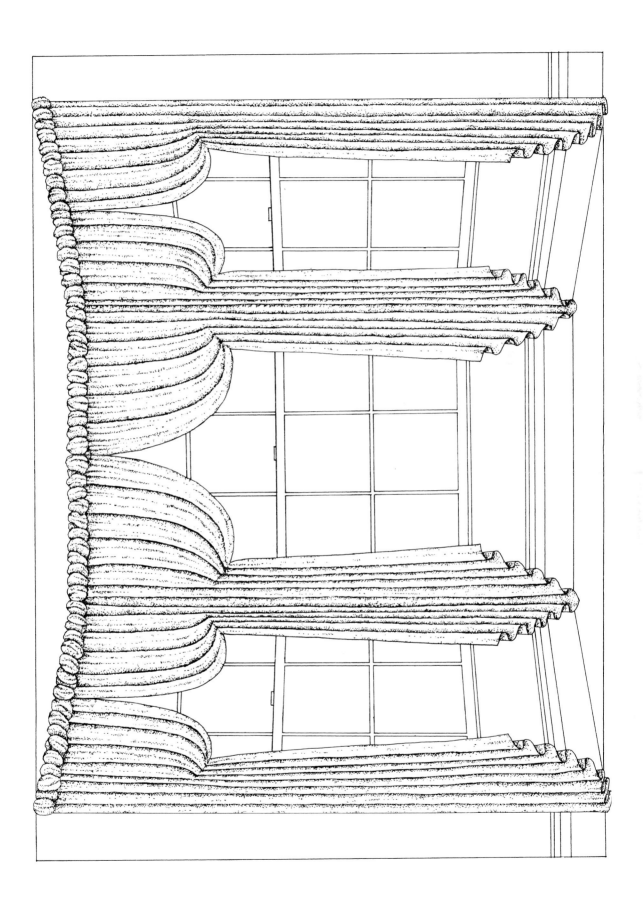

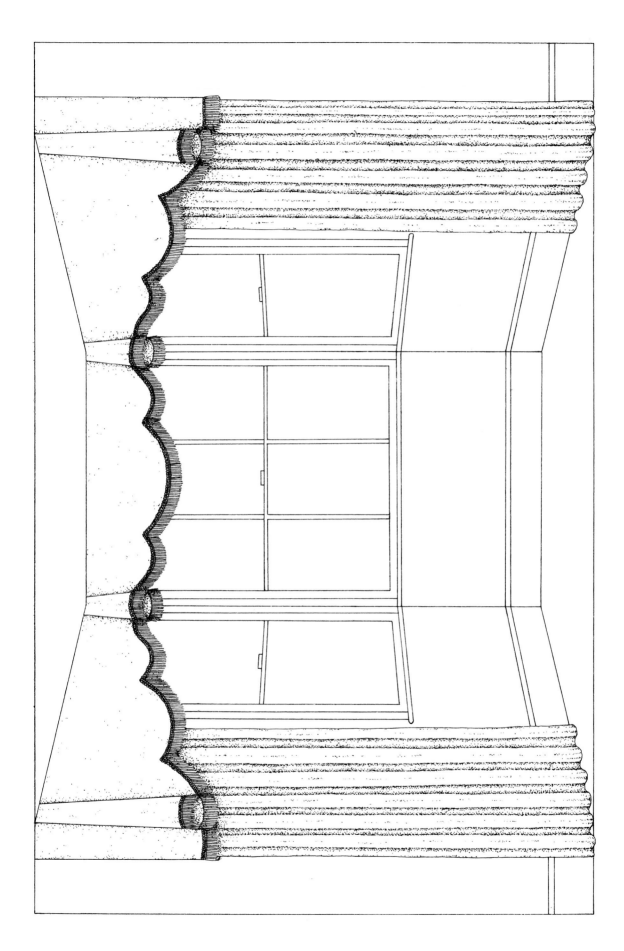

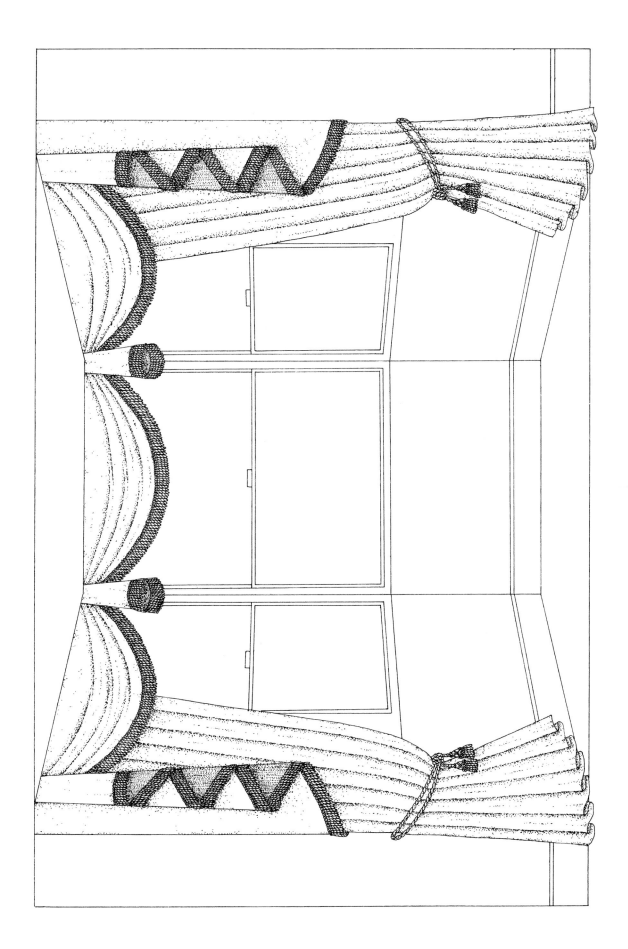

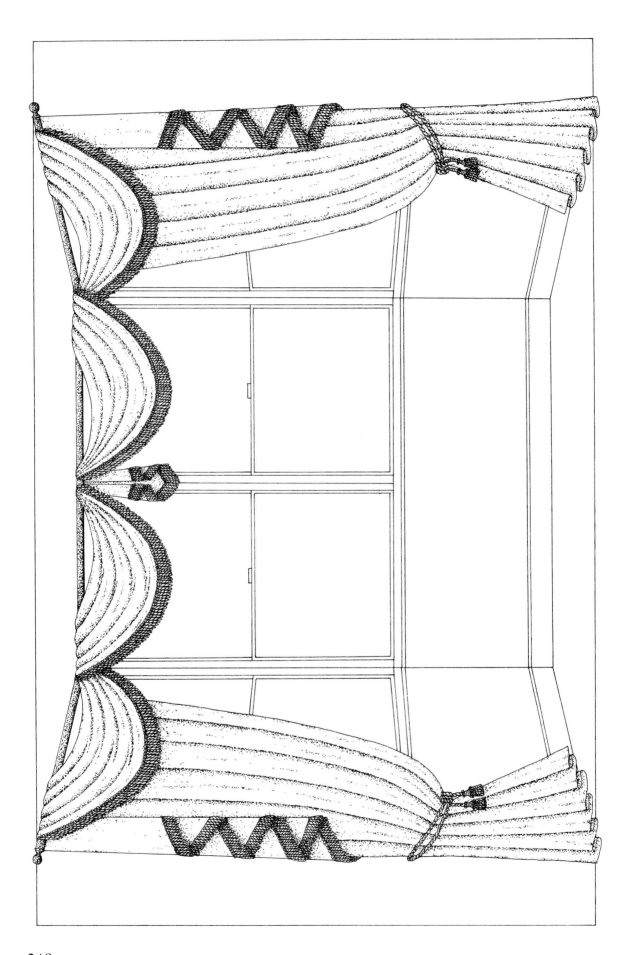

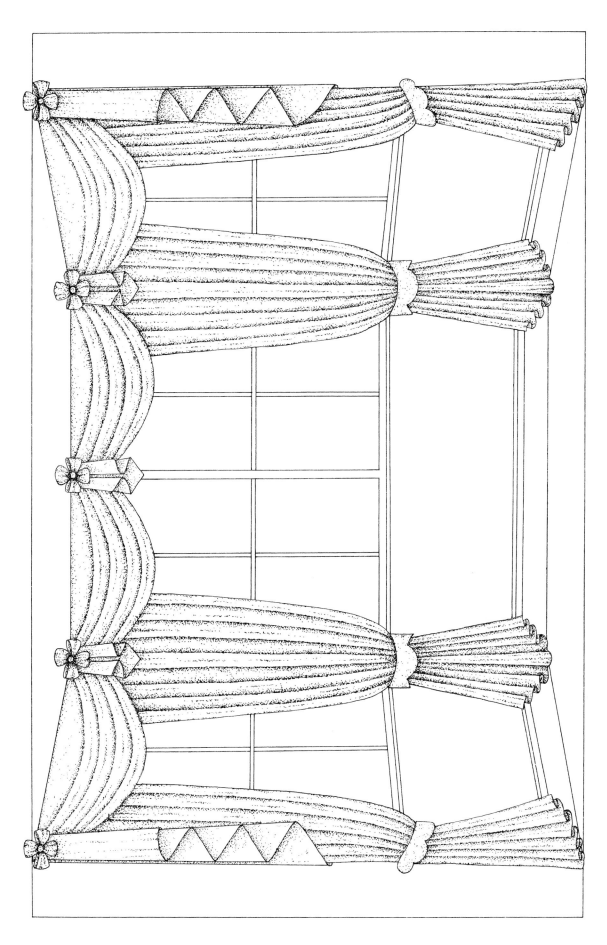

Tall and narrow windows
INCLUDING ARCHED WINDOWS

These are elegant windows which allow a lot of light into a room. Most types of window treatment are suitable, and they also present an opportunity to use static or fixed headings, with the curtains held open by tie-backs, ombras or Italian stringing. Arched windows also require fixed headings and again the curtains will need to be held open.

To Italian-string curtains, six or more rings are sewn into the lining side of the curtain, set in from the leading edges. Cords are threaded through the rings up to screw eyes on the underside of the pelmet board and secured onto a cleat hook at the side of the curtain.

Curved pelmet boards are described on page 86. Curtains are hung from the board in the same way as a valance.

For arched windows either fit a pliable plastic track or bend a metal track to the shape of the window. To fit swags in front of the curtains it may be necessary to make a wood or fibreboard arch-shaped pelmet board.

ILLUSTRATION NOTES

Page 252
Italian-strung goblet-headed curtains.

Page 255
Goblet-headed curtains with 1cm (½in) contrast-bound top joined in the middle with false goblet. Two rows of rope are looped across the swags from knots beneath alternate goblets. Tasselled rope hangs from clovers at the outer and central

goblets. The curtains are Italian-strung and hung from a pole.

Page 256
Channel-headed curtains slotted onto a pole with ball end finials. A striped fabric cut on the true cross is used on the leading edges, for the frill above the channel and on the edges of the ruched tie-backs. The heading is permanently fixed.

Page 257
Channel-headed curtains held by acanthus curtain bands, slotted onto a pole with decorative finials. The top of the frill, leading edges and hems of the curtains are contrast-bound, the heading permanently fixed.

Page 258
Italian-strung, puff-headed curtains with rope sewn at the base of the gathers. They are hung from a curved board with a roller blind set behind.

Page 259
Italian-strung goblet-headed curtains with a 1cm (½in) contrast top, knotted rope at the base of the goblets, a central rope clover with tassels, and fringe along the hem. They are hung from a curved board.

Page 260
Italian-strung curtains with a tiara-shaped deep smocked heading finished with a central Maltese cross and hung from a curved board.

Page 261
Italian-strung curtains with a deep pencil heading finished with a trefoil and tassels at the centre and hung from a curved

board. The leading edges and the hem are trimmed with bullion fringe.

Page 262
Italian-strung arch-shaped curtains with a dropped-down gathered heading permanently joined at the centre.

Page 263
Italian-strung arch-shaped French-headed curtains with fan edging on-set on the leading edges. The curtains are permanently joined at the centre.

Page 264
Two asymmetrical arch-shaped swags with a central double tail, all trimmed with fan-edged fringe. The curtains are trimmed with fan edge on the leading edge and held by scallop-shaped tie-backs.

Page 265
Curtains hung from a straight track behind an arch-shaped flat pelmet, with scalloped and fringed lower edge. Pelmet is finished with tasselled rope looped between choux with central rope clover.

Page 266
Goblet-headed arch-shaped Italian-strung curtains, with a rope clover and tassels hung at centre on a false goblet.

Page 267
Gathered Italian-strung curtains with asymmetric fringed swags. Fringed tails and central decorative tail, all finished with small choux.

Page 268
Straight pelmet board placed across the top of an arched window. Pair of curtains with valance with arch-shaped fringed lower edge, and 1cm (½in) contrast-bound top and drop-down gathered heading. Fabric trefoils at either side, with rope clover and tassels placed on top.

Page 269
Three arch-shaped swags trimmed with fringe. The curtains are held by plain tie-backs. The curtains are hung from a straight track.

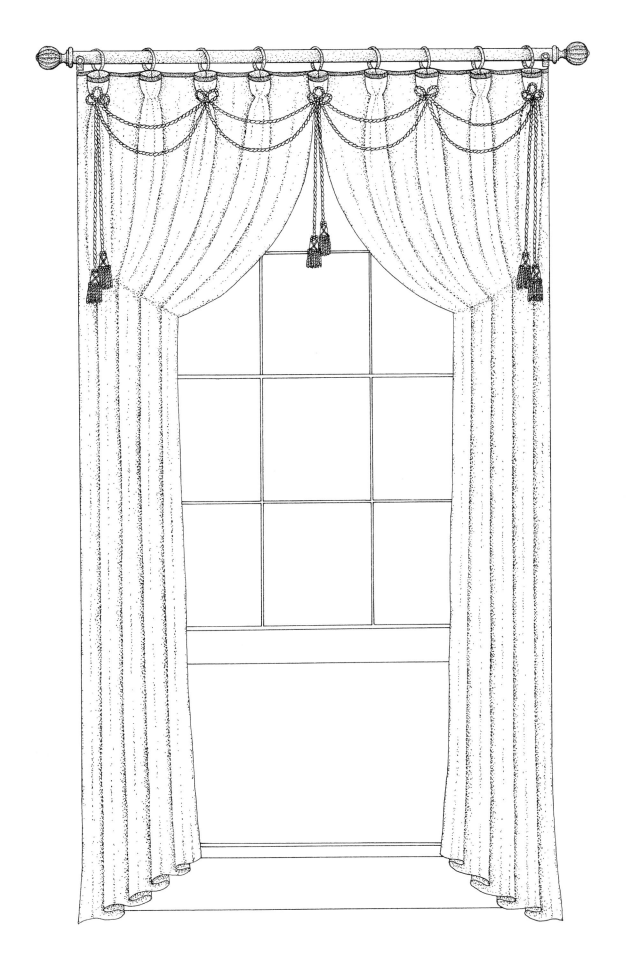

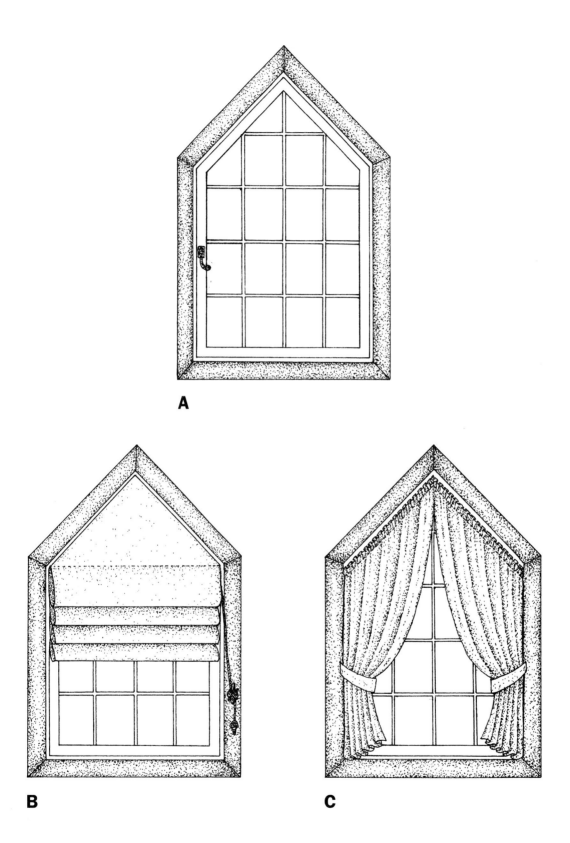

A

B

C

PROBLEM WINDOWS

When a window presents a challenge because of its unusual shape or because there are fitting constraints, this very often results in an exciting and unusual treatment. With a little ingenuity, most window treatments can be successfully adapted for problem windows.

DORMER WINDOWS AND SKY-LIGHTS

Dormer windows are upright windows built out from a sloping roof. As these windows are often small, it is important that the treatment does not obscure light. If possible, dress the wall area around the window to make the window appear larger. If space is restricted, then plastic or brass swing arms fitted into the window recess are a sensible solution. They are a neat way to hang curtains inside the recess, and they dress the side wall when not in use. A swing arm pivots from a bracket placed in the corner of the window to lie both against the window and the side wall. Note that the curtains must be double-sided as the back of the curtain is visible when the arm is swung open onto the wall.

A skylight is set in the line of the roof or ceiling. Special roller or Roman blind systems with tracking down the sides of the window are used for skylights. These blinds are usually needed to filter sunlight rather than provide privacy.

ILLUSTRATION NOTES

Page 270
A A Gothic-shaped dormer window.

B A recess-fitted shaped Roman blind.

C Gathered headed curtains held open by small tie-backs.

Page 274 Swing arm solutions for dormer windows.

A A double-sided channel-headed curtain slotted onto the swing arm. The curtains are held in small tie-backs.

B A double-sided curtain hung from the swing arm with rings. The curtains have a set-down tape heading and are held back in tie-backs. This heading may let light filter between the rings and swing arm.

Page 275 Curtains hung from a pole placed on the sloping wall above a dormer window. They are held back to the wall behind a second pole. Dressing the ceiling and wall area around the window makes it possible to use full-length curtains, which makes the treatment more impressive. Most types of headings would be suitable for this fitting method.

A French-headed curtains.

B A drop-down frill is a soft heading design which counterbalances the linear effect of the poles.

Page 276 Blinds for skylights.

A A roller blind set in the skylight recess covered by a lambrequin pelmet fitted flush to the wall. The pelmet hides the blind mechanism and softens the square shape of the window opening.

B A Roman blind with tracking down the

sides of the window. It could be unlined to allow light into the room.

Page 277 As the ceiling comes down to the top of this attic window, the curtains are hung from a track set onto the wall concealed by a pelmet set onto the ceiling. The pelmet is covered with box-pleated fabric, edged at the top and bottom with piped box-pleated frilling. Dressing the ceiling area above the window will add height to the treatment.

Design solutions

The shape and size of a problem window is not always ideal for standard curtain designs, but these difficult windows usually give rise to an opportunity to create dramatic design statements. The design solution may need unconventional fitting methods with improvised hardware but this should not be a deterrent from trying a new design.

ILLUSTRATION NOTES

Page 278
A-B Two windows close together present an opportunity for a three-curtain treatment. Swags and tails are wrapped over a pole which is set in front of curtains hung from a track. The pole brackets must be mounted on wooden blocks to allow the curtains free movement on the track.

Page 279
A-B
Two dissimilar-shaped windows are treated with three French-headed curtains hung from a pole. The centre curtain hides the wall space, and so hides the variation in the windows' shape. The result is elegant because the windows have been treated as a whole rather than individually.

Page 280
A A window with a lot of dead wall space above it.

B Two layers of fabric slotted onto a pole set high above the window form two swags which are looped around ombras at the sides of the window. The remaining fabric falls into tails. A roller blind is placed behind.

C A tented effect anchored to a curved pelmet board is held above the board by a chou trim. A small scalloped pelmet is set onto the front edge of the pelmet board The curtains are hung from a curved track that follows the shaping of the board.

D Asymmetrical swags are finished at the central point with a Maltese cross. A small central underswag hides the window's soffit or architrave. The cone-shaped tails are finished with Maltese crosses.

Page 281
A A window with no stack-back area on one side. This could be due to a wall, for example, or to a wardrobe or a bookcase.

B A goblet-headed curtain hung from a pole fitted with a recess bracket on the left-hand side. The curtain is held open with a cord secured onto the pole.

C A single curtain secured onto a board which has been covered in pleated fabric, with choux trims. The curtains are held open with choux-covered ombras.

D A symmetrical swag, flute and tail wrapped around a pole fitted using a recess bracket on the left-hand side. A curtain hung from a track set behind the pole is held in a barrier rope tie-back.

Page 282

A A Gothic-shaped window.

B A shaped pelmet echoing the shape of the window, emphasising the pretty Gothic lines. The simple design enhances rather than detracts from the window.

C Pencil-headed curtains joined in the centre with a Maltese cross. The curtains are held open by barrier rope tie-backs which are placed high enough to allow the Gothic shaping to be seen.

D A pair of curtains with a tab heading hung from a pole and held in fabric tie-backs set high on the wall.

Page 283

A A round or porthole window.

B An informal swag wrapped over a pole falling into dress curtains at the sides. The pole is placed across the centre of the window. A sheer fabric is most suited to this treatment.

C A pair of Italian-strung curtains with a pencil heading that follows the shaping of the round window. The curtains are finished with a rope clover with tassels.

D An arch-shaped pencil-headed valance with a pair of curtains.

Page 284

A A rectangular-shaped window which not only has a lot of dead wall space above it but is also small in size.

B A Roman blind trimmed with braid set high above the window, giving the illusion of covering a further area of glass.

C A shaped pelmet set high above the window with a roller blind concealing the wall area above the window. The full-length curtains also heighten the effect of the window treatment.

D Informally draped swags wrapped around a pole and falling into dress curtains. The pole is set high above the window. The functional roller blind covers the dead wall area above the window.

Page 285 Café curtains can be used for overlooked windows or glass doors.

A A scallop-headed café curtain hung from a pole.

B A set-down gather-headed café curtain hung from a pole on rings. The dead wall area above the window is covered by a valance.

C A channel-headed and hemmed sheer curtain slotted onto small rods attached to the door.

D A channel-headed and hemmed sheer curtain slotted onto small rods attached to the door. The curtain is tied in the centre with a bow.

DORMER WINDOWS

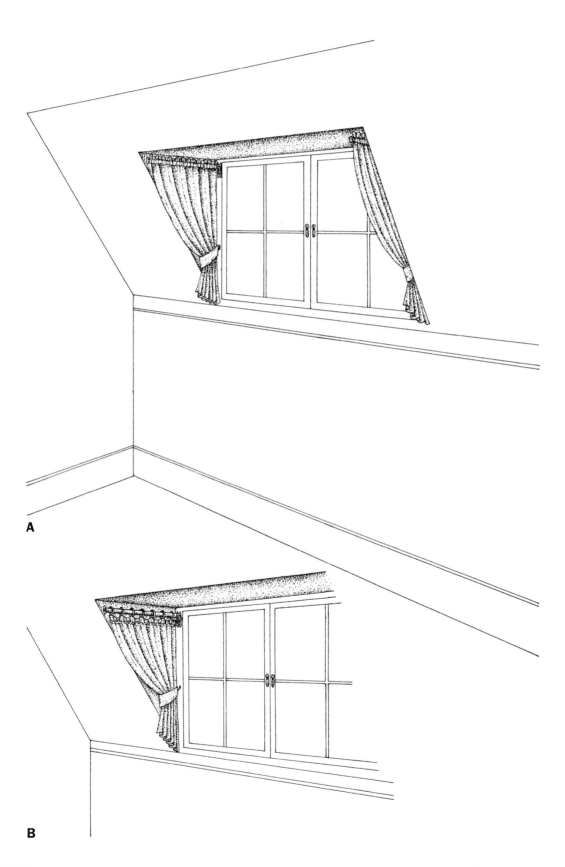

A

B

DORMER WINDOWS

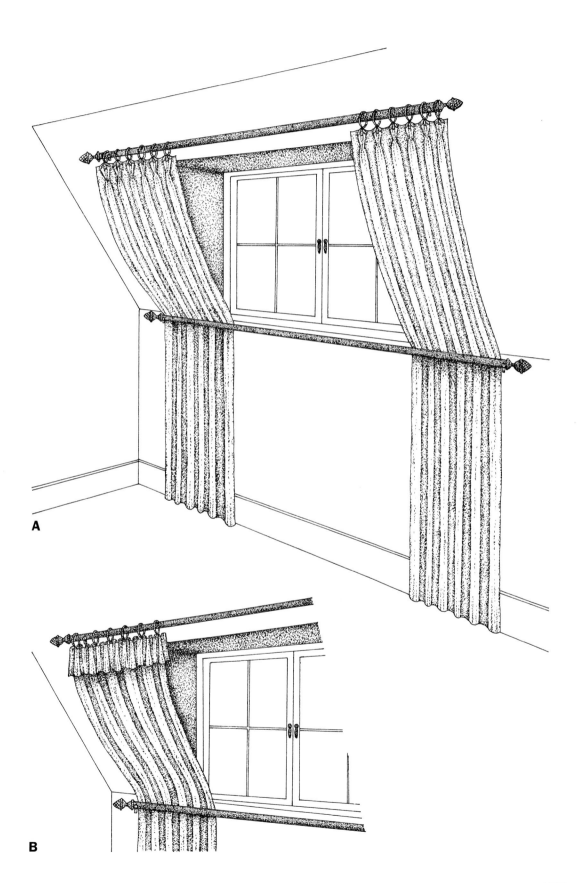

A

B

SKYLIGHTS

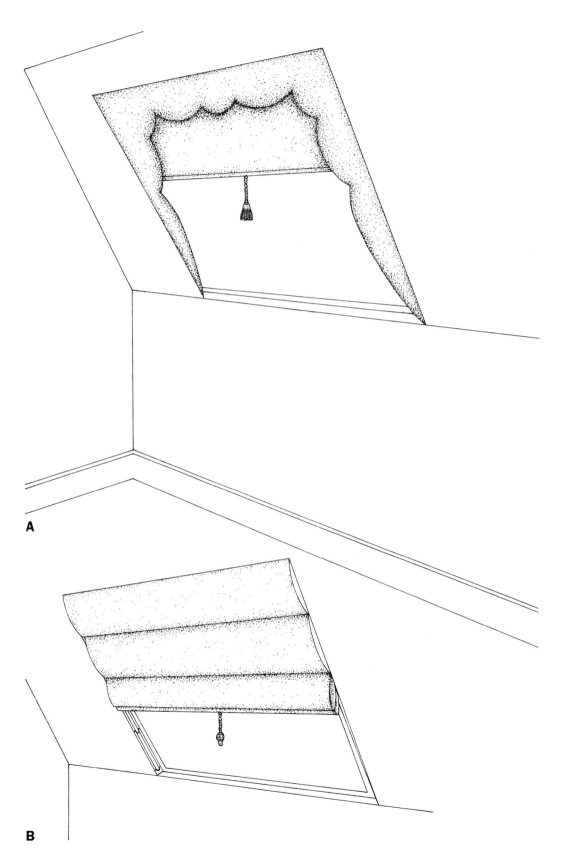

A

B

ATTIC WINDOW

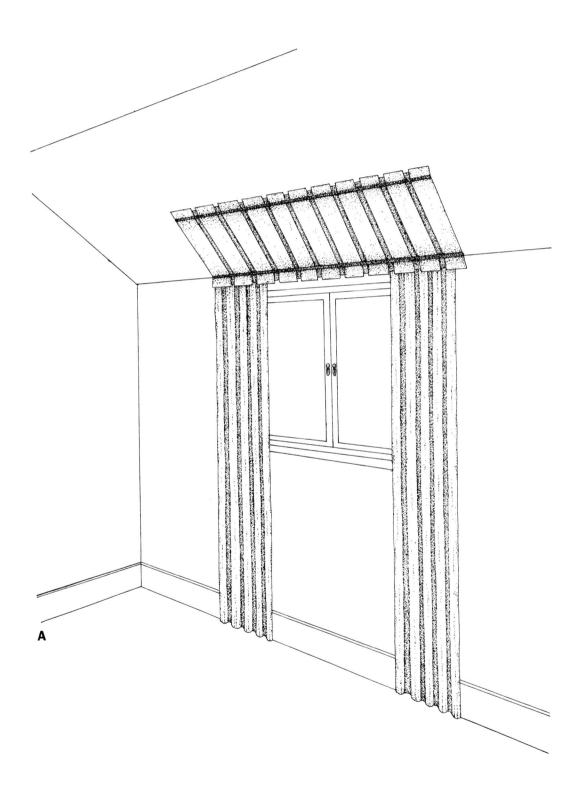

A

DESIGN SOLUTIONS

A

B

DESIGN SOLUTIONS

A

B

DESIGN SOLUTIONS

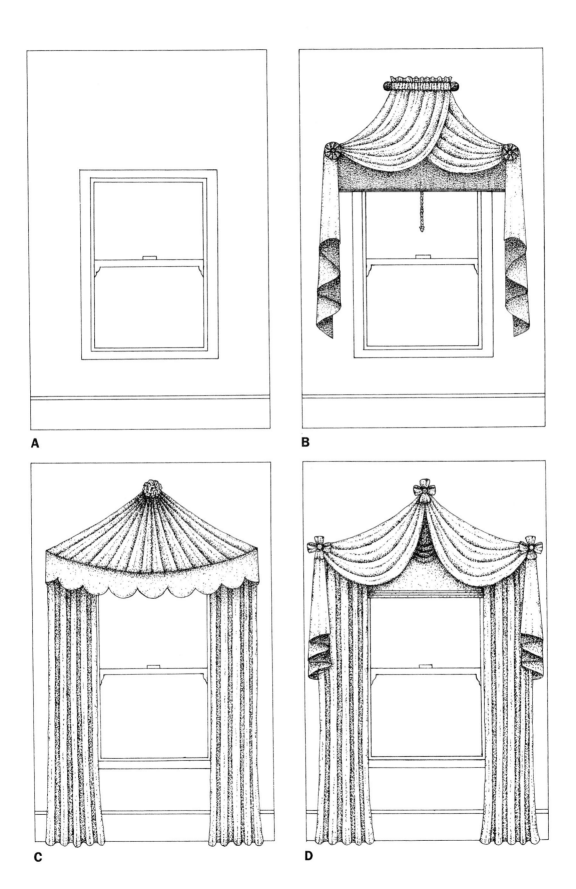

A

B

C

D

DESIGN SOLUTIONS

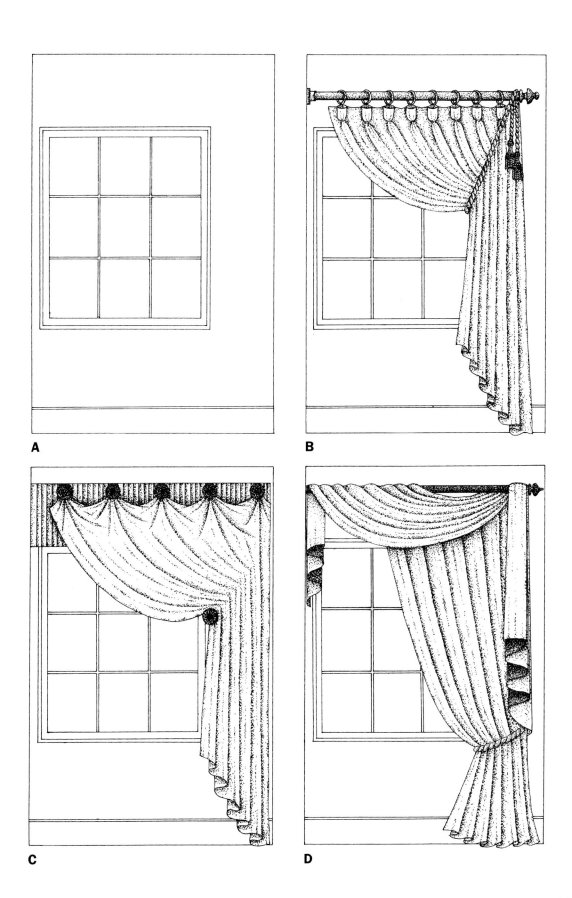

A

B

C

D

DESIGN SOLUTIONS

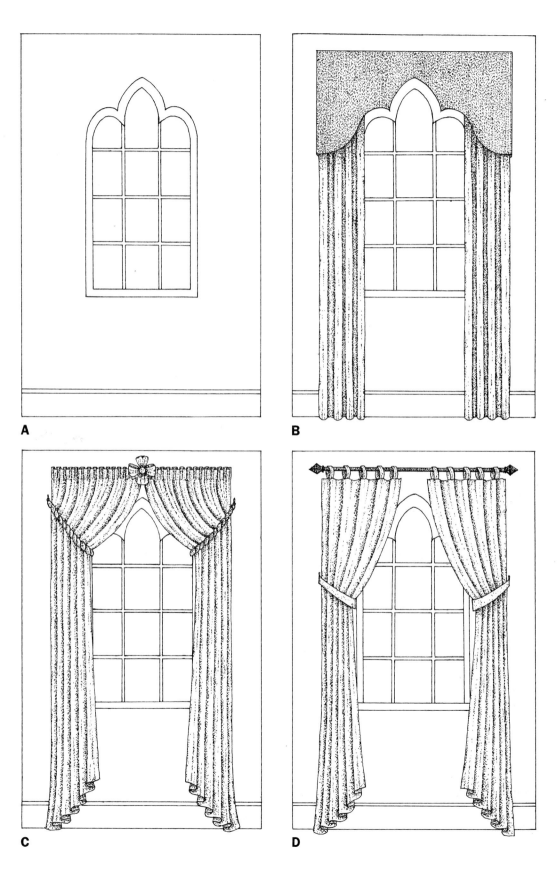

A

B

C

D

DESIGN SOLUTIONS

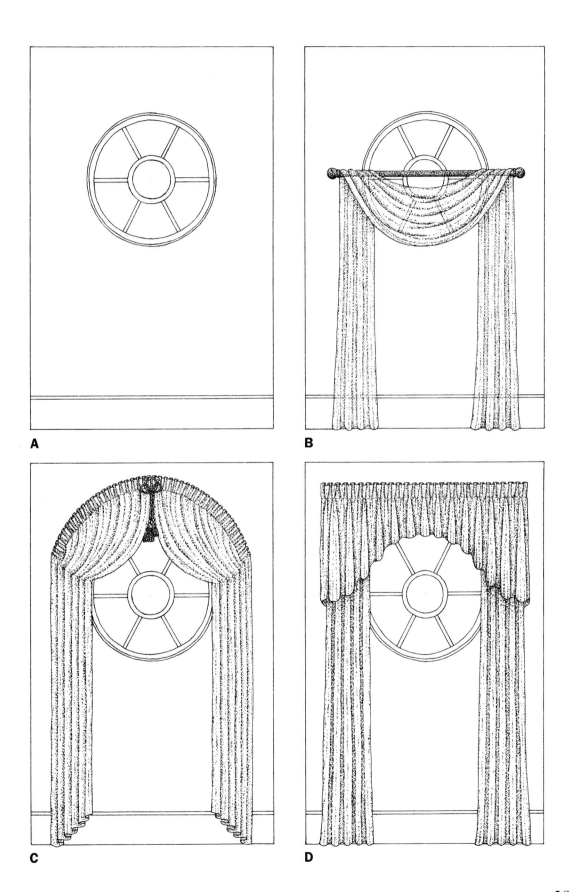

A

B

C

D

DESIGN SOLUTIONS

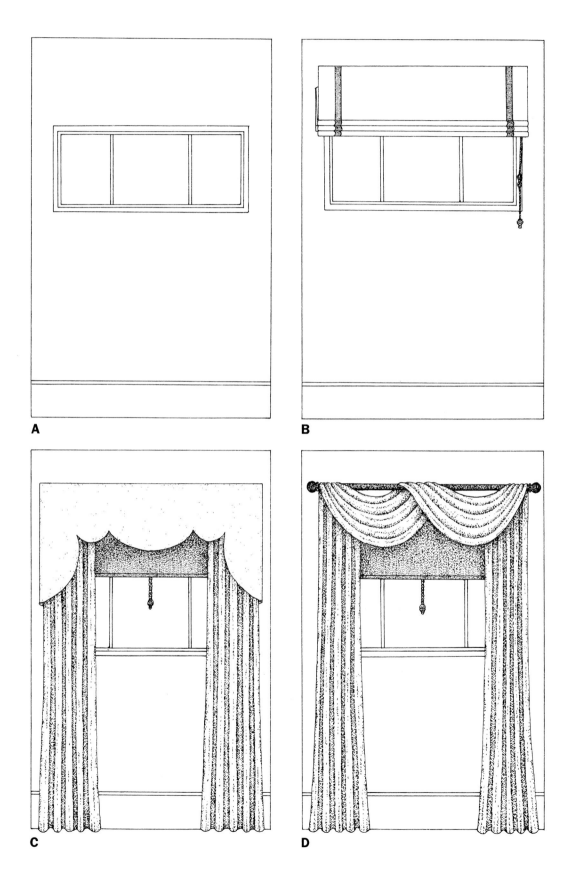

A

B

C

D

DESIGN SOLUTIONS

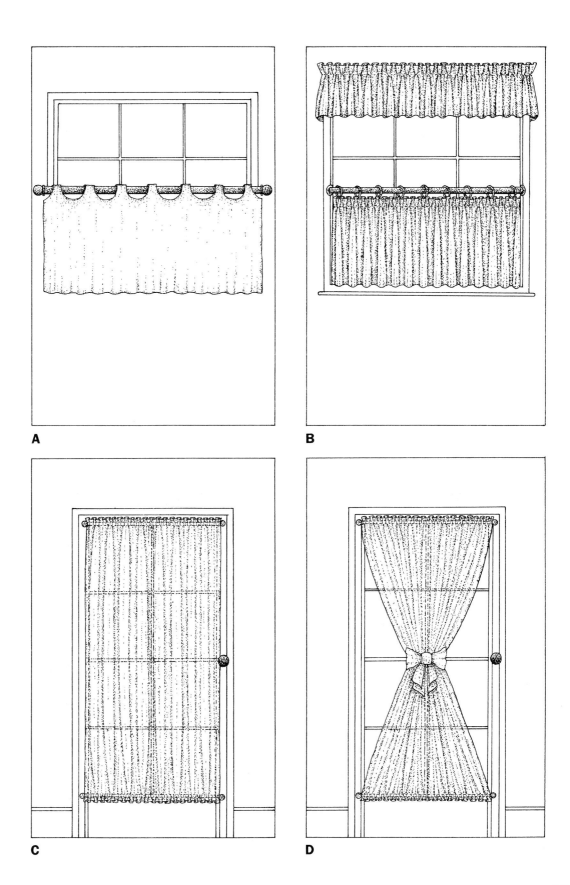

A

B

C

D

QUILTING STITCH DESIGNS

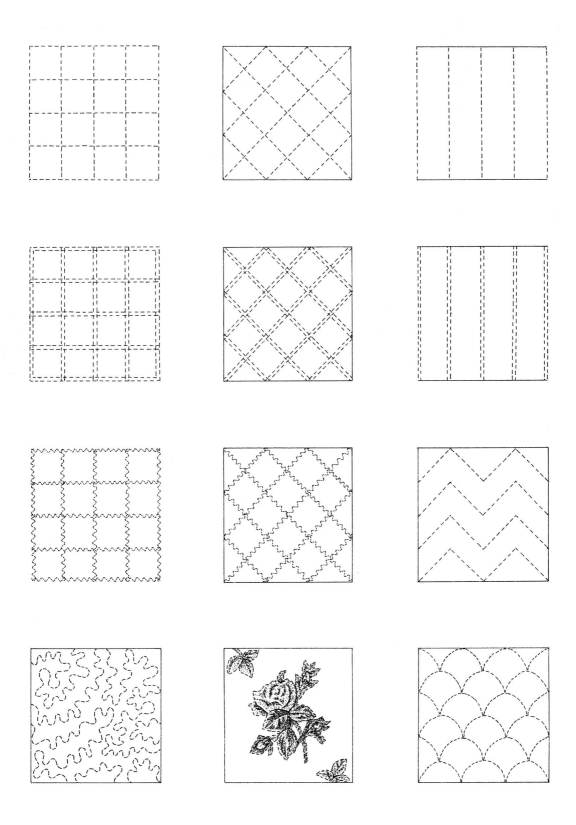

BEDS

The bed is usually the focal point of a bedroom and should be dressed to look comfortable and to link in with the window treatment. Upholstered headboards, quilts and bed valances are all important in the overall treatment.

Bed dressings can range from simple treatments made up in muslin dressing the wall behind the bed to a four-poster bed fitted with curtains and swags.

Baths can also be dressed with curtains and canopies. Depending on the style chosen, the effect can range from the light-hearted to the sumptuous and sophisticated. Cotton main fabrics lined with waterproof material (such as a shower curtain fabric) are the most suitable types of fabrics for use in bathrooms.

CORONAS AND HALF-TESTERS

A corona is a small semicircular-shaped pelmet board covered in fabric. A back curtain and two side curtains hang from the board and frame the bed. The side curtains are held by tie-backs or ombras. If required, a small valance or swags can also be hung from the board.

The side curtains can be made up in the main fabric used in the window treatment, and lined in a plain or small patterned fabric. The back curtain could then be made up in the lining fabric.

Half-tester boards can be dressed in the same way as coronas, although they are larger (as wide as the bed) and rectangular in shape. For corona or half-tester bed curtains, allow 1½ widths of fabric for each side curtain. To accommodate the take-up of the leading edge, the side curtains should be made 20cm (8in) longer than the top of the board to floor measurement. If there is a back curtain it can be unlined, with an allowance of two widths of fabric for a single bed and three widths for a double bed.

For a double bed, a corona board would be 50cm (20in) across the back and 30cm (12in) in depth. For a single bed the corona board would be 30cm (12in) across the back and 20cm (8in) in depth. Half-tester boards would be the width of the bed and 20-30cm (8-12in) in depth. The boards should be covered in fabric. Corona and half-tester boards can be fitted at the same height as the window treatment. For rooms with low ceilings they can be fitted to the ceiling.

A back curtain should be gathered and fitted to the board at the top and have a batten slotted through the bottom of the curtain. The batten should then be attached to the wall just above the skirting. For coronas and half-testers, the back curtain is joined to the side curtains: the seam should be left open up to the height of the tie-backs to allow the ombras or tie-back hooks to be fitted to the wall. Sometimes ombras have short stems and need to be blocked out on wood to get the required distance away from the wall.

FOUR-POSTERS

These are very varied in style and can be made out of wood or metal. The beds have a post at each corner, often with a fabric-covered ceiling and curtains at each corner. The curtains are usually decorative rather than functional. Whatever the style they are large and would need to be placed in a suitably sized bedroom.

Four-poster beds are individual and the way the bed dressings are attached depends on the design of the framework. However, it is important that any tracks or fittings are concealed. This sometimes means having a second valance or pelmet inside the framework.

ILLUSTRATION NOTES

Page 286
Stitch designs for bed quilts.

Page 291
A-L Upholstered headboards are the focal point of the bed, are decorative as well as comfortable, and are available in various shapes. Padded headboards can have ruched borders, plain borders with piping, or deep buttoning.

Page 292
A Three-quarter-length contrast-bound bed cover showing gathered valance beneath.

B A full-length contrast-bound bed cover.

C A three-quarter-length contrast-bound bed cover showing box-pleated valance beneath.

D Three-quarter-length contrast-bound diamond-quilted bed cover, showing valance with kick pleats.

E Bed cover with a piped, gathered full-length skirt.

F Full-length bed cover with separate pillow cover.

G Full-length contrast-bound bed cover with contrast-binding at the seams.

H Full-length square-quilted bed cover.

Page 293
Valances are placed over the bases of divans to hide them. They can also be used on wooden or metal framed beds for decorative reasons, but this is not essential. Valances can be made out of the main window treatment fabric or a co-ordinating one.

A A gathered valance with piping in the seam.

B A gathered valance with piping in the seam and a contrast-bound hem.

C A smart straight valance with kick pleats at each corner.

D A straight valance with kick pleats at each corner and at the centre of each side.

E A straight valance with kick pleats at each corner and a contrast-bound hem.

F A straight valance with kick pleats at each corner and an inset contrast border.

G A box-pleated valance with piping in the seam.

H A box-pleated valance with piping in the seam and a contrast-bound hem.

Page 294
Two swags and a pair of tails looped through large rings which are fixed to the back wall. A gathered back curtain is set behind the swags and tails. In a sheer fabric this could look informal.

Page 295
French-headed curtains, permanently

joined at the centre, hung from a pole fixed to the back wall. The gathered back curtain is secured to a batten behind and below the pole.

Page 296
Goblet-headed curtains with a 1cm (½in) contrast top and 2cm (¾in) contrast-bound leading edges with a gathered back curtain all hung from a corona board. The bed curtains are held by fabric-covered ombras.

Page 297
Pencil-headed curtains with 1cm (½in) contrast-bound leading edges, finished with a Maltese cross at the centre and a gathered back curtain all hung from a corona board. The bed curtains are held back by ombras.

Page 298
Three swags trimmed with fan-edge fringe hung from a corona board, with gathered back and side curtains with fan-edge fringe sewn down the leading edges, held by fabric-covered ombras.

Page 299
A serpentined valance trimmed with fringe with a 1cm (½in) contrast-bound top and set-down gathered heading. The gathered side and back curtains are hung from a corona board, trimmed with fringe on the leading edges, and held by ombras.

Page 300
Puff-headed side curtains and a gathered back curtain hung from a corona board. The side curtains are held by ombras finished with choux. A single bed is placed sideways against the wall.

Page 301
Gathered side curtains with a wide contrast binding hung from a corona board which is covered by a contrast-bound pelmet. The curtains are threaded through large rings. The single bed is placed sideways against a wall.

Page 302
A half-tester with gathered side and back curtains. The side curtains are held in contrast bound tie-backs. The valance has a 1cm (½in) contrast top with set-down smocking. The serpentined hem is finished with a contrast-piped frill with a contrast base.

Page 303
A tiara-shaped half-tester with gathered side and back curtains. The valance has a 1cm (½in) contrast top with a set-down gathered heading trimmed with rope. The lower edge of the valance has been trimmed with fringe. The valance is straight but looks arch-shaped because of the shape of the board. The side curtains have in-set fan-edge fringe on the leading edges and are held by tassel tie-backs.

Page 304
A four-poster bed with a pair of gathered side curtains and a gathered back curtain. The side curtains have 2cm (¾in) contrast-bound leading edges and are held by tie-backs. The straight valance has a 1cm (½in) contrast top with a set-down gathered heading and is finished with a fan-edged block fringe. The shape of the bed frame makes the valance appear serpentined.

Page 305
Four-poster bed with two side curtains with wadded edges and held by tassel tie-backs. A back curtain, and contrast-bound gathered valance hung round by the bed from the architraved top.

Page 306
Two side curtains with fringed edges held by tassel tie-backs. Back curtain, and

serpentined gathered valance with fringed lower edge hung round the bed from the architraved top. Plain bed cover and gathered bed valance.

Page 307

Two side curtains with fringed edges held by tassel tie-backs. Back curtain with vents at each side to allow wall lights through. Box-pleated fringed valance hung round the bed from the architraved top.

Page 308

Two side curtains held by tassel tie-backs. Back curtain with vents at each side to allow wall lights through. Flat fringed pelmet hung around the top of the bed.

Page 309

A four-poster bed with a pair of gathered side curtains and a gathered back curtain. The side curtains are trimmed with fan-edge fringe on the leading edges and are held by tassel tie-backs. The top frame of the bed is fitted with six swags, three decorative tails, a pair of side tails and a pair of double tails over the posts, all trimmed with fringe.

Page 310

A bath fitted into an alcove with a cornice box placed across it. The gathered valance has a 2cm (¾in) contrast-bound hem, and the side curtains have 2cm (¾in) contrast-bound leading edges and are held by tassel tie-backs.

Page 311

A bath with a tent-shaped canopy with side curtains tied with rope concealing the supports. The canopy has a short zigzag pelmet and is trimmed with rope, a central ball and tassels at the corner.

HEADBOARDS

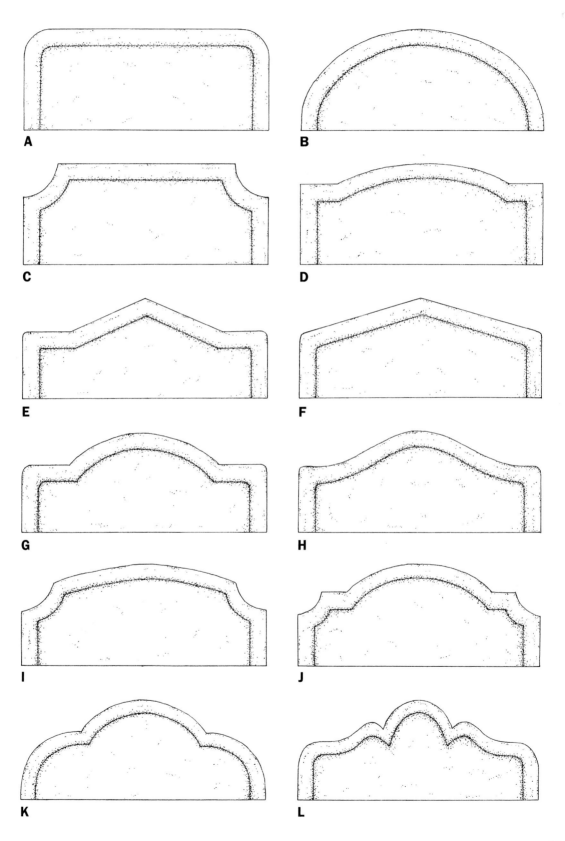

A

B

C

D

E

F

G

H

I

J

K

L

BED COVERS

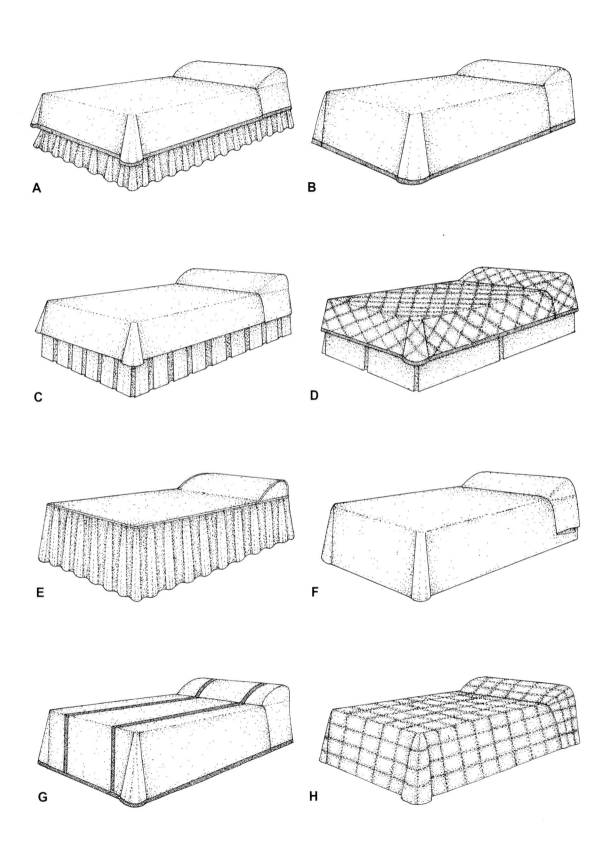

A

B

C

D

E

F

G

H

BED VALANCES

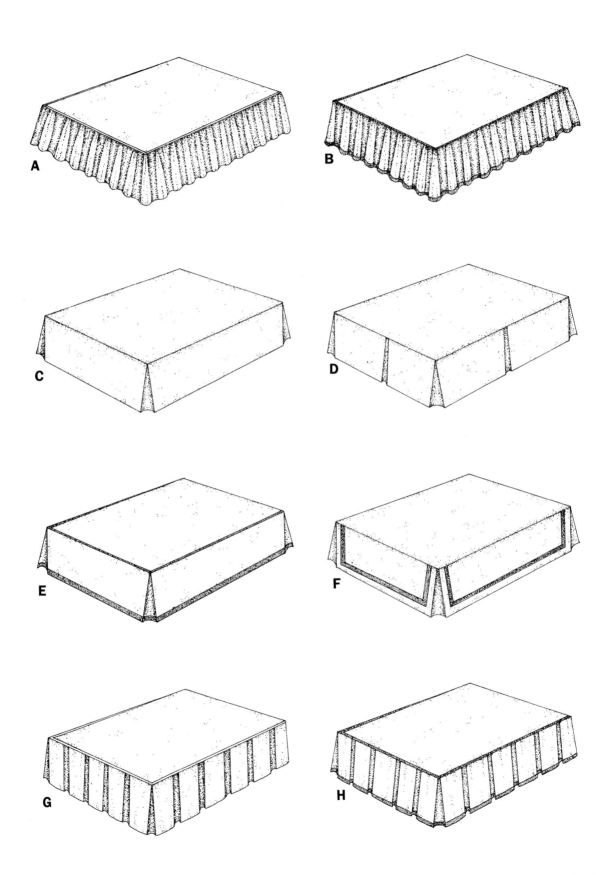

A

B

C

D

E

F

G

H

WALL DRESSINGS

WALL DRESSINGS

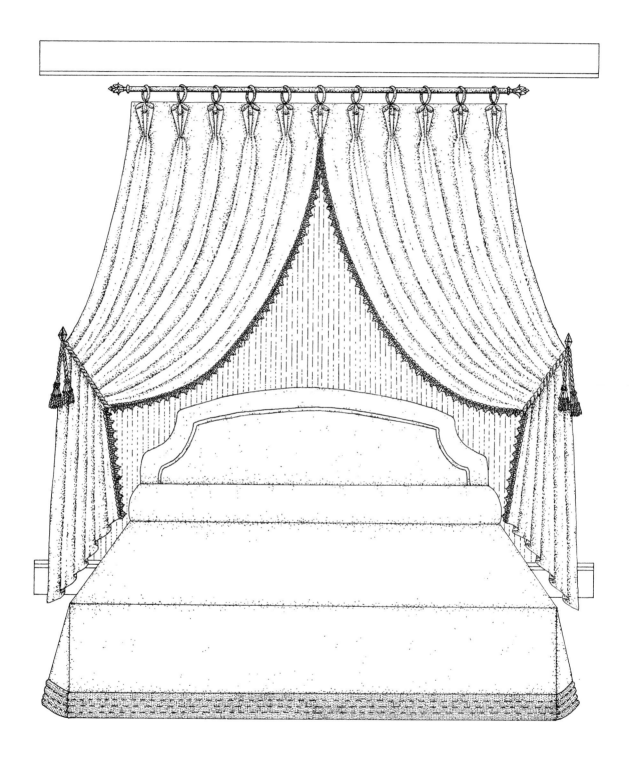

CORONAS

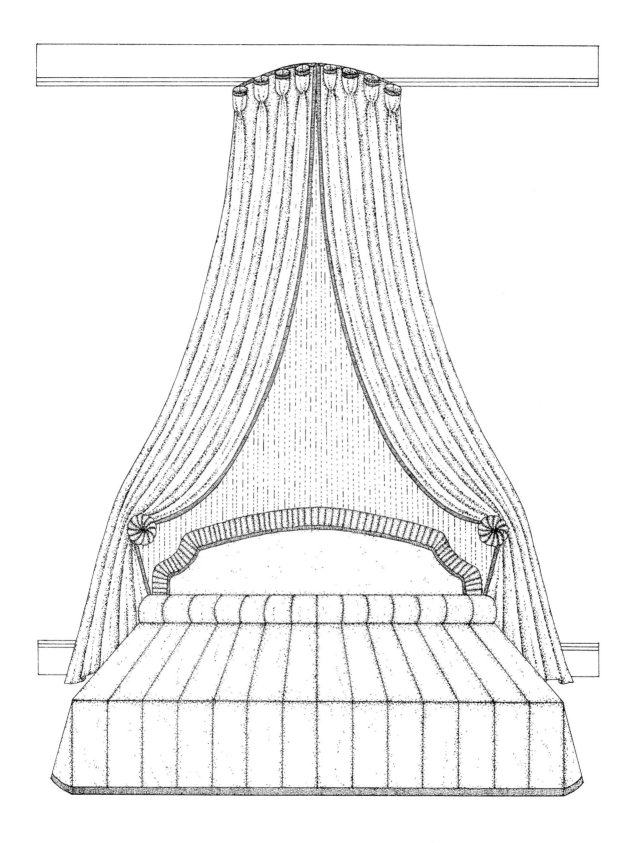

CORONAS

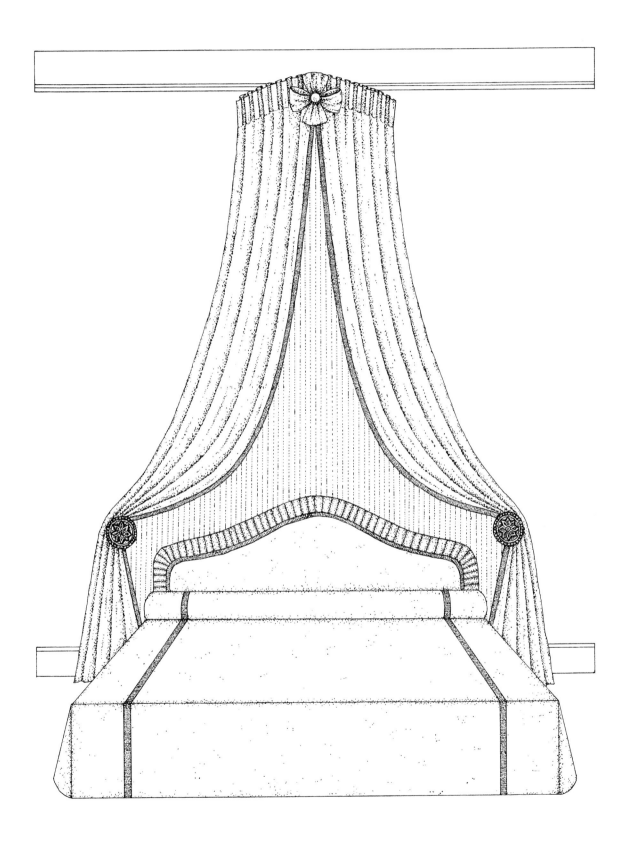

CORONAS

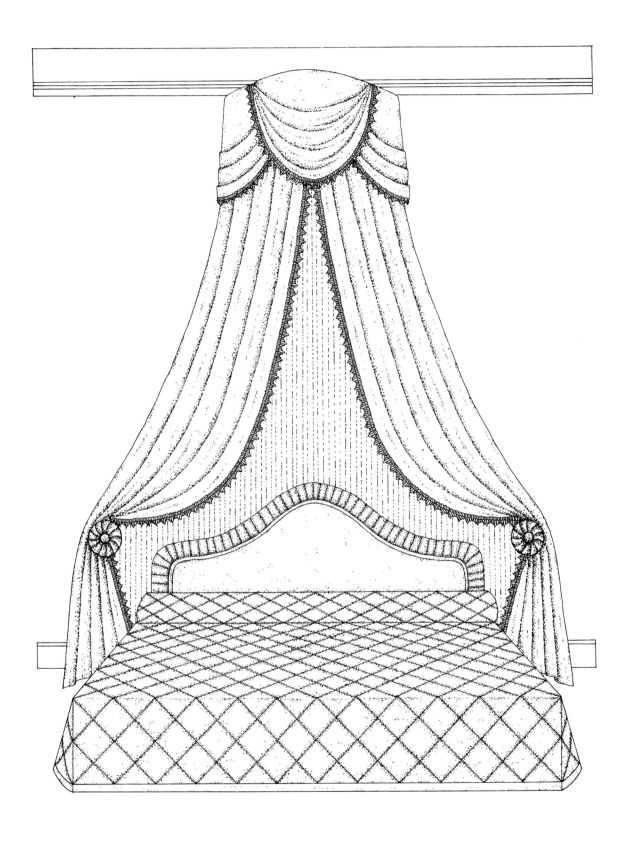

CORONAS

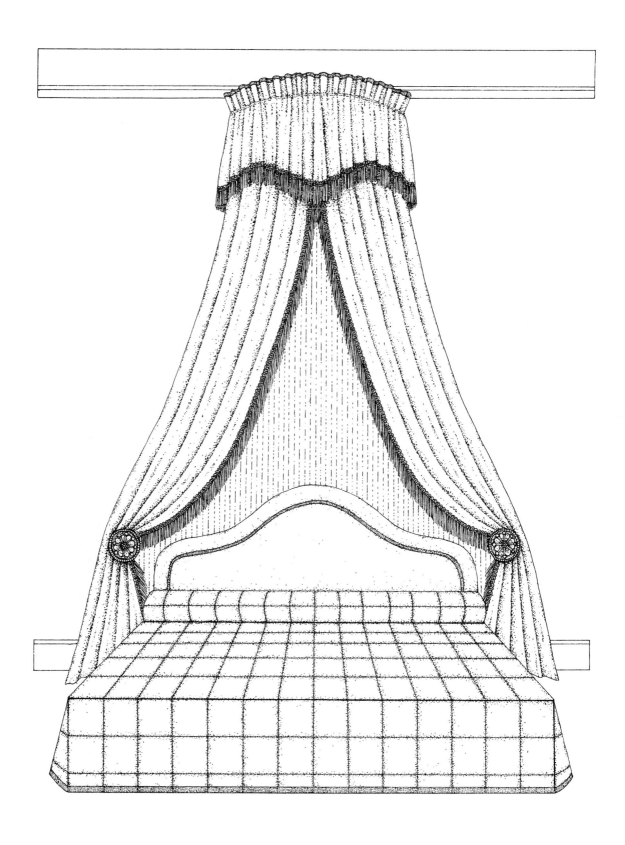

CORONAS

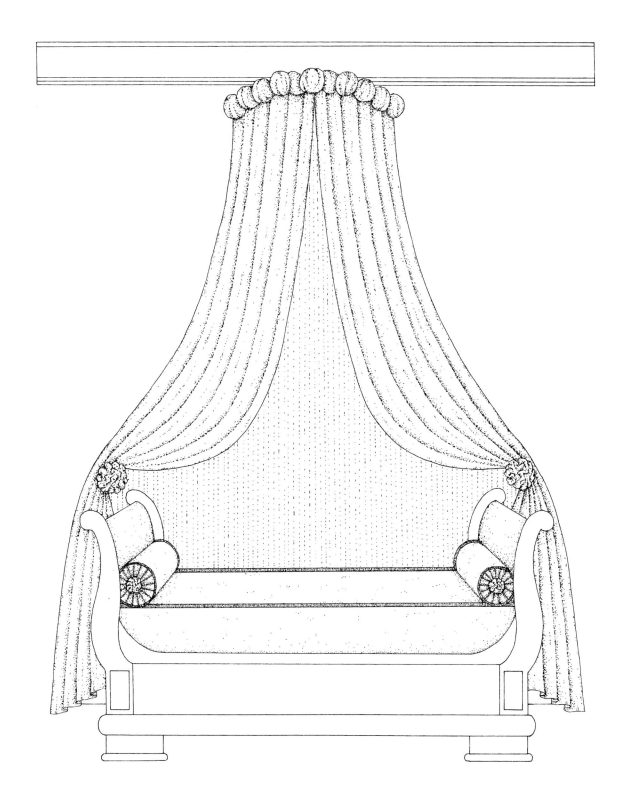

CORONAS

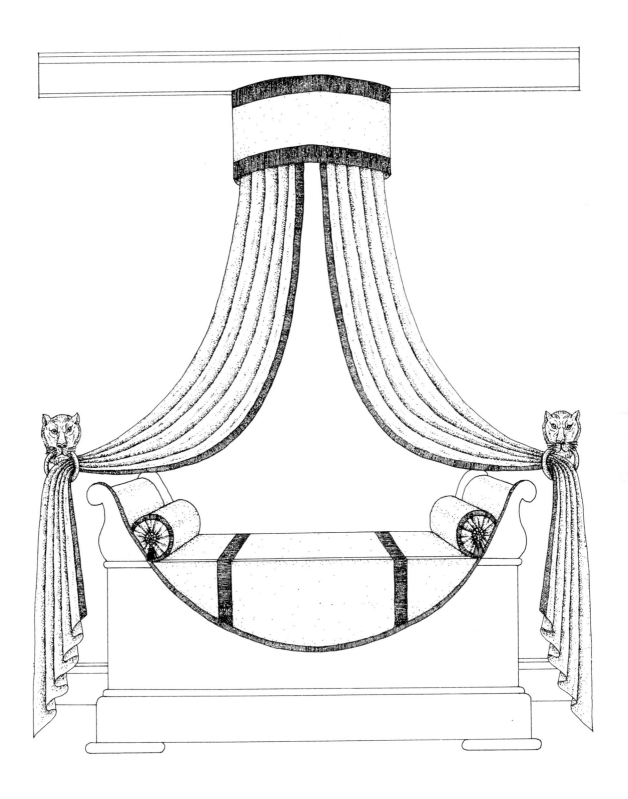

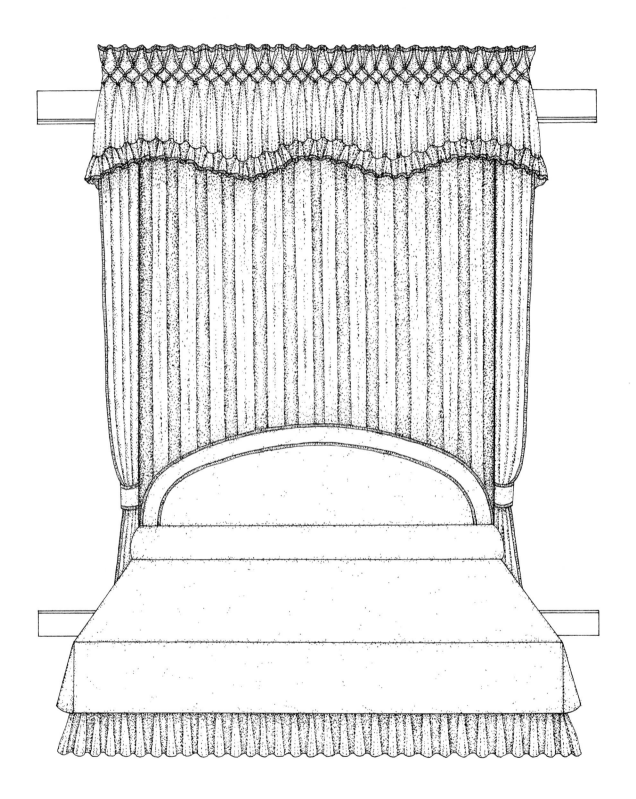

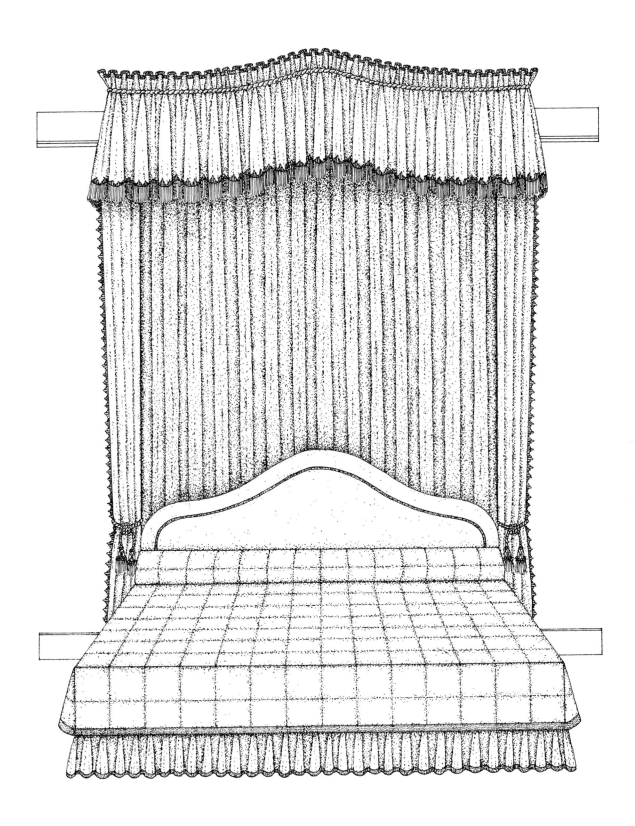

FOUR-POSTERS

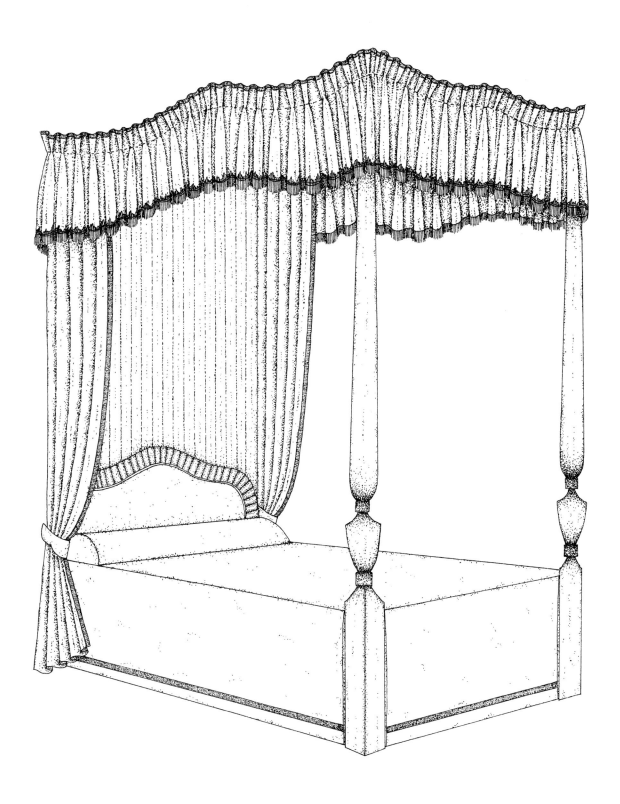

FOUR-POSTERS

FOUR-POSTERS

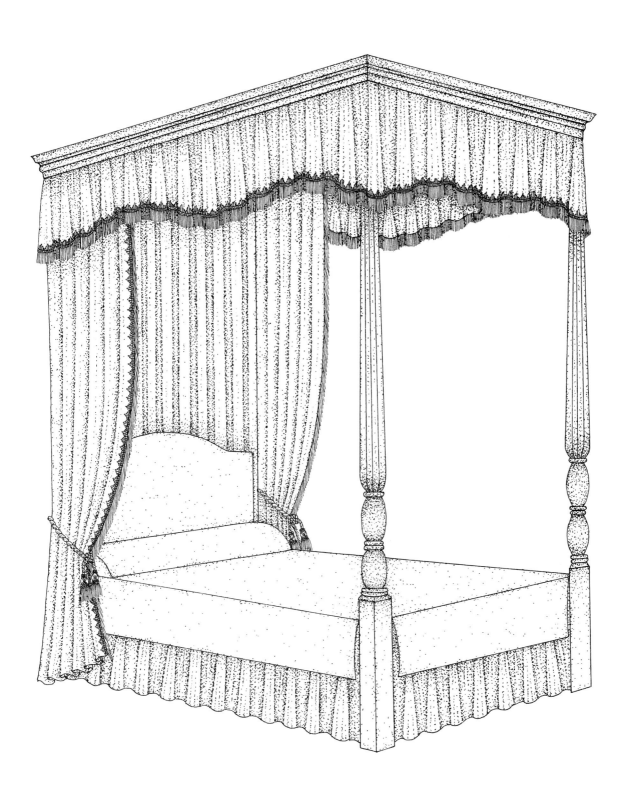

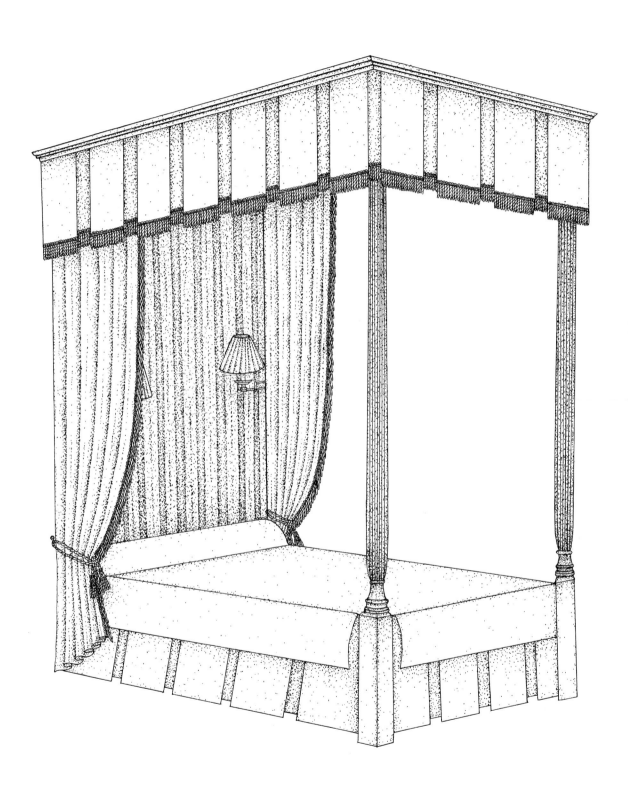

FOUR-POSTERS

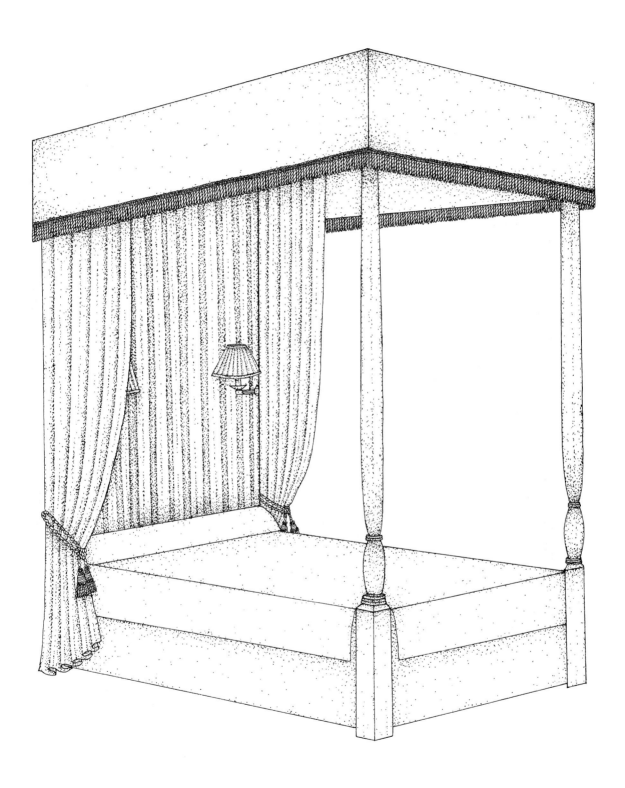

FOUR-POSTERS

BATH CURTAINS

ACCESSORIES

Tablecloths and cushions provide an opportunity to add colour, texture and patterns into a scheme They are important soft-furnishing elements, particularly in sitting-rooms and bedrooms. As they require only small amounts of fabric, they are an economical way of adding interest.

Tablecloths can be used to conceal inexpensive furniture and make a statement in a room Floor-length tablecloths should either just graze the floor or fall generously onto it. Lining and interlining a tablecloth will add extra weight and make it drape well.

TV tables have a shelf underneath the round table for a television. When it is not in use it is concealed by the skirt of the tablecloth which is hung from a curtain track fitted to the underside of the table. A cloth with a frill covers the top of the table and also conceals the curtain track.

Cushions should always be plump, and work better in groups rather than singly. The choice and shapes is varied, and the trimmings and embellishments endless.

ILLUSTRATION NOTES

Page 312
A selection of piped cushions and cushions with contrast borders.

Page 314 Tablecloth shapes.
A Plain round.
B Round, contrast bound.
C Round, on a hexagonal table.
D Hexagonal with a ruched yoke.
E Rectangular with kick pleats on a rectangular table.

F Rectangular with contrast-bound kick pleats finished with bows and on a rectangular table.

Page 315 A choice of frill designs, shown on floor-length round tablecloths.
A Contrast-piped gathered frill.
B Contrast-piped knife pleated frill.
C On-set gathered frill, contrast-bound at the top and bottom.
D On-set knife pleated frill, contrast-bound at the top and bottom.
E Double frill pinked at the top and bottom.
F Contrast-piped double gathered frill.

Page 316 Fringes, top cloths and quilted hems all add interest.
A Bullion fringe on the lower edge.
B Bullion fringe on the lower edge, with rope looped around the top.
C Small square top cloth trimmed with fringe and tassels at the corners.
D Small square tartan top cloth with frayed edges making the fringe.
E Padded quilted hem with three rows of machine stitching.
F Padded and diamond quilted hem.

Page 317
A-F Design details such as frills and scallops on the top cloths of TV tables can echo or contrast with those used in the window treatment. For example, cloth F echoes a scalloped pelmet trimmed with braid.

Page 318
A selection of cushions of various shapes, trimmed with rope or fringe.

Page 319
A selection of quilted cushions.

TABLECLOTHS

A

B

C

D

E

F

TABLECLOTHS

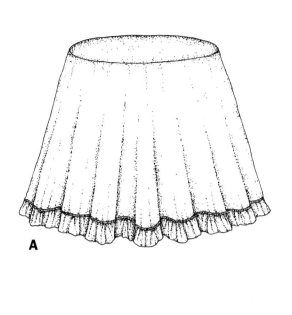

A

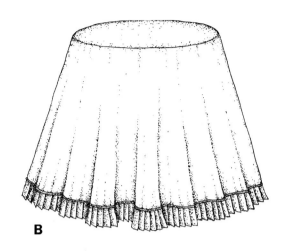

B

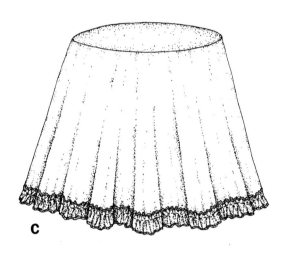

C

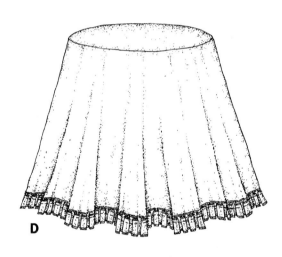

D

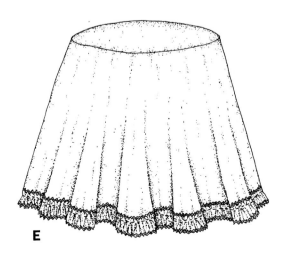

E

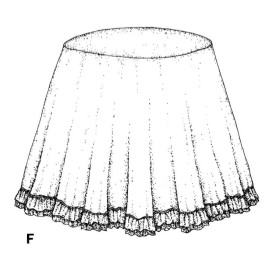

F

TABLECLOTHS

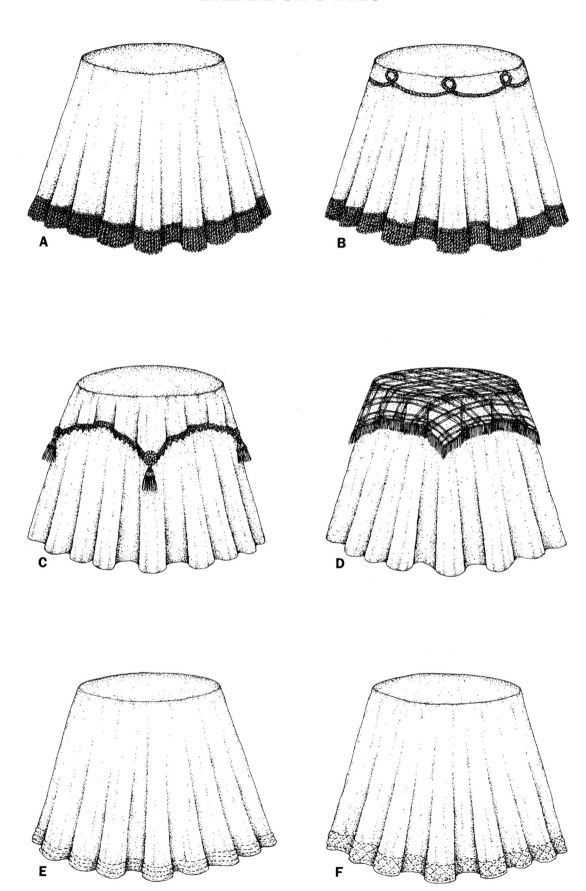

A

B

C

D

E

F

TV TABLECLOTHS

A

B

C

D

E

F

CUSHIONS

CUSHIONS

AMERICAN GLOSSARY

UK	US
Bedcovers	Bedspreads, quilts
Bed valances	Dust skirts/ruffles
Binding	Banding
Blinds	Shades
Curtains	Drapes
Curtain track	Travers rod
Cushions	Pillows
Frill	Ruffle
Pelmet	Upholstered cornice board
Pelmet board	Cornice board
Piping	Cording/welting
Tails	Cascades/jabots
Trumpet	Trumpet/bell